Gems from Martyn Lloyd-Jones

Ramsey.

Gems from Martyn Lloyd-Jones

An Anthology of Quotations from 'the Doctor'

with thanks to
Tony Chapman and Phillip Hudson
*ever in your deb*t

and the loving and generous
congregation of Worthing Tabernacle
1970–1998
always in my thoughts

Tony Sargent

I thank the Good LORD for your quality ministry

Paternoster:
thinking faith

MILTON KEYNES ● COLORADO SPRINGS ● HYDERABAD

(Ecclesiastes 12 √8–12) March 08

13 12 11 10 09 08 07   7 6 5 4 3 2 1

This edition first published 2007 by Paternoster
Paternoster is an imprint of Authentic Media,
9 Holdom Avenue, Bletchley, Milton Keynes, Bucks,
MK1 1QR, UK
1820 Jet Stream Drive, Colorado Springs, USA
OM Authentic Media, Jeedimetla Village
Secunderabad 500 055, A.P., India
www.authenticmedia.co.uk

Authentic Media is a division of IBS-STL U.K., limited by guarantee, with its
Registered Office at Kingstown Broadway, Carlisle, Cumbria CA3 0HA.
Registered in England & Wales No. 1216232. Registered charity 270162

British Library Cataloguing in Publication Data

A catalogue record for this book is available from the British Library

ISBN-13: 978-1-84227-494-1

Design by James Kessell for Scratch the Sky Ltd (www.scratchthesky.com)
Print Management by Adare Carwin
Printed in Great Britain by J.H. Haynes & Co., Sparkford

Index

FOREWORD

If there was ever warrant for labelling Thomas Aquinas *Doctor Angelicus*, as some have done for many centuries, there is comparable warrant for labelling David Martyn Lloyd-Jones *Doctor Evangelicus*. Doctor in both cases means *teacher*. There were contrasts, of course: Thomas taught in university lecture rooms, and by voluminous writings; Lloyd-Jones taught entirely by oral discourse from platforms and pulpits and informally. His only paper qualifications were those of a physician (that is why he was addressed as 'Doctor' to his face and referred to as 'the Doctor' in his lifetime). Yet he was a great, even momentous teacher of the truths of the gospel and the realities of the life of faith. And he, more than anyone, gave his generation of English evangelicals a concern for theology that was not there before, and so led them from juvenility to adulthood. Puritans of the seventeenth century, Jonathan Edwards of the eighteenth, Charles Hodge of the nineteenth and B.B. Warfield of the twentieth, all fusing with the Welsh Calvinistic Methodist heritage of his youth, gave him the evangelical understanding which he expounded with such clarity and power, plus masterful personal magnetism, throughout his ministry. He had a quick, sharp, probing, intuitive, logical mind and an easy flow of simple, energetic, non-technical, well-paced, passionate speech; you always felt he was totally absorbed in whatever line of exposition, persuasion, or application he had in hand; and on his day there was no one to touch him.

Because he believed so strongly that the true heart of evangelistic and pastoral Christian communication was God's ordinance of preaching, and that the direct impact of the preacher, living each moment in the power of his message, was the true heart of preaching, he was at first unwilling to be taped; and when finally he gave in on this point he constantly insisted that listening to a speaker 'canned', if one may so speak, on tape was spiritually far less fruitful than being in the same space with a live expositor of God's Word. But we should be very glad that, now that he is gone, the tapes remain, and loving labour gives us books in which we can almost hear the Doctor speaking as he relays and enforces his biblical wisdom. This book is one such.

Culling elegant extracts, nuggets of truth and wisdom and arrows of application, from the taped and transcribed utterance of one whose stock-in-trade was lawyer-like cumulative argument, is not the easiest of tasks; but Tony

Sargent has worked faithfully at it, and we owe him a deep debt of thanks for what he gives us here.

J.I. Packer
Professor of Systematic and Historical Theology,
Regent College, Vancouver

INTRODUCTION

It is to Iain Murray, one time assistant to Dr Lloyd-Jones, that we owe a detailed account of the Doctor's 'pilgrimage' (his favourite description of everyone's journey through life). Often in his final prayer he invoked the blessing of God on the congregation and 'their short, uncertain earthly life and pilgrimage'. Murray's two volumes reveal extraordinary detail. I attempted a synopsis of his life in my earlier book. Since then a work of first class scholarship has been made available by Dr John Brencher which is more thematic, analytical and objectively critical of this remarkable ministry.[1] Both authors should be consulted by any reader whose interest has been aroused in Lloyd-Jones' life as well as his preaching.

In a fascinating preface to *Liberty and Conscience*, the final volume in the Romans series, Murray tells the story behind this publishing venture. Writing in 2003 he noted that the million sales mark was passed 'many years ago', and he goes on to state that the proliferation of Lloyd-Jones' works and the interest of several publishers makes the total world sales impossible to compute. Though the Banner of Truth have published the majority of Lloyd-Jones' books there have been a range of other publishers involved in making his work available.

Twenty-six years have elapsed since Martyn Lloyd-Jones was taken to his eternal reward. It could well be said 'his works live after him'. The demand for the books has been so high and the readership so widespread this must be one of the great publishing feats for religious books in the 20th and 21st centuries. The Banner of Truth's step of faith has been vindicated. Those who have tolled the death knell of preaching have acted prematurely.

More than ten years ago, in a personal interview with John Brencher, The Revd Dr John Stott said that it was a pity that Lloyd-Jones had not abridged his sermons. Stott predicted 'I cannot imagine that all these works will still be in print in twenty or thirty years' time.' Uncharacteristically Stott, a redoubtable preacher himself and an admirer of Lloyd-Jones, seems likely to be proved wrong.[2]

---

[1] J. Brencher, *Martyn Lloyd-Jones (1989–1981) and Twentieth Century Evangelicalism*. Milton Keynes: Paternoster, 2002.

[2] J. Brencher, *Martyn Lloyd-Jones*, 198. Stott was asked by Lloyd-Jones to consider succeeding him to the pulpit of Westminster much to the Anglican minister's surprise.

I commenced working on this volume some ten years ago after publishing *The Sacred Anointing*.[3] The latter was one of the first of a number of books to attempt an evaluation of the extraordinary ministry of Martyn Lloyd-Jones. In it I examined his controversial approach to the doctrine of the Spirit and its importance in empowering the ministry of preaching. Gratifyingly it was well received in the UK and also published in the USA. A special edition was made available in India and it went on to be translated into Korean. Now the book has again been reprinted by Paternoster. In the preface of the first edition I promised another volume sampling the content of his teaching. I had been so impressed by material culled in my researches that I began to compile an anthology. I confess I was triggered to do this having come across a book which was the result of a trawl through the sermons of C.H. Spurgeon, one of the most quoted and quotable preachers of the nineteenth century.

An unexpected request to go to Scotland to help establish the Scottish-based International Christian College caused me to leave the church I had served for twenty eight years on the south coast of England. Somewhat naively I imagined this would give me more time to write and travel. I was wrong. Eight years have elapsed and I have returned to the task, having been chided by the late Professor Neil Hood who welcomed me to his country and made my life easier by establishing contacts in the academic world. Sadly he died before seeing that his pressure for me to write seriously again bore fruit.

I used my earlier volume as a text book for students who attended my homiletics (preaching) courses. In compiling this I have preachers in mind – though not exclusively. In his day Charles Spurgeon published *Feathers for Your Arrows* – a quaint book of helps in the form of illustrations and quotations for preachers. Hopefully there are some feathers for the choosing in this volume too which might become the stimulus for sermons.

My concern is not to encourage preachers to copy Lloyd-Jones – he often enjoined younger ministers, 'be your own man'. My hope is for an up-and-coming generation of preachers to identify with Lloyd-Jones' commitment to declare the living word of God through the exposition of Scripture and to do it with clarity and passion. This is the essence of true preaching. Lloyd-Jones' famously defined preaching as, 'Logic on fire'. Calvin was as daring: 'Preaching the word of God *is* the word of God.'

It is also my hope in compiling this anthology that non-preachers will find benefit and that it may be a compendium of theology, albeit in short capsules. One of my organists picked up some stray pages of an earlier manuscript which I had left in my Worthing church. He read them and asked for more. He said the quotes had prompted him to think and had given him a short course in theology. A similar experience was mine when I came across the writings of A.W.

---

[3] A. Sargent, *The Sacred Anointing*, London: Hodder & Stoughton, 1994. Reprinted, Milton Keynes: Paternoster, 2007.

Tozer.[4] My prayer is that non-preaching readers will be as blessed with Lloyd-Jones as I have been with Tozer.

My method of compilation follows a personal and simple track. I perused volume after volume, occasionally returning for a second reading. When something struck a particular chord I extracted it and endeavoured to slot it into a category. The latter evolved as I read. Sometimes it was a tussle to decide where to place a particular quotation. Many would fit into several groupings. Where there are multiple quotations under one heading, I attempted the more difficult task of sub-divisions. I crave the reader's forgiveness if I am marked down for my choices. Obviously my approach represents an inexact science, but I hope this anthology and its structure will be useful and inspirational.

I have borne in mind the main emphases within Lloyd-Jones' ministry and tried to reflect them. He was very definite on his view of the atonement, the love and the wrath of God. He preached strongly on heaven and hell and the doctrine of election. His commitment to Scripture, its authority and its inspiration, is a constant throughout his sermons, as is his belief in creation over against evolution. Occasionally I caved in to personal concerns. For example, I quote him several times on the subject of animals simply because of my interest in their welfare and what I consider to be a lack in our churches of biblical teaching on animal husbandry.[5] Nevertheless, this was hardly one of the Doctor's main themes![6]

Would Lloyd-Jones have approved of what I have attempted? In some respects I have been prompted by him. Any reader of his celebrated *Joy Unspeakable* (originally two books now printed as one) will be aware of his proclivity for quotations. This emerges particularly as he traced the history of religious experience and gives samples. He wished to support his theology of the baptism in the Holy Spirit which (claiming to follow Spurgeon, *et al*) he believed to be distinct from regeneration. He takes us to Whitefield, Edwards, Wesley, Moody, Pascal and many others.[7] A similar example is found when he

---

[4] Dr Lloyd-Jones and George Verwer helped to make Tozer's slender paper backs available in the United Kingdom and Verwer encouraged their wide-scale distribution.

[5] J.A. Sargent, *Animal Rights and Wrongs: A Biblical View of Animal Welfare*. London: Hodder & Stoughton, 2000.

[6] Some years ago I came across a picture of Lloyd-Jones about to mount a horse. An explanatory comment referred to his love for these creatures. If this is accurate, he had something in common with John Wesley who sometimes prayed for his beast when it was sick. It was, after all, vital to his itinerant ministry. What would we do if stuck in the south west corner of England with a pressing engagement in Bristol and only equine means of transport? Wesley preached a remarkable sermon on animal immortality (*The Great Deliverance*. Sermon 60, John Wesley, 1872 edition), the theology of which might not have impressed the good Doctor!

[7] I work through the far reaching implications of this in *The Sacred Anointing*.

departs from the text midway through his Romans series and engages in a *tour de force* of church history – 'Good knock-about stuff,' as J.I. Packer once affectionately dubbed it. Frustratingly, the Doctor does not give his sources, but then he was engaged in preaching and not writing a book in the fashion of academic authors.

I have meticulously given references throughout. I have not resorted to the practice followed in my previous volume of using a code but have each time given the full title. I have done my best to supply readers with an exhaustive list in the bibliography at the end of this book. My reason for consistent and full referencing is obvious. I have tried to accurately reflect Lloyd-Jones but where a quote prompts great interest I urge the reader to go to the context; particularly if the subject matter seems controversial. He could be controversial; check the quotations on, for instance, demon possession. He certainly was his own man!

There are advantages in extracting pithy quotations which seem to stand on their own. But sometimes they do need buttressing by considering what straddles them. In preaching, Lloyd-Jones consistently gave the sense of Scripture. He usually compelled his hearer to work through the context and introductory verses to a particular doctrine. Once he urged his listeners to stay 'in the porch' with Paul in order to be better prepared to enter the 'main building'. We can be helped in reading difficult passages of Scripture by considering the run up to more doctrinal verses. In similar fashion I have made it possible for readers to 'enter the porch' of Lloyd-Jones' quotations if they find the reference abstruse. Hopefully this will help the gist of his reasoning to be clearer.

My admiration for his wife and his elder daughter – Lady Elizabeth Catherwood (and her son Christopher) – overflows for taking on the editing task after Dr Lloyd-Jones's death. I have similar appreciation for Tony Rushton for making the tapes available to thousands through the superbly organised Martyn Lloyd-Jones Recording Trust. Modern technology has meant that defective tapes can be upgraded to an acceptable quality.[8]

Responsibility for the writing and compilation of this book is mine. But it could hardly have been achieved without the help of others down the years. I am glad to acknowledge assistance from Chris Howie who was my personal secretary during my final years at Worthing Tabernacle and to Gina Trim who easily adapted her skills in financial administration to handling material she feels represents a better investment. I am particularly indebted to Joan Hall who spent hours checking and rechecking my sources. My move to Scotland brought with it the blessing of a brilliant personal assistant, Sandra McSporran. Thanks

---

[8] Bear in mind that Dr Lloyd-Jones never wrote a book. (Yes he is the author of more than fifty volumes.) Providentially the advent of the tape recorder coincided with much of his period at Westminster Chapel. Critical of the now popular tape ministries, he allowed the recordings of his sermons, but ruled out distribution. He feared that people might stay at home to listen to his sermons on a Sunday rather than grace a local church.

too to Ailsa Bell who worked so quickly on a number of items in this project. One of my post graduate students Aileen Pender spent hours too on checking my material and now is a self confessed addict to Lloyd-Jones' sermons.

I am immensely grateful to Lady Elizabeth Catherwood and the Lloyd-Jones' family for generously waiving copyright restrictions and giving me liberty to quote from their beloved Father. Elizabeth encouraged me many years ago when we had coffee together in Cambridge and I discussed the idea behind this volume.

Rev Dr James Packer endorsed my first volume and when I sent him the anthology manuscript nervously requesting some comment he wrote a fulsome, perceptive and gracious foreword – something I was too timid to request and for which I now thank him.

Finally I express thanks to the Lord who continues to endow his Church with pastor-teachers of whom Martyn Lloyd-Jones is an outstanding example.

Tony Sargent
International Christian College
Glasgow
anthony.sargent@ukonline.co.uk
Summer Term 2006

– A –

ACHIEVEMENT
The men who have accomplished most in this world have always been theo-
logically-minded.
The Unsearchable Riches of Christ, 222

ACTIVITY (Age)
I have seen men who have been indefatigable in the work of the kingdom suddenly laid aside by illness, and scarcely knowing what to do with themselves.
What is the matter? They have been living on their own activities. You can be so
busy preaching and working that you are not nurturing your own soul. You are so
neglecting your own spiritual life that you find at the end that you have been living on yourself and your own activities. And when you stop, or are stopped by illness or circumstances, you find that life is empty and that you have no resources.
Studies in the Sermon on the Mount (2), 278

ACTS OF APOSTLES
Do you not feel [the warmth resulting from the Spirit's presence] as you read
that most lyrical of books, the Acts of the Apostles? Live in that book, I exhort
you; it is a tonic, the greatest tonic I know of in the realm of the Spirit.
The Christian Warfare, 274

There is no more exhilarating book than that; I always regard it as a kind of spiritual convalescent home, a book to which tired Christian people should always
go to be really invigorated and built up. If you are feeling tired and therefore in
need of a spiritual tonic, go to the book of Acts and there you will find this irre-
pressible joy that these people had in confirmation of the Lord's promise!
Fellowship with God, 24

Anatole France, an infidel French novelist, used to say that when he felt jaded and
tired in Paris in the height of the season and at other times, he never went into the
country to find refreshment, but into the eighteenth century. I understand that
very well. I have often gone into the eighteenth century myself – to the Evangelical
Awakening, the blessing of God in revival – but *the* place to go to is the book of the
Acts of the Apostles. Here is the tonic, here is the place to get refreshment, where
we feel the life of God pulsating in the early Christian Church.
Authentic Christianity (1), 225

ADAM

Understand Adam and in a sense you will begin to understand Christ. The relationship of mankind to Adam is a picture of the relationship of the redeemed to the Lord Jesus Christ.
Assurance, 179

before the Fall

Adam was perfect, sinless, completely innocent. Even God could not make a more perfect man than Adam, for Adam was made 'in the image of God'.
The Final Perseverance of the Saints, 360

Adam by creation was in a condition which was already immortal, and that he would continue as such to all eternity. He was perfect, but he was not glorified. Adam had still to achieve immortality, but there was no principle of death in him; and he would not have died if he had not sinned. To be glorified and to become immortal his body would have to be changed to make it correspond to that glorified body of the Lord Jesus Christ, but if he had not sinned he would not have died.
Assurance, 195

Unfallen Adam was righteous, but it was his own righteousness as a created being, it was the righteousness of a man. Adam never had the righteousness of Jesus Christ upon him. What he lost was his own righteousness. But you and I are not merely given back a human righteousness, the righteousness that Adam had before he fell – we are given the righteousness of Jesus Christ.
Assurance, 262

after the fall

Entire humanity was resident in him.
Great Doctrines of the Bible (1), 194

Adam's sin is imputed to us in exactly the same way that Christ's righteousness is imputed to us. We inherit, of course, a sinful nature from Adam; there is no dispute about that. But that is not what condemns us. What condemns us, and makes us subject to death, is the fact that we have all sinned in Adam, and that we are all held guilty of sin.
Assurance, 210

It is our union with Adam that accounts for all our trouble. It is our corresponding union with Christ that accounts for our salvation.
Assurance, 210

There is a sense in which we were all 'in the loins' of Adam and therefore were acting in Adam.
Assurance, 216

Adam and Christ
A race started in Adam; another race started in Christ.
The Final Perseverance of the Saints, 227

We are put into a position in which, as Isaac Watts says so rightly, we have a better status than that of Adam. We have something that Adam lacked; for we are 'in Christ'. Adam was not in Christ. Adam was made in God's image but he was, as it were, outside the life of God. But we are 'in Christ'. God the Son came down to earth; He took human nature unto Himself; and we are 'in Him'. Adam was never in that position. We are incorporated into Christ. We are members of the household of God. Not so, Adam.
Assurance, 235–36

We are partakers of the divine nature. Adam was not. Adam was given a positive righteousness, but he was not a partaker of the divine nature. He was made in the image and likeness of God and no more; but the man who is in Christ, the man who is a Christian, the man who is born again is a 'partaker of the divine nature'. Christ is in him and he is in Christ.
Faith on Trial, 103

Every true Christian is related to Christ, as every natural man was related to Adam. In other words, it means that if we are Christian, if we believe in the Lord Jesus Christ, we are incorporated into him, we become a part of him, we share his life, and we are born of him. We are in him in exactly the same way as we were in Adam.
Saved in Eternity, 146

That is the simple, primary, truth about the Christian: he is 'in Christ' and not 'in Adam'. The old man that I once was has gone and gone for ever. Now you notice that I am saying 'the old man'. I am not saying that the sin that is in the body and in the flesh has gone; I am simply saying that as the entity that was in Adam, I am no longer there; I am an entity in Christ now.
God's Way of Reconciliation, 119

ADULTERY
This adulterous mentality is ruled by curiosity.
Spiritual Blessing, 166

That is the characteristic, is it not, of every adulterous person? 'Oh, this is too tame! We want something fresh, something new, something exciting!' This is our Lord's own description of a generation of people that are always seeking after signs. And ultimately, of course, it comes to this: animated by such a spirit, and moved and controlled by it, adulterous people eventually take their life into their own hands and decide what to do.
Spiritual Blessing, 167

Is it not a shameful thing that infidelity in marriage should be regarded as a matter for jokes and for laughter, that a man who is not loyal to his wife should be regarded as a subject for jesting.
The New Man, 281

ADVOCACY

There are two kinds of advocacy from which we benefit as Christian people. We know that the Lord Jesus Christ is our Advocate with the Father; He is there in Person pleading for us. We are not there; He is doing it for us. But this advocacy of the Spirit is within us. He does not do it instead of us, but He tells us what to say. Both are advocates but in a different manner. The parallel is quite perfect. The solicitor I am using as an illustration does the two things; he not only tells us what to say, he can also address the court himself. When he is addressing the court the picture is that of our Lord's advocacy for us with the Father. But when the solicitor preparing the case tells us in his office what to say, and puts words into our mouth, he is acting as the Spirit does in this matter of prayer.
The Final Perseverance of the Saints, 137

AFTER LIFE (Death, Heaven)

When God proclaims Himself to be the God of Abraham and of Isaac and of Jacob, He is proclaiming that Abraham, Isaac and Jacob are to go on living in resurrected form. It is His proof of the resurrection.
Great Doctrines of the Bible (3), 230

May I venture to add, therefore, that because of this doctrine we shall know one another. You will not lose your identity, though you will be absolutely changed by an amazing miracle. Your identity will be preserved, it will be *you*, your salvation completed, your spirit already saved, your body then also perfectly redeemed, the whole person entirely delivered from sin and evil. Oh blessed, oh glorious day! Oh wonderful redemption! Oh ineffable Redeemer!
Great Doctrines of the Bible (3), 238

There are certain things we can say. One is that the Scripture teaches very clearly that our identity will be preserved. My body will always be recognisable as my body.
Great Doctrines of the Bible (3), 235

The body is not static, it is constantly changing in its elements, in its constitution, yet the body remains a constant. That is what will continue and that is what is asserted by the Scripture when it asserts the resurrection of the body . . . When I have received this resurrection body I shall no longer be subject to disease; I shall no longer be subject to age; I shall no longer be subject to death. My body will never decay, it will never change in any way. This body is corruptible; that body will be incorruptible. What a glorious prospect!
Great Doctrines of the Bible (3), 236

AGE

We do not find such divisions in the early church; they were all one. Age differences did not count; and they should not count now. An old man may be a babe in Christ; and a young person can be spiritually mature.
Christian Unity, 89

There are some advantages in being old, my friends!
Authentic Christianity (2), 151

Many Christians get into trouble along that line as they get older, and their faculties naturally and inevitably begin to fail. They say, 'I am not as I once was, I seem to be losing something, I am slipping.' It may be spiritual; all I am suggesting is that *sometimes* it is purely physical; and we must be very careful, therefore, lest we condemn one another unfairly, and do great harm to one another in our ignorance. It is important that, as Christians, we should realise that we are still in the body, that we carry the body with us, and that the interactions of these various parts are very intimate and very important.
The Christian Warfare, 210

The words of an old man are always worthy of respect and consideration; they are words that are based upon a long lifetime's experience.
Life in God (5), 193

Old Age tests us, for when we enter that stage our natural powers are failing. So many of us in this life and world live on our own activity. That is why many a man dies suddenly after he has retired from business; and often a wise doctor will advise such a man not to give up altogether, but to go two or three times a week to his business . . . That also applies in connection with Christian work. A man may live on his own preaching instead of on Christ, just as a man can live on his business. But when old age has come he cannot do these things; his powers are failing him, and he cannot appreciate the things of the world. And there he is, left to himself! That is the test. How does one face old age, how are we going to die?
Expository Sermons on 2 Peter, 49–50

Great attention is being paid to young people today, and a considerable amount of attention is being paid to old people; but I am perfectly convinced that the most difficult period of all in life is the middle period, and, if you like, of middle age.
Spiritual Depression, 192

AMBITION

My desire should not primarily be to be happy, but to be holy.
The Christian Soldier, 52

You notice that ambition came into it (the Fall] and ambition taking on a particular form: a desire for a short road to divine knowledge.
Great Doctrines of the Bible (1), 183

ANGELS

There is a very clear and specific teaching that there are indeed such beings as guardian angels.
The Life of Joy, 26

I fear that we neglect the ministry of angels; we do not think sufficiently about it. But whether we realise it or not, there are angels who are looking after us; they are round and about us. We do not see them, but that does not matter. We do not see the most important things; we only see the things that are visible. But we are surrounded by angels; and they are appointed to look after us and to minister to us – guardian angels. I do not pretend to understand it all; I know no more than the Bible tells me – but I do know this, that His servants, the angels, are my servants. They are surrounding us all, they are looking after us, and they are manipulating things for us in a way we cannot understand. And I further know that when we come to die they will carry us to our appointed place.
Life in the Spirit in Marriage Home and Work, 205–06

We have also the great comfort, taught in the parable of Dives and Lazarus in Luke 16, of knowing that we shall be 'carried by angels into Abraham's bosom' when we die. Because we are Christians the angels of God are at our service; they are 'ministering spirits' sent forth by God to serve and to minister to you and to me. Though we are unconscious of this they are exercising this ministry. We are surrounded by them, they are unseen, but they are there, and they minister to us because we belong to Christ, because we are married to Him and are thereby 'the heirs of salvation'. We sadly neglect and forget the service of the angels; but if ever you feel lonely and bereft, and feel that you do not know what to do nor where to turn, remind yourself that your heavenly Father, the Father of the Lord Jesus Christ, has sent angels to minister to you as He did to Him in the hours of His greatest crises and His greatest agony.
The Law: Its Functions and Limits, 59

The suggestion is [it has been put forward many times in the history of the Church] that our Lord, when He returned to heaven and in the fullness of this redemption, made Himself the head of all the angelic host.
Great Doctrines of the Bible (1), 364

Whether you and I realise it or not, the angels are doing this for us. It may be that we shall go through this life without seeing an angel in any form, but whether we see them or not, we can be absolutely certain that this is the work which they are doing for us. They are caring for us, they are watching over us, they are protecting us, and sheltering us. They often deliver us, and they are used by God to help us in this way.
Great Doctrines of the Bible (1), 114

The cherubim are undoubtedly the highest form of being, and [that] their special function is to worship God, and to present to Him the worship of the entire universe.
Great Doctrines of the Bible (1), 119

In other words, the Scripture teaches that when Christians meet together, and when they gather together in prayer, then the angels of God are present, and the women are to be covered when they take part in public prayer because of the presence of the angels.
Great Doctrines of the Bible (1), 110

fallen angels (Devil, Demons)
. . . [T]hose whom the Bible refers to as demons or as devils, or as unclean spirits, are undoubtedly fallen angels, these angels that sinned against God with the devil, the angels that followed him, that 'kept not their first estate' (Jude 6). These are the devil's angels, his emissaries, his agents, the instruments that he uses to do his work. These are the principalities and powers and 'rulers of the darkness of this world', the 'spiritual wickedness in high places' (Eph. 6:12). All these are fallen angels. They must be – what else can they be? The devil cannot create; he cannot produce such followers; he cannot produce his own angels, because he is only a created being himself. No. The demons or the devils are those who followed this 'anointed cherub' and have been cast out by God.
Great Doctrines of the Bible (1), 125

ANIMALS (Consummation)
The animal at its best is essentially different from the lowest type of man; he belongs to a different order, to a different realm altogether. Man is unique, he is made in the image of God. So though the animals are wonderful there was not one that could make a companion for man, the companion that man needs.
Life in the Spirit in Marriage Home and Work, 189–90

While possessing many of the same instincts and powers as the animal, man was to differ by having the high power of reason and therefore of discipline and control. To him alone was given the power of being able to think, to regard even himself objectively and to ponder and in a measure to understand the whole meaning of life, being and existence.
Old Testament Evangelistic Sermons, 246–47

Sin is not possible for an animal.
Great Doctrines of the Bible (1), 184

From the start the Bible emphasises – and we can substantiate and corroborate what it teaches – that these are peculiar qualitative differences between man and all types of animals, even the highest type.
Great Doctrines of the Bible (1), 156

[Adam] was obviously intelligent and able to understand. God brought the animals to him and asked him to name them, and it was Adam who gave the names to all these animals and creatures (Gen. 2:19-20). He could differentiate and distinguish; he knew the right type and kind of name to give, and they are names that carry meanings and tell us something about the character of each animal. So he was obviously gifted with a high intelligence.
Great Doctrines of the Bible (1), 175–76

We are told that you and I who are children of God are destined to dwell in that kind of world, under those new heavens and on this new earth, while the animals that have been such bitter enemies, attacking and destroying and eating one another, will now eat and lie down peaceably together, and a little child shall lead them.
The Final Perseverance of the Saints, 80

The animals were created, the flowers and the plants and so on, but men and women were made in the image of God; they are like God.
Love so Amazing, 212

As you look out upon the whole of the world of nature what you see is a great confusion: depravity, animals killing one another, ferocity, living on one another, cruelty! Do you not see it everywhere? Watch the insects, beetles, spiders and others, watch this tremendous activity. Here it is, 'Nature red in tooth and claw'! Do you think that this is how God made our world? Of course not! That is what it has become; that is why it needs to be reconciled. It is not man and woman alone who went wrong; but because they have gone wrong, everything else has too. This is the result of the fall as you see it in brute creation. You see it everywhere, animate and inanimate, right through the whole cosmos. The fall has led to this further collapse and this terrible calamity.
Love so Amazing, 272

ANNIHILATIONISM (Hell)
If we adopt the modern philosophy and attitude of not believing in hell and in eternal punishment, and believe that, because God is love, everybody will somehow be all right in the end, if we believe that after death our souls are annihilated and go out of existence after a limited infliction of punishment which mercifully comes to an end, and that the whole thing is conditional – well, we must see that, as we detract in that way from our belief in the punishment of sin, so we are detracting from the good news of the gospel.
The Gospel of God, 59

ANOINTING (Assurance, Baptism in the Spirit)
We are told that we receive 'an anointing of the Holy One'; and this anointing of the Spirit is a very practical matter, and particularly so in this context of the battle of the Christian life . . . This 'anointing' always leads to power. It is a particular aspect of the work of the Holy Spirit. The Holy Spirit is a seal. He is also

'the earnest of our inheritance'; but there is an anointing aspect of the work of the Holy Spirit in the Christian believer by which he is enabled to do various things.
The Christian Soldier, 115

ANTICHRIST
We can, I think, be certain that the Antichrist will ultimately be concentrated in one person, who will have terrible power, and will be able to work miracles and do wonders in a way that will almost deceive the elect themselves.
Great Doctrines of the Bible (3), 118

John says there were many antichrists, and yet the teaching is clear that there is going to be an ultimate antichrist, one person, a person having terrible power, able to work miracles and do such wonders that he almost deceives the elect themselves.
Walking with God, 101

ANTINOMIANISM
True preaching of the gospel in its fullness always exposes itself to the charge of antinomianism.
The Sons of God, 228

Means that as long as you are a Christian and claim you know God in Christ, it is immaterial what you do, because you do not sin, it is the flesh or body that sins.
Fellowship with God, 118

ANXIETY
If you want to seek anything, if you want to be anxious about anything, be anxious about your spiritual condition, your nearness to God and your relationship to Him. If you put that first, worry will go; that is the result.
Studies in the Sermon on Mount (2), 145

APOLOGETICS
I am not sure that apologetics has not been the curse of evangelical Christianity in the last twenty to thirty years.
Authority, 14

APOSTASY
We must never be surprised if the church is to be found in a state of apostasy . . . If the nation of Israel could be apostate, then it is possible for anybody to be apostate. The fact that the church is the church does not prove that she is always right. The visible people of God can go all wrong . . . The church must always put herself under the judgement of the word of God.
God's Sovereign Purpose, 325

APOSTLES
An Apostle is one chosen and sent with a special mission as the fully authorised representative of the sender.
The Gospel of God, 38

It follows, then, that once you have the New Testament Scriptures – the New Testament Canon – you have here the authoritative teaching, and henceforth, of course, an apostle is not necessary.
The Gospel of God, 48

It [the Bible] cannot be added to because there cannot be any successors to the Apostles. By definition they can have no successors. We assert this as against Roman Catholicism and Anglo Catholicism, and all who teach the spurious doctrine of 'apostolic succession'. If an Apostle is a man who must have seen the risen Lord and who is therefore able to witness to the fact of the resurrection, there cannot be successors.
Authority, 59

The man who is in the direct line from the Apostles is the man who preaches the doctrine of the Apostles, the man who has the spirit of the Apostles in him.
God's Sovereign Purpose, 324

John is sometimes described as the Apostle of love. People say that Paul is the Apostle of faith, John the Apostle of love, and Peter the Apostle of hope; but I dislike these comparisons, because nothing on the subject of love has ever been written to compare with Paul's 1 Corinthians 13.
The Love of God, 38

The Apostles and prophets are a class apart, and therefore for people to claim that they are as uniquely and directly and divinely inspired as the Apostles and prophets is to contradict the plain teaching of Scripture.
Walking with God, 124

ARMINIANISM (Calvinism)
Is there not a real danger of our becoming guilty of a very subtle form of Arminianism if we maintain that correct doctrine and understanding are essential to our being used by the Spirit of God . . . I said that John Wesley was to me the greatest proof of Calvinism. Why? Because in spite of his faulty thinking he was greatly used of God to preach the gospel and to convert souls! That is the ultimate proof of Calvinism, predestination and election.
The Puritans, 297

ASSURANCE (Baptism in the Spirit)
Lloyd-Jones taught that there are three levels of assurance; he was aware that his view departed from the general Reformed position. He works this through particularly in Joy Unspeakable and his series on 1 John.

With Paul, I am persuaded. Are you?
The Final Perseverance of the Saints, 457

So let us be clear about this. It is no sign of humility, no mark of saintliness, to go into the presence of God doubting whether God is forgiving you.
Great Doctrines of the Bible (1), 355

I sometimes think there is no better proof of a knowledge of God and knowledge of the love of God than that. You know, if you hate sin, you are like God, for God hates it and abominates it.
The Love of God, 152

So when people claim to have heard an audible voice we have a right to be suspicious. It is not the Spirit's way of working. But though it is not through an audible voice, the assurance is quite as definite and as unmistakable as an audible voice. Many can testify that 'It was as if I had actually heard it with my very ears.' It is the Spirit speaking to the inner man, to the inner ear.
The Sons of God, 306

In some amazing and astounding manner we know that we are partakers of the divine nature; that the being of God has somehow entered into us. I cannot tell you how; I cannot find it in the dissecting room. It is no use dissecting the body, you will not find it, any more than you will find the soul in dissecting the body, but it is here, it is in us, and we are aware of it. There is a being in us – 'I live; yet not I, but Christ liveth in me' (Gal 2:20) – how, I do not know. We will understand in glory.
Fellowship with God, 81

Assurance is a matter of deduction in the first instance. Apart from the ultimate assurance that is given immediately by the Spirit.
Assurance, 314

If the postmark of the Heavenly Post Office is on you, thank God for it, even though it may appear to be very faint by contrast with other examples you may have come across in the Scriptures or in the literature of the Church throughout the centuries.
The Sons of God, 330;

Barthianism
There is no certainty, no assurance in the Barthian teaching; and it is at this point that we see most clearly that that teaching cannot be regarded as evangelical in the true Protestant and Reformed sense.
The Sons of God, 286

The Barthian school of thought which, in its rejection of the old Liberalism, appears to resemble the evangelical position, is nevertheless radically different,

and particularly for this reason, that it dislikes assurance. It teaches that a Christian can never be sure.
God's Ultimate Purpose, 372

need
We should all be concerned about our assurance of salvation, because if we lack assurance we lack joy, and if we lack joy our life is probably of a poor quality.
The Sons of God, 16

We are meant to have assurance, we are meant to know certainty.
The Christian Warfare, 222

The greatest need at the present time is for Christian people who are assured of their salvation.
Joy Unspeakable, 41

reception
. . . [I]f you want to have assurance of salvation, the place to start is not with your feelings, but with your understanding; then the feelings will follow. The way to get assurance is not to try to feel something, but it is to grasp this objective truth.
Assurance, 274

The common teaching concerning assurance of salvation is that the way to give people assurance is to take them to the Scriptures and then ask them, 'Do you believe this to be the Word of God?' If they say that they do, it is then pointed out to them that the Scripture says, 'He that believeth hath everlasting life', with many other such passages, for example, 'He that believeth shall not come into condemnation'; 'God so loved the world that he gave his only begotten Son, that whosoever believeth in him should not perish, but have everlasting life' (John 3:16). They are then asked, 'Do you believe in Him?' If they do, they are again told: 'The Word says that if you believe in Him you have everlasting life.' So if they believe they must have everlasting life, and that becomes the basis of their assurance of salvation. It is deduced in that way from the Scriptures. But that is not the sealing of the Spirit, though it is quite right as far as it goes.
God's Ultimate Purpose, 262–63

salvation
There is a difference between assurance and full assurance. What I stipulate and postulate is that there is always some assurance. You can be a Christian, you can be justified by faith, and have an assurance of justification without knowing what Paul has in mind when he says, 'The Spirit beareth witness with our spirits that we are the children of God'. You can be a Christian without this full assurance of faith; but you cannot be a Christian without being justified by

faith, and that always means an element of assurance, the ability always to come to a place of rest.
Assurance, 24

sealing
Have you been 'sealed' with the Spirit? I am not asking you if you are a believer in the Lord Jesus Christ; I am not even asking if you have that type of assurance which is based on the first or second grounds; I am asking whether you know anything about the experience of being overpowered in your soul by the direct witness and testimony of the Spirit?
God's Ultimate Purpose, 275

The sealing with the Holy Spirit is primarily a matter of assurance of salvation. It is that which gives us a direct and immediate assurance that we are the children of God, and heirs of God, and that the inheritance is ultimately to be ours.
The Unsearchable Riches of Christ, 157

If you identify the baptism with the Spirit with belief in the Lord Jesus Christ unto salvation, you are automatically saying that there is no difference between saving faith and an assurance of faith, and this is a very serious matter.
Joy Unspeakable, 41

Let me use an illustration that I once heard an old preacher use. He pointed out that two men may arrive at the end of a journey with their clothes wet all through. But if you enquired as to how it happened to the two men, you might find that it happened in a different way in each case. One man might say that he set out on the journey with the sun shining brilliantly. He had not brought an umbrella or a macintosh as there was no suggestion it was going to rain; but halfway along the road, suddenly the clouds gathered and a veritable downpour took place, and in a moment he was soaked through. The other man's story is a very different one. There was a kind of drizzle all the way through the journey, so he could not tell you when he got wet. The first man could, and the second man could not, but what really matters is not *how* the two men got wet, but the fact that they *are* both wet all through. Whether it happened suddenly or imperceptibly is utterly irrelevant.
Life in God, 106

ultimate
There is a third type of assurance which is the highest, the most absolute and the most glorious, and which differs essentially from the other two. How? Like this. You notice, in the first two types of assurance, what we are doing is to draw distinctions, as we read the Scriptures perhaps. We arrive at the assurance by a process of reading, understanding, self examination or self-analysis . . . But the glory of this third and highest form of assurance is that it is neither anything that we do, nor any deduction that we draw, but an assurance that is given to us by the blessed Spirit Himself.
Joy Unspeakable, 101

This is something beyond believing, beyond trusting, even beyond being sealed with the Spirit. The difference is that in the sealing with the Spirit we are given to know that we are His; the Holy Spirit 'bears witness with our spirit that we are the children of God' (Romans 8:16). It is God saying to us, 'Thou art my son, my child'. Is there anything beyond that? Yes; to know God Himself! That is the summit, the *'summum bonum'*. It is wonderful to know that I belong to God; it is an infinitely greater privilege and blessing to know God Himself.
God's Ultimate Purpose, 347

This is something beyond understanding, beyond reason, indeed beyond comprehension, and yet it is absolute certainty, it is light, knowledge, the truth itself, for it is God; Father, Son, and Holy Spirit. Such is the light and the knowledge and the understanding that is given to a man who is baptised with the Holy Spirit of God.
Joy Unspeakable, 121

This is what our Lord is speaking about in the fourteenth chapter of John's gospel, where he says, 'I will manifest myself unto you'. It is His promise concerning what is going to be true when the Holy Ghost comes. He had not yet come in that way, but He tells His unhappy disciples that He is going to come, this 'Other Comforter' whom He is going to send to them. This is what Paul calls elsewhere 'the sealing of the Spirit'. Another expression concerning it is 'the earnest of the Spirit'. It is God through the Holy Spirit giving us this absolute certain knowledge that we are His children, that we are heirs of the glory that is coming. He gives it in the form of an 'earnest', He gives us 'foretastes' of that glory, samples of it, instalments of it in order to make it real to us.
Assurance, 83–84

Over and above your intelligent apprehension of it, over and above your intelligent and intellectual deduction of it, there is a direct and immediate assurance given by the Holy Ghost who sheds abroad the love of God in your heart. You are overwhelmed by it, it is poured out in your heart, and there is no uncertainty any more.
Assurance, 80

ATHEISM
It is the mark of a fool always to draw important deductions from inadequate evidence and anyone who says that 'there is no God' is guilty of that.
Enjoying the Presence of God, 15

ATONEMENT (Cross, Salvation)
We have been giving an exposition of what has always been the traditional Protestant interpretation of the doctrine of the atonement, namely, that it is substitutionary and penal and that our sins were actually punished in our Lord, in His body upon the cross.
Great Doctrines of the Bible (1), 338

If you believe at all in the doctrine of the wrath of God against sin, then obviously sin must be punished. What comes in and that leads to the necessity of substitution.
Great Doctrines of the Bible (1), 332

Ah! you may admire the life of Jesus Christ and feel that His words and works were wonderful; you may shed tears as you think of Him as the babe born in that manger, or as you watch Him at the end forsaken of all and crucified; you may feel a great desire to follow Him and to imitate Him and His life, but you will never feel your whole soul and entire being going out to God in gratitude, wonder and adoration, until you are conscious of the fact that He died for you and until you have experienced His life and power flooding your own, changing it and transforming it, infusing power into it, turning your defeats into victories and liberating you from the power of sin. And that is offered to you tonight in the gospel of Jesus Christ.
Evangelistic Sermons, 201

You and I must realise that; that before we see the love of God in the cross we must see His wrath. The two things are always together and you cannot separate them. It is only as you have some conception of the depth of His wrath that you will understand the depth of His love. It was God Himself who found the way whereby His own wrath could express itself against sin, and yet the sinner not be destroyed but rather justified, because His own Son had borne the punishment.
The Gospel of God, 349

Jesus Christ offered himself. God took him as his own lamb and took our sins and put them upon him, and punished them in him.
Authentic Christianity (2), 182

He [God] made Him [Jesus Chris] sin, *He* imputed the guilt of our sins to Him; *He* put them upon Him; and then *He* tells us that *He* punished them in Him. Any idea or theory of the atonement must always give full weight and significance to the activity of God the Father.
Great Doctrines of the Bible (1), 326–27

God took our trespasses and laid them on his Son. Think of it in terms of ledgers: here is the list of my debts, my trespasses, my transgressions against God. They are taken out of my record and put on to his record. My guilt is transferred to his account and he pays the bill. He bears the punishment.
Authentic Christianity (3), 86

If I understand the New Testament aright, there is no place where we should be more careful to go with our minds fully operating as to the cross on Calvary's hill.
Great Doctrines of the Bible (1), 308

'The Son of God became the Son of Man, that the sons of men might becomes the sons of God,' as John Calvin once said.
God's Ultimate Purpose, 45

Our Lord was conscious of being forsaken of God. His communion with the eternal Father was temporarily broken. He, who had come from the eternal bosom and had been with God from the beginning, for the one and only time in all eternity was not able to see the face of God.
Great Christian Doctrines (1), 329

The only explanation for Christ's death is that it was an absolute necessity. It was the only way in which, if I may so term it, the eternal character of God could be reconciled with itself and could be vindicated, not only before the whole world of men, but before the principalities and powers in heavenly places, indeed, even before the devil and all the citizens of hell. God proclaims His eternal justice and yet can forgive the sins of those who believe in Jesus – a most amazing, a most profound statement.
Great Doctrines of the Bible (1), 331

There is only one answer to the question as to why Christ had to die – the holiness of God! The holiness of God is such that He cannot deal savingly with a sinner unless sin has been dealt with; nothing less than the death of His Son can satisfy the holy demands of this righteous God. So on the Cross He has 'set him forth as a propitiation to declare His righteousness.'
God's Ultimate Purpose, 134

God, being God, cannot just forgive sin.
Saved in Eternity, 99

There is only one doctrine of the atonement, not only in the Bible, but which is true to the biblical revelation concerning the character of God. God's love, let us never forget, is a holy love. I say it to the glory of God – that God cannot forgive anybody by just saying, 'I am going to forgive'. He cannot. There was only one way in which God could forgive: it was by putting our sins on His Son and by punishing them in Him. He poured out the vials of His wrath against sin on His own Son. He has 'set him forth as a propitiation'. God has done it. That is His severity working with his goodness – the two together. It is a holy love; It is a righteous forgiveness.
To God's Glory, 135

The cross is not something that influences the love of God; no, the love of God produced it. That is the order. Were it not for His love, God would have punished sin in us, and we should all suffer eternal death. Indeed, I do not hesitate to go so far as to say this: nothing anywhere in the Scripture in any way approaches the substitutionary and penal doctrine of the atonement as an exposition and an

explanation of the love of God. Is there anything greater than this, that God should take your sins and mine and put them on His own Son and punish His own Son, not sparing Him anything, causing Him to suffer all that, that you and I might be forgiven? Can you tell me any greater exhibition of the love of God than that?
Great Doctrines of the Bible (1), 335

No one can bear the penalty of man's sin except someone who is man Himself; it is the only way to redeem man.
Great Doctrines of the Bible (1), 282

Thank God for imputation!
Assurance, 212

We must underline in a very special way the substitutionary aspect and element of the atonement, the penal, piacular element.
Knowing the Truth, 349

AUTHORITY (Bible, Inspiration)
So that [human reason] is not the basis of authority, because if it is, then every man is his own authority and if I cannot believe a thing, it is not true. But then if another man can, it is! So anybody can believe anything at all and there is no authority whatsoever – chaos!
Love so Amazing, 41

There are only two ultimate positions; we either regard the Bible as authoritative, or else we trust to human ideas, to what is called philosophy. The whole case of the Bible is that this is the unique revelation of God and that finally I am shut up and shut into this particular revelation.
Fellowship with God, 104

'Christianity is Christ.' It is not a philosophy, indeed not even a religion. It is the good news that 'God hath visited and redeemed his people' and that He has done so by sending His only begotten Son into this world to live, and die, and rise again. Our Lord Jesus Christ is 'the Alpha and Omega, the First and the Last'. In other words, He is the one Authority.
Authority, 29

No man can truly believe in and submit himself to the authority of the Scriptures except as the result of the *'testimonium Spiritus internum'*. It is only as the result of the work, and the illumination of the Holy Spirit within us that we can finally have this assurance about the authority of the Scriptures. This is just to say in other words what the Apostle Paul states so clearly in 1 Corinthians 2;14: 'The natural man receiveth not the things of the Spirit of God: for they are foolishness unto him: neither can he know them, because they are spiritually discerned.'
Authority, 39

[Our Lord] continually says, in effect, 'Check me and what I am saying. Check me by the Old Testament Scriptures. Go through them, search them. Pick them all out'. In addition, He Himself uses them, illustrates His teaching and shows the truth concerning Himself by means of them. The whole of His own teaching is set against the background and the context of the Old Testament Scriptures.
Authority, 52

There is no inherent authority in an office. The authority is the presence of the Holy Spirit in the man.
The Gospel of God, 236

The chaos in the world is due to the fact that people in every realm of life have lost all respect for authority, whether it be between nations or between parts of nations, whether it be in industry, whether it be in the home, whether it be in the schools, or anywhere else. The loss of authority! And in my view it all really starts in the home and in the married relationship. That is why I venture to query whether a statesman whose own marriage has broken down really has a right to speak about the world's problems. If he fails in the sphere where he is most competent, what right has he to speak in others? He ought to retire out of public life.
Life in the Spirit in Marriage Home and Work, 111

– B –

BACKSLIDER

Surprising things can happen to a Christian, and a Christian can do surprising things. But the doctrine concerning the backslider teaches that, though he may fall, he is not utterly cast down. In other words, he always comes back; he does not remain in sin. He is a man who has what is called 'a temporary fall' . . . It is only of the true Christian that the term 'backslider' can be used.
Faith on Trial, 91

When we sin we should not feel that we are back under the wrath of God, but that we have hurt a loving Father. What a difference! 'There is no condemnation', but we have wounded and hurt a loving Father. So we go back to Him as the prodigal son did, and find that all is well.
The Final Perseverance of the Saints, 100

I venture to assert that even falling into sin, or backsliding, because of our relationship to God can work for our ultimate good, and help to produce our final glorification.
The Final Perseverance of the Saints, 171

Christians do not spend their lives walking in and out of the kingdom of God; we are all by nature in the kingdom of darkness, and by becoming Christians we are translated, put into, the kingdom of God. Let me say this, and it is a daring statement in a sense, yet it is scriptural: if I fall into sin I am still in the kingdom of God. I am not walking in darkness because I have sinned; I am still in the realm of light and in the kingdom of God even though I have sinned – the shed blood of Jesus Christ put me there. And it is this shed blood of Christ that still delivers me from the guilt of my sins in the kingdom of God.
Fellowship with God, 142

. . . [W]e are married to the Lord Jesus Christ. For how long am I married to Him? Is it only until I fall into sin? Does my falling into sin mean I drop out of the relationship and have to be married again to Him, and then sin and drop out and be married again and again? What utter nonsense! No, let us realise that the relationship is legal and lasting. I am married to Him, and I remain married to Him until one or the other of us dies; but neither the One or the other of us can ever die! Says the Apostle in chapter 6:9: 'Knowing that Christ being

raised from the dead dieth no more; death hath no more dominion over Him.'
(Romans) He cannot die again. There is my Husband, He cannot die, and I am
joined to Him.
The Law: Its Functions and Limits, 53

BALANCE
Oh, there is nothing so tragic as this foolish lack of balance. The history of the
Church, the history of revivals, shows so clearly that when people go off at tan-
gents, as it were, and are monopolised by one thing, the Spirit is always
quenched and the work is always hindered.
Revival, 61

We are all creatures of extremes. It is most difficult to avoid going either to one
extreme or the other. It always seems to be easier to be at an extreme, does it
not?
Great Doctrines of the Bible (2), 244

For myself, as long as I am charged by certain people with being nothing but a
Pentecostalist and on the other hand charged by others with being an intellectual, a man who is always preaching doctrine, as long as the two criticisms come, I
am very happy. But if one or the other of the two criticisms should ever cease,
then, I say, is the time to be careful and to begin to examine the very foundations.
The Love of God, 18

BAPTISM in the Spirit (Assurance)
Dr. Lloyd-Jones believed that the Baptism of the Spirit is a distinct experience from con-
version. One can be filled with the Spirit without being baptised in the Spirit; indeed,
being filled with the Spirit is vital to salvation. He considered the terms 'sealing',
'earnest' and 'anointing' as synonyms. As worked out in my book The Sacred
Anointing *he traced unction in the act of preaching back to the Baptism in the Spirit.*
It is also vital in the area of assurance.

Got it all? Well, if you have 'got it all' I simply ask in the name of God, why are
you as you are? If you have got it all, why are you so unlike the New Testament
Christians? Got it all! Got it at your conversion! Well, where is it, I ask?
Westminster Record, September 1964

The earnest of the Spirit gives me an instalment of my inheritance, a first down-
payment of what I am later to receive in its fullness. If you buy a house, for
example, and you do not have sufficient money to pay for it, you pay the seller
an agreed lesser amount saying, 'I give you this as an earnest that I will pay the
remainder; I pay this on account, as a deposit'. That is to say, you pay him an
earnest. It can also be thought of as a foretaste, or the first-fruits of a harvest, a
portion of a fullness that is to come. The 'sealing' and the 'earnest' are both concerned with sonship, and especially with 'heirship'; the earnest being that

which is given to us 'until [the time of] the redemption of the purchased possession' (Ephesians 1:14).
The Sons of God, 301

It is an occasion in which the reality of divine things becomes plain, in a way that it has never been before and, in a sense, never is again, so that they can look back to it; it stands out in all its glory. And, therefore, this is something which we should seek. But so many, because of their fear of the excesses, have never even sought it and have felt that it is wrong and dangerous to seek it and thereby they have put themselves out of the category that includes these great men of God whose experiences we have just been considering.
Great Doctrines of the Bible (2), 251

Seek not an experience, but seek Him, seek to know Him, seek to realise His presence, seek to love Him, Seek to die to yourself and everything else, that you may live entirely in Him and for Him and give yourself entirely to Him. If He is at the centre, you will be safe. But if you are simply seeking an experience; if you are looking for thrills and excitement, then you are opening the door to the counterfeit – and probably you will receive it.
Great Doctrines of the Bible (2), 253

God then as we are told here, provides this amazing chariot for us which takes us to the very heavens and gives us this glorious experience of the reality of the Son of God, the manifestation of Christ according to His promise, which moves us and grips us to the depths of our being and we are lost in a sense of wonder, love and praise.
Great Doctrines of the Bible (2), 254

You cannot take the baptism of the Spirit by faith. You cannot take sanctification by faith. It is a sheer impossibility because of this fundamental personal relationship . . . You can bombard the door, but he alone can open it.
Spiritual Blessing, 200

affects
Truths which he has believed before and which he has accepted and relied on, suddenly become luminous and plain with a clarity which is heavenly and divine. In love, even human love, there is always an element which cannot be put into words. It is much more so with this, because it is an experience of God's love, and in turn of our love going out to Him! We love Him because He first loved us, and there is something almost inexpressible about the experience. Yet it is the most real thing that can ever happen to us.
God's Ultimate Purpose, 289

This is what happens when a man is baptised with the Holy Spirit – this immediacy. This is not reason, or faith; but action taking place upon us and to us. It

is a manifestation, God – Father, Son, and Holy Spirit – making themselves real to us and living in our very experiences.
Joy Unspeakable, 97

Men and women can be advocates of these things without the Holy Spirit. I mean that they can have an understanding of the doctrine; they can receive the truth, and can present it, argue for it and defend it. Yes, they are acting as advocates. But primarily, as Christians, we are called upon to be witnesses, to be witnesses of the Lord Jesus Christ as the Son of God and as the Saviour of the world, as our own Saviour, as the Saviour of all who put their faith and trust in Him. And it is only the Holy Spirit who can enable us to do that. You can address people and act as advocates for the truth but you will not convince anybody. If, however, you are filled with the Spirit and are witnessing to the truth which is true in your life, by the power of the Spirit, that is made efficacious. So this filling is essential to all our Christian service.
Great Doctrines of the Bible (2), 242

Now this is to me a most remarkable thing. Would you know the Christian truth, would you know the Christian doctrine? Would you have a firm grasp and understanding of God's great and glorious purpose? The highway to that is the baptism with the Holy Spirit.
Joy Unspeakable, 119

distinction
You cannot be 'baptised with the Spirit' without being 'filled with the Spirit'; but you can be 'filled with the Spirit', and full of the Spirit, without experiencing 'the baptism with the Spirit'. Baptism is a distinct, concrete, special experience; whereas this, as I am going to show, is meant to be a continuous state, a condition in which one should always be.
Life in the Spirit in Marriage Home and Work, 42

I deduce that this [being 'filled with the Spirit'] is not something that happens to us; this is something which we control, and which we determine. As a man decides and controls whether he is going to be filled with wine or not, so it is he himself who controls and decides whether he is going to be controlled by the Spirit or not. He is therefore given a commandment, an injunction, an exhortation. We must therefore cease to think of it [being 'filled with the Spirit'] in terms of 'having an experience'.
Life in the Spirit in Marriage Home and Work, 49

When you are baptised with the Spirit you are 'filled' with the Spirit; but you can be 'filled with the Spirit' in the sense of Ephesians 5:18 without being baptised by the Spirit. We ourselves are responsible for being filled with the Spirit, and the Apostle tells us in the passage in Ephesians how to do that. But we are not responsible for the baptism with the Spirit which is something that we receive in a passive manner; it is given to us.
The Sons of God, 273

It is most important that we should remind ourselves again that the 'Spirit of adoption' is not essential to salvation.
The Sons of God, 246

If you take what happened to our Lord at His baptism, and which can be described as His 'sealing' with the Spirit, as your standard or norm, there is only one possible conclusion, namely, that this is something that is given to, and done to, those who are already believers and regenerate, and who already have the Holy Spirit in them.
The Sons of God, 326

A man may be a Christian, a good one too, 'growing in grace and in the knowledge of the Lord', a man may be progressing in sanctification and still not know the baptism with the Holy Spirit.
Joy Unspeakable, 140

. . . [S]ealing does not immediately and automatically happen at believing – I would not be understood as saying that there must always be a long interval between the two. It may be a very short interval, so short as to suggest that the believing and the sealing are simultaneous; but there is always an interval. Believing first, then sealing. It is only believers who are sealed; and you can be a believer without being sealed; the two things are not identical. It is believing that makes us children of God, that joins us to Christ; it is the sealing with the Holy Ghost that authenticates that fact. Sealing does not make us Christians, but it authenticates the fact, as a seal always does.
God's Ultimate Purpose, 253–54

early church
I must then ask the question – was this [the event at Pentecost] therefore something once and for all? The answer is that it was once and for all in one sense only, in that it was the first time it ever happened; but it is not once and for all in any other sense, as I am now going to try to prove to you. When something happens for the first time – well, you cannot go on repeating the first time, but you can repeat what happened on that first time.
Joy Unspeakable, 433

It seems to me that the vast majority of the early Christians had received the baptism with the Holy Spirit. So when the Apostles come to write their letters to them they can assume that, they can act on that assumption and supposition.
Joy Unspeakable, 341

. . . [M]ost of the early Christians, if not all, had full assurance of salvation, the reason being that in New Testament times the Holy Spirit had been poured forth in unusual profusion.
The Sons of God, 248

experience
You cannot be 'baptised' or 'filled' with the Spirit without knowing it. It is the greatest experience one can ever know.
The Sons of God, 271

Not conscious! The Apostles were as men who appeared to be filled with new wine; they were in a state of ecstasy. They were rejoicing, they were praising God; they were moved, their hearts were ravished; they experienced things which they had never felt or known before. They were transformed, and were so different that you can scarcely recognise them as the same Peter and James and John and the rest as they once were. Not experimental! Nothing can be more experimental; it is the height of Christian experience.
God's Ultimate Purpose, 269–70

. . . [T]hough the intensity or the degree may vary considerably, the experience itself is always unmistakable. It is always distinct, and different from everything else we have known.
The Sons of God, 328

. . . John Flavel says that during the greater part of a day he did not know where he was; he was so enjoying a visitation of God that he even forgot his wife and children in his ecstasy. Is it therefore correct to say that we have not been sealed with the Spirit until we have had some such overwhelming experience?
God's Ultimate Purpose, 286

It is a wonderful thing to tell someone whom you love that you love him or her, but still more wonderful is the experience of being told by the other that he or she loves you. That is the greatest desire and yearning of every lover, and it is the exact difference here. In Romans 8:15 we tell God that we love Him. We have 'the Spirit of adoption, whereby we cry, Abba, Father', the child's cry of love to the Father. Ah, but here it is God, through the Spirit, telling us that He loves us, and doing so in a most unmistakable manner. It is personal and secret.
The Sons of God, 302

Old Testament
Sometimes Christian people speak very wrongly of the kind of spiritual experience that was enjoyed by the Old Testament saints. There is a tendency to say that we have this experience but that they had nothing. You would be very surprised to hear that the psalmist is further on spiritually than you are! The type and kind of blessing is exactly the same in both Testaments. Notice that I am referring to the *type* and *kind* of blessing; there is a difference . . . But the same blessing is in the Old Testament; it is a spiritual blessing and Psalm 51 alone is proof.
Great Doctrines of the Bible (1), 236

reception
Unless we are satisfied with regard to the doctrine we are never likely to experience it.
God's Ultimate Purpose, 255

When we are sealed with the Holy Spirit of God we shall know it. It is not to be accepted by faith, apart from feelings. You must go on asking for it until you have it, until you know that you have it . . . But when God blesses the soul, the soul *knows* it.
God's Ultimate Purpose, 295

It is a false teaching that urges people to let themselves go. If you do that, you are letting yourself go to a riot of the imagination and of the feelings, you are letting yourself go to evil spirits and powers that are around about you and ever ready to possess you and to use you and to fool you.
Authentic Christianity (2), 209

Faint heart never won fair lady. Of course not! And faint heart has never won this blessing of the baptism with the Holy Spirit. If you really want something, you are persistent and you cannot be put off. You keep on and on and on until you almost make a nuisance of yourself. I say, with reverence, we must become like that in the presence of God if we really understand this and truly desire it. Keep on! Be persistent! Be importunate! 'I will not let thee go!'
Joy Unspeakable, 383

When the Holy Spirit is operating you do not need to work it up, you do not need to organise it; he does it all. It is the vision of him, the knowledge of him, this immediacy, and this is the inevitable result – a joy which is unspeakable and full of glory, though we do not see him.
Joy Unspeakable, 116

If you really desire the blessing, prove that you do so by living a life of obedience.
The Sons of God, 282

The Holy Spirit is a Person! He is God, the third Person in the blessed Holy Trinity; and we Christians cannot take Him just as we breathe in the air, whenever we like, and whenever we choose. What we are taught is that we have to be subject to the Spirit, we have to surrender to the Spirit, and we have to be very careful not to 'grieve' or to 'quench' the Spirit. But there is never any suggestion anywhere in Scripture that we can take Him in this simple and almost casual manner.
The Sons of God, 253

I am not saying that a man cannot have the gift of being able to give the gift to others. I am not excluding it, but I am saying that we must be careful.
Joy Unspeakable, 349

sanctification

Imagine a farmer or a gardener sowing seed in the ground. He digs or ploughs and harrows, and then puts in the seed. He covers it over and flattens it out. Then he waits for some sign of growth. But weeks pass and nothing happens. There may be a particularly dry spell of weather. At long last the seed begins to sprout and just appears above the ground. Then growth seems to stop at that stage and there seems to be no development, so the man begins to wonder whether there is life or not. Then suddenly there comes a wonderful burst of sunshine and a good shower of rain. The man returns and looks at the plot which had seemed to be quite dead in the morning and finds that by evening all is green. He can almost see the shoots growing. What is the explanation? It is that life was there all along, but it was feeble. But there was life in the seed, though it did not seem to be much in evidence. But the sunshine comes and the shower comes, and the life springs up immediately. More happens in one afternoon than had happened in the previous weeks. That is a picture of the relationship. The sunshine and the rain are the Spirit 'bearing witness with our spirits', 'the love of God shed abroad in our hearts'. And some men have testified that they received more in one hour of this experience than they had felt and learned in fifty years. The effect of the rain and the sunshine on the seed in the ground is to stimulate, to draw out the life that is present in the seed. It is precisely the same in the Christian life. The moment we are born again the process of sanctification has started, the seed of life and of holiness is implanted in us, and nothing so causes that seed of life to spring up, to grow and to develop and to show itself in a manner that amazes everyone, as this baptism or sealing with the Spirit, this testimony that the Spirit bears with our spirits. Such, then, is the relationship between the testimony of the Spirit and our sanctification. It is not direct, it is not immediate: it is indirect. It is the greatest stimulus to sanctification, but it is not sanctification itself.

The Sons of God, 383

What then is the true relationship between this experience of the 'sealing of the Spirit', or 'baptism of the Spirit', or 'the testimony of the Spirit with our spirit', and sanctification? My answer is that it has no direct association or relationship; but it has a very important indirect relationship.

The Sons of God, 381

terminology

There are many different particular usages with regard to this word 'baptism', and the statement in 1 Corinthians 12:13 is but one of them. We are all placed into the realm of Christ by the Holy Spirit and into His body which is the Church. All Christians are in that way made members in particular of the body of Christ. But it does not follow that that is the only possible meaning of the expression 'baptised with the Holy Ghost'.

God's Ultimate Purpose, 268

There is a sense in which I, for my part, am not concerned about the terminology with regard to 'sealing' with the Spirit or 'baptism' with the Spirit. To me it is very regrettable that many are so much concerned about the terminology, and especially about the word 'baptism', that they fail to face the real question. That question is, Do we know that we have been sealed with the Holy Spirit? . . . Terminology has its place and it is important that we should have ideas clearly in our minds; but it is the experience itself that matters most.
God's Ultimate Purpose, 280

There is nothing, I am convinced, that so 'quenches' the Spirit as the teaching which identifies the baptism of the Holy Ghost with regeneration. But it is a very commonly held teaching today, indeed it has been the popular view for many years.
The Christian Warfare, 280

I am suggesting . . . that the 'baptism with the Spirit' is the same as the 'sealing with the Spirit'.
God's Ultimate Purpose, 264

BAPTISM in Water

Dr Lloyd-Jones was neither a Baptist nor a paedo-baptist by practice. He sprinkled water on believers after their profession of salvation. Surprisingly this sacrament did not feature in his ministry.[9]

However, we surely cannot arrive at any finality and, therefore, the only view, it seems to me, which one is justified in taking is that one should allow both methods. The mode of baptism is not the vital thing. It is the thing signified that matters; it is the sealing that counts, and, for myself, I would be prepared to immerse or to sprinkle a believer. If there is an adequate supply of water such as a river, I think the best method is to stand in the water and to baptise in that way. I would not refuse even to immerse completely. What I am certain of is that to say that complete immersion is absolutely essential is not only to go beyond the Scriptures, but is to verge upon heresy, if not to be actually heretical. It is to attach significance to the mode, a view which can never be substantiated from the Scriptures, and certainly it is out of line with the practice that was consistent throughout the Old Testament.
Great Doctrines of the Bible (3), 45

Clearly it [water baptism] represents our being washed from the guilt of sin. There we were, sinners, and in sin, under the wrath of God. We have been delivered from that by our faith in the Lord Jesus Christ, by what He has done for us. Baptism reminds us of that deliverance. Secondly, it reminds us of the fact that we are being cleansed from the power and pollution of sin. It is a sort of 'washing', a symbolical representation of a process of cleansing. It includes that

[9] Brencher *op cit* 70ff.

idea also. And thirdly, it stands for the whole concept of our being baptised into Christ by the Holy Spirit.
Life in the Spirit in Marriage Home and Work, 159

BEHAVIOUR

To expect Christian behaviour from people who are not Christians betokens a colossal ignorance of sin and its ways as they are revealed in the Bible.
God's Ultimate Purpose, 197

Indeed, I do not hesitate to say that according to the New Testament it is rank heresy to recommend Christian behaviour to people who are not Christian. They are incapable of it! Before people can live the Christian life they must be made a new creation; if they cannot keep the moral law and the Ten Commandments, the ancient law given to the Children of Israel, how can they live according to the Sermon on the Mount? How can they follow Christ? It is ridiculous!
Fellowship with God, 70

If only we realised who we are, then the problem of conduct would almost automatically be solved. This is how parents often deal with this problem in instructing their children. They say to them, 'Now remember who you are.' In other words it is our failure to realise who we are that causes us to stumble on this whole question of moral conduct and behaviour.
Children of God, 24

BELIEF

I once heard a man use a phrase which affected me very deeply at the time, and still does. I am not sure it is not one of the most searching statements I have ever heard. He said that the trouble with many of us Christians is that we believe *on* the Lord Jesus Christ, but that we do not *believe* Him.
Studies in the Sermon on the Mount (2), 128

A belief that does not lead to love is a very doubtful belief.
Joy Unspeakable, 360

It is better to believe nothing than to believe a lie.
Old Testament Evangelistic Sermons, 185

No man can believe the gospel in and of himself; the power of the Spirit alone can lead anyone to belief; without it we are spiritually dead and lost and ruined, and under the wrath of God.
The Unsearchable Riches of Christ, 311

BIBLE

There are other great books, of course – the works of Shakespeare, for example. But put them by the side of this, and though Shakespeare's language and

pictures are marvellous, and though his dramatic intensity is sometimes almost overwhelming, his plays cannot for a moment compare with the sublimity of the Bible's concepts, the way in which it lifts one up and conveys a sense of God.
God's Way Not Ours, 10

It is a very interesting point to notice about *The Screwtape Letters* that C.S. Lewis does not deal with this question of not reading the Word. That is a significant point which reveals a real defect in his teaching. The chief of the evil spirits of whom Lewis writes does not give any instruction to his underlings to prevent the believers from reading the Bible. But this is one of our main weapons.
The Christian Warfare, 152

I have sometimes been almost tempted to say that the Bible itself is a Book for the children of God and for the Church only. The unbeliever as such does not understand it, and he cannot understand it unless and until he is born again. We need to remember our Lord's phrase in the Sermon on the Mount about 'casting pearls before swine'.
The Final Perseverance of the Saints, 202

If you want realism, come to the Bible.
Love so Amazing, 81

Do we realise, I wonder, what a privilege it is that we have these Scriptures, New Testament as well as Old? Do we realise the advantage of having an open Bible? Do we realise the advantage and the privilege of having these living oracles of God?
The Righteous Judgement of God, 171

The promise of Jesus Christ to the disciples when He said the Holy Spirit would guide them into all truth was fulfilled in the writing of the New Testament Scriptures; and the wisdom given to the Church to deliver the canon of Scripture is that which can be traced back to the Apostles and which therefore can be regarded as the Word of God.
The Love of God, 123

The Word of God does not merely give us general comfort. There is nothing I so dislike and abominate as a sentimental way of reading the Scriptures . . . there are many people who read the Scriptures in a purely sentimental manner. They are in trouble and they do not know what to do. They say, 'I read a Psalm – it is so soothing . . .' That is not the way to read the Scriptures. We can never bring too much of our intelligence to our reading of them. They are not merely meant to give general comfort and soothing – follow the argument; let them reason it out with you.
Spiritual Depression 253

approach

It is a good and a wise thing to gather together everything that Scripture has to tell us about the subject. We must never base our doctrine upon one statement only; or to put it in another way, our doctrine must never be so formulated as to be in conflict with any other statement of Scripture or to contradict any other clear and obvious scriptural teaching.
Life in God, 116

Let us remind ourselves that when we are reading the Scriptures we must never take anything for granted; we must always be alert and alive, and always ready to ask questions. How easily one can miss the great blessings found in the very introduction to an Epistle . . . by simply sliding over the terms as if they did not matter!
God's Ultimate Purpose, 138

If ever you come across a difficult passage, then try to find something similar that will help to cast light upon it.
Great Doctrines of the Bible (3), 220

If the apparent meaning, the first meaning that suggests itself to you, is in obvious contradiction to some plain teaching of the Scripture it cannot be the truth and therefore you will have to seek for another explanation.
The Law: Its Functions and Limits, 148

Every bit of intelligence we possess is needed as we read the Scriptures; all our faculties and propensities must be employed. Even that is not enough; we must pray for the illumination and inspiration of the Holy Spirit.
The Unsearchable Riches of Christ, 266

What often amazes me is how anyone can possibly read the Bible without a shudder and without an awful fright, for while it displays God in all his perfection, it most certainly displays man as he is and at his worst.
Old Testament Evangelistic Sermons, 236

How easy it is to listen to a sermon or an address or to read the Scriptures and just pick out what we like and leave the rest. Some people do that even in their regular reading of the Bible; they only read certain parts of the Bible, and they say they find it very comforting, very nice. It never disturbs them, of course, because they want only comfort, that is what they go for, and they get nothing else. They take parts of the Scripture and leave the rest.'
The Righteous Judgement of God, 8–9

My main advice here is: read your Bible systematically. The danger is to read at random, and that means that one tends to be reading only one's favourite passages. In other words one fails to read the whole Bible.
Preaching and Preachers, 171

If you really want to enjoy your reading and studying of the Bible, always ask it questions. So, when Paul says 'Wherefore', you ask, 'Why did he say "wherefore"? What was his purpose and object in doing so here?' You then try to work out the answer.
Assurance, 171

Our reading of the Scriptures is often far too superficial.
Assurance, 160

You do not take up your Bible as you take up Shakespeare or a book of history or politics. It is not a textbook, among textbooks, but God's word. It is a unique word.
Love so Amazing, 94

Here is the only book in the world that tells me the truth about myself.
Love so Amazing, 129

I do not hesitate to say that nothing gives me greater comfort than to know that behind, me, little creature as I am passing through this world of time, there is this doctrine of the eternal decrees of God Himself.
Great Doctrines of the Bible (1), 94

There is no other book which is the voice of God.
Evangelistic Sermons, 25

Here in this Book is a message that would solve every single problem of the human race.
Old Testament Evangelistic Sermons, 130

I have often commended the importance of staying a little time in the porch, as it were, before you come into the building. Paul's vestibules are always very wonderful.
Saving Faith, 223

authority

So we are entirely confined to the Scriptures, and we can add nothing to them. Neither must we take anything from them. We are in no position to pick and choose from them. We cannot say, I believe this and I reject that, I rather like the teaching of Jesus, but I do not believe in miracles; I admire the way in which He died, but I do not believe that He was born of a virgin or that He rose in the body from the grave. The moment you begin to do that you are denying revelation. You are saying that your unaided human intellect is capable of judging revelation, and sifting it and finding what is true and what is false. That is to deny the whole principle of revelation, of the apostolate, and of this unique work of the Holy Spirit.
The Unsearchable Riches of Christ, 37

Lay hold on every word here; do not yield anything, not a single letter of any word.
The Final Perseverance of the Saints, 388

There are no contradictions in the Scripture.
The Final Perseverance of the Saints, 362

Every term is important, every word counts, and therefore we must look at them and examine them carefully.
Assurance, 230

Let us follow our fathers, who always talked about 'The Book'.
Great Doctrines of the Bible (1), 242

benefits
Think of its ennobling and elevating character, of how you feel when you read it – truly as if you had a spiritual bath – how you are searched and examined and made to feel ashamed; and how good and noble desires are stimulated within you, and a longing after a better life.
I am not Ashamed, 47

If we want to be 'strong in the Lord, and in the power of his might', one of the first things we have to do is to read and to take in and to masticate thoroughly this Book.
The Christian Soldier, 77–78

There is no other book which is the voice of God.
Evangelistic Sermons, 25

I have no knowledge of God apart from what the Bible tells me.
Great Doctrines of the Bible (1), 36

Here in this Book is a message that would solve every single problem of the human race.
Old Testament Evangelistic Sermons, 130

difficulties
Eventually, I believe, in glory we shall be given an understanding of some of these things that baffle us now.
Assurance, 251

There are certain final antinomies in the Bible, and as people of faith we must be ready to accept that. When somebody says, 'Oh, but you cannot reconcile those two,' you must be ready to say, 'I cannot. I do not pretend to be able to. I do not know. I believe what I am told in the Scriptures.'
Great Doctrines of the Bible (1), 95

I am not big enough to be an authority; I am too fallible to be an authority. No man is capable of being such an authority. I either submit to the authority of the Scriptures or else I am in a morass where there is no standing.
Assurance, 221–22

. . . [I]nstead of rejecting it because you cannot understand it, get your spirit right, come back to the Word, try to consider it again, pray God to give you understanding and enlightenment. Nothing is more important, as you come to Scripture, than your spirit; it is much more important than your intelligence, or your training.
God's Sovereign Purpose, 147

When a difficult section of Scripture like this confronts us, it is always good to stand back, as it were, and look at it as a whole first. Do not get immersed in the details immediately or you will be confused. Stand back; get hold of the main principle, and having seen that, it will be easier for you to master the various particular statements.
Assurance, 189

In athletics, if you come up against a particularly high hurdle that you have to jump, you take a longer run! If you want to vault over it, you go further back. You do not try to lift yourself up over this very high hurdle from where you are on the ground. The further back you go, the longer your run, and the momentum will carry you over. That is a very valuable principle in the exposition of Scripture and the elucidation of some [of these] problems with which it present us.
Saving Faith, 253

Do not be impatient with yourself when you are studying a difficult passage in Scripture; keep on, hold on, reading or listening; and suddenly you will find that not only do you know much more than you thought you knew, but you will be able to follow and to understand. It is necessary that one should say things like that from time to time, because the devil is ever at hand to say to us, 'This or that is of no use to you, you cannot follow it, leave it to the theologians.' Do not listen to him, but say, 'I belong to the Christian family and I intend to listen and to read until I do understand it.' Do that, and you will not only defeat the enemy, but you will soon find that you have an understanding.
The Law: Its Functions and Limits, 189

As I understand the meaning of the word 'faith', it means that I am content not to understand certain things in this life and in this world.
Assurance, 250

True understanding . . . teaches us . . . that we must be content to 'believe where we cannot prove', to accept where we cannot understand, and to realise that the final synthesis is to be found in God's holy Being and character.
Assurance, 252

I think the New Testament does teach very clearly that our knowledge always follows our belief. It is like a horse drawing a carriage; they are bound together, and they are never separated, but the horse is always in front, and the carriage is being drawn by him. Belief, then knowledge – that is the position.
The Love of God, 147

inspiration

The doctrine of verbal inspiration does not mean a mere mechanical dictation. The personality of the writer is left as it was, and the individual characteristics of style and mode of thought remain, whereas the truth is guaranteed and controlled.
Life in God, 130

To me one of the profoundest arguments for the unique inspiration of the Scriptures is the truth of prophecy, the fulfilment of prophecy.
Knowing the Times, 342

Shake my faith in the facts and you shake my faith in the teaching.
Old Testament Evangelistic Sermons, 255–56

It is God's word, and the terms you will find in the New Testament are always used interchangeably: 'God said'; 'the Spirit saith'; 'the scripture saith'; 'the Holy Ghost saith'.
God's Sovereign Purpose, 166

The Old Testament is primarily a revelation of the holiness of God, and of what God has done as a result of that.
Great Doctrines of the Bible (1), 70

pulpit

I am one of those who like to have a pulpit Bible. It should always be there and it should always be open, to emphasise the fact that the preacher is preaching out of it. I have known men who have just opened the Bible to read the text. They then shut the Bible and put it on one side and go on talking. I think that is wrong from the standpoint of true preaching. We are always to give the impression, and it may be more important than anything we say, that what we are saying comes out of the Bible, and always comes out of it. That is the origin of our message; this is where we have received it
Preaching and Preachers, 75

purpose

But the whole case of the Bible is that God is searching for man, and that he has revealed himself to man, because man by searching cannot find God.
Revival, 39

The first thing the Bible does is to make a man take a serious view of life.
Banner of Truth, Issue 275

The Bible in the first instance is a terrible exposition and a graphic delineation of the effects of sin. That is why it gives all that history in the Old Testament; why, for instance, it shows a man like David, one of its greatest heroes, falling into gross sin, committing adultery and murder. Why does it do that? It is to impress upon us the effects of sin, to teach us that there is something in all of us that can drag us down to that, that we are all by nature false and foul and vile.
Studies in the Sermon on the Mount (2), 307–8

reading

The most difficult thing in the world is to read the Bible with an open mind.
The Heart of the Gospel, 86

I verily believe that the main trouble of most evangelical people today is that they read their Bibles too devotionally, which means, I say, subjectively.
Revival, 96

Do you, when you come to this Book, read it, as a matter of custom or of practice, because you have decided to have a quiet time in the morning and read a few verses before you run off to something else – is that the way you approach it? Or do you say, 'Here God is speaking to me, speaking to man and I am reading because it is God's direct word'.
The Righteous Judgement of God, 171

I would say that all preachers should read through the whole Bible in its entirety at least once every year.
Preaching and Preachers, 172

I regard the Scripture and these great statements in it as being comparable to a great art gallery where there are famous paintings hanging on the walls. Certain people, when they visit such a place, buy a catalogue from the guide at the door, and then holding it in their hands walk round the gallery. They notice that Item number 1 is a painting by Van Dyck, let us say; and they say 'Ah, that is a Van Dyck'. Then they pass on hurriedly to Item number 2, which is perhaps a portrait by Rembrandt. 'Ah,' they say, 'that's a Rembrandt, a famous picture'. Then they move on to further Items in the same way. I grant that that is a possible way of viewing the treasures of an art gallery; and yet I have a feeling that when such a person has gone through every room of the gallery and has said, 'Well, we have "done" the National Gallery, let us now go to the Tate Gallery', the truth is that they have never really seen either of the galleries or their treasures. It is the same in regard to the Scriptures. There are people who walk through this first chapter of this Epistle to the Ephesians in some such manner as I have described, and they feel that they have 'done' it. It is surely better to stand, if necessary, for hours before this chapter which has been given to us by God Himself through His Spirit, and to gaze upon it, and to try to discover its riches both in general and in detail.
God's Ultimate Purpose, 171

I am shut up to this Book; anything that I may say that I believe apart from the Bible will be sheer imagination. That is why this talk about going directly to Christ [without reference to the Scriptures] is, according to the New Testament, the most dangerous position we can be in.
The Love of God, 123

textual criticism
It is important of translation that we should get as accurate a manuscript as is available and, beyond any question, much excellent work has been done in that direction during the past one hundred and fifty years or so. Higher criticism, on the other hand, is the approach to the Bible which says that the Bible is only a book like any other book. It is a view that denies a unique inspiration, and that certainly denies infallibility. It says that the Bible must be approached in its historical setting and from the grammatical standpoint, and that in this way you will find that you must arrive at conclusions different from those of the men who translated the Authorised Version and different from the teaching of the church throughout the long centuries of her history.
God's Sovereign Purposes, 80

As Christians we must recognise textual criticism, which is very different from higher criticism. We do not recognise higher criticism because it is simply the introduction of man's mind and opinion and philosophy, man deciding whether a thing should or should not be there according to whether or not he agrees with it.
Liberty and Conscience, 95

'Are you not suddenly becoming a higher critic?' No, I am not! I am a textual critic, and there is all the difference in the world between these two things. It is right that you should know the relevant texts and their relative value . . .
Saving Faith, 292

unity
The real division of the Bible is this: first, everything you get from Genesis 1:1 to Genesis 3:14; then everything from Genesis 3:15 to the very end of the Bible.
Great Doctrines of the Bible (1), 228

The light of truth is like the natural light; it can be broken up by prism into a large number of subsidiary colours which together form that perfect light. And so it is with the Scriptures, all from God, all in-breathed by the Holy Spirit, all perfectly inspired, and yet differing in these many ways, and thereby reflecting different aspects of the one glorious, ultimate truth. There is a unity, a wholeness about it all.
Fellowship with God, 10

It can never be pointed out too frequently that the great message of the Old Testament, and the great message of the New Testament, are really one.
Old Testament Evangelistic Sermons, 33

This Book is one. We call them Old Testament, and New Testament, but it is only one book. Some people say this is a library of books – that is a terrible fallacy. This is not a library, this is one book, sixty-six sections in it, but only one book, as there is only one theme, only one message.
Old Testament Evangelistic Sermons, 128

That is the glory of our Bible, we have the Old and New Testaments, and may I emphasise again the vital importance of taking *both*. It is quite wrong to take the Old Testament alone, and there is a sense in which it is almost equally wrong to take the New Testament alone. It was the Holy Spirit that guided the early church to interpret the two together.
Saved in Eternity, 143

I feel increasingly that it is very regrettable that the New Testament should ever have been printed alone, because we tend to fall into the serious error of thinking that, because we are Christians, we do not need the Old Testament.
Studies in the Sermon on Mount (1), 191

I mean that there is no contradiction between the New Testament and the Old Testament. This needs to be emphasised at the present time because of the common attitude towards the Old Testament. People say glibly and superficially, 'Ah well, of course, we are not interested any longer in anything said in the Old Testament; we are New Testament people'. Some are foolish enough to say that they do not believe in the God of the Old Testament.
Life in the Spirit in Marriage Home and Work, 89

It is the same God who was operating in the Old Testament as in the New, and one of the great functions of the Old is to be a prophecy and a picture of the New.
God's Sovereign Purpose, 255

versions
Some people seem to be conservative evangelicals simply because they will not examine anything other than the contentions of their own school of thought. The type of person who says that he believes the whole Bible in the Authorized Version 'from cover to cover including all the commas as well.' is certainly one who is unaware of the problems of a translator and is probably equally oblivious of the nature of the writings in the earliest manuscripts and their lack of punctuation marks.
Knowing the Times, 40

We believe in the absolute control of the Spirit over the minds and thinking and style and everything else of the writers. He so controlled them that they were kept from error, but the Holy Spirit did not dictate to them mechanically, otherwise there would be no variation in the style. Incidentally, in connection with

this matter, any translation of the Bible that does away with the variations in the styles of the authors is a bad translation. There are several such at the present time.
The Final Perseverance of the Saints, 159

Incidentally, the *Revised Version* is a bad translation; the *Authorised Version* is altogether superior.
Great Doctrines of the Bible (1), 285

We believe that the Word of God is definitely inspired, but that does not mean that every translation is definitely inspired.
Children of God, 74

I refer to the Revised Standard Version because it is so popular, many people, indeed, give me the impression that they think it is perfect. But let us never forget that the men responsible for that translation are all men who are liberal in their theology, and it is interesting to notice how that comes out even in places like this (Romans 1:10) in their translation.
The Gospel of God, 196

The *New* English Bible – I am increasingly of the opinion that that is a very accurate title!
Banner of Truth, Issue 275

BIRTH
The moment you come into this world you begin to go out of it; your first breath is linked with your last.
The Final Perseverance of the Saints, 51

There is no divine spark in anybody born into this world; all born into this world, because they are children of Adam, are born dead, born dead spiritually.
God's Way of Reconciliation, 105

BLESSING
I believe that Isaac Watts is right when he says that the blessings of salvation exceed the losses consequent on Adam's fall.
Assurance, 232

There is no blessing that ever comes to man from God without coming through the Lord Jesus Christ.
Assurance, 237

'He brought me to the banqueting house . . .' – and that is where he always brings us. It is not to some kind of 'soup kitchen'.
Spiritual Blessing, 98

We are so anxious for blessings, that we forget the one who gives them.
The Life of Joy, 94–95

Many Christian people miss so many blessings in this life because they do not seek God diligently. They do not spend much time in seeking His face. In His courts they drop on their knees to pray, but that is not of necessity seeking the Lord. The Christian is meant to be seeking the face of the Lord daily, constantly. He takes and makes time to do so.
Studies in the Sermon on the Mount (2), 143

The most terrible thing about a man who is in sin, and who is not a Christian, is that he is cut off from the blessings of God. That is much worse than the misery and all the suffering to which sin leads, and all the subjective elements in which people are so interested today.
The New Man, 135

. . . [N]egative mercies and blessings must never be despised.
The Sons of God, 233

When am I to enjoy all these great and rich and wondrous blessings? The answer is, Here and now! Obviously all this comes to us in a progressive manner, for if 'the fullness of the Godhead' came into us suddenly we would crack and break; so it comes in instalments progressively.
God's Ultimate Purpose, 67

BOOKS
I again plead guilty to this. It is possible to live a kind of second-hand spiritual life on books. It happens in the following manner. Feeling dissatisfied and disturbed, and having a consciousness within that our life is not what it should be, and that there is something much greater possible, we begin to read certain books, for example, the biography of a saint or a book which deals with the higher reaches of the Christian life. We greatly enjoy doing so and we are moved. Though we have not had the experience itself of which we are reading, we feel happier and better. We may do this for years without realising that we are living on books instead of living on Christ.
The Unsearchable Riches of Christ, 261

We often say that we have not the time to read – shame on us Christian people! – the truth being that we have not taken the trouble to read and to understand Christian doctrine. But it is essential that we should do so if we really desire to worship God.
God's Ultimate Purpose, 52

I have made it a practice now for many years, whenever I see a book on the doctrine of the Holy Spirit which I have never seen before, to look first at the

synopsis or the table of contents at the beginning, and the index at the end. I look for 'Revival' and I do not find it.
Joy Unspeakable, 430–31

CALVINISM (Election: Sovereignty of God)

Lloyd-Jones was a Calvinist by conviction but rarely described himself as such. Committed to the principles of the Reformation he found no contradiction in attempting to arrest the will of men by pleading and persuading them to become Christians. Any success was to be attributed to the power of the Holy Spirit working on the hearers and the preacher. The gospel thus can be scattered like the seed in the Lord's parable and the news of salvation freely offered.

I recall how a good friend once told me that he was somewhat disappointed, because in my exposition of the second chapter of this Epistle to the Ephesians I had not once mentioned Calvinism as I worked through the chapter. My simple reply to him was, 'The text does not mention that term.' My friend was so much in the grip of a party-spirit that he was becoming doubtful of my position!
Christian Unity, 251

We do not believe in the infallibility of John Calvin any more than we believe in the infallibility of the Pope. And any man who makes John Calvin a pope is denying Scripture and is really not doing a service even to John Calvin.
God's Sovereign Purpose, 18

The more powerful Calvinism is the more likely you are to have a genuine revival and reawakening. It follows of necessity from doctrine . . . I regard the term 'dead Calvinism' as a contradiction in terms. I say that a dead Calvinism is impossible and that if your Calvinism appears to be dead it is not Calvinism.
The Puritans, 210–11

It is important for us to be clear about this matter. There are some who have misunderstood the doctrine of the great reformers and who say . . . that the gospel is only to be offered to those who are chosen and elect. Many in their ignorance regard that as Calvinism. But it is hyper-Calvinism. John Calvin taught that the general call, the offer, should be made to everyone, to all creatures.
The Final Perseverance of the Saints, 188

hyper Calvinism

If you were asked to define the difference between a Calvinist and a hyper-Calvinist, how would you do it? It is a question that is worth asking for this reason; I know

large numbers of people who, when they use the term 'hyper'-Calvinist, generally mean Calvinist. In other words, they do not know what a hyper-Calvinist is. A hyper-Calvinist is one who says that the offer of salvation is only made to the redeemed, and that no preacher of the gospel should preach Christ and offer salvation to all and sundry. A hyper-Calvinist regards anyone who offers, or who proclaims, salvation to all as a dangerous person. For what it is worth, there is a society in London at the moment that has described me as a dangerous Arminian because I preach Christ and offer salvation to all!
Great Doctrines of the Bible (2), 50

The gospel is to be offered to all. That is where what is called 'hyper-Calvinism' is so terribly wrong and unscriptural. The gospel is to be offered to all. It is to be preached to all.
God's Sovereign Purpose, 285

CHANGE
It is a small and narrow mind that is afraid to change; it is a sign of greatness that one is prepared to admit at times that one has been mistaken, and that therefore you have had to change your position.
The Law: Its Functions and Limits, 177

CHARACTER
The blood that is in us will show itself; we cannot help it.
Children of God, 97

CHARISMATIC GIFTS (Healing, Miracles, Prophecy)
The Scriptures never anywhere say that these things were only temporary – never!
Joy Unspeakable, 159

There are people today . . . who say that the baptism with the Spirit is always accompanied by certain particular gifts. It seems to me that the answer of the Scripture is that that is not the case, that you may have a baptism with the Spirit, and a mighty baptism with the Spirit at that, with none of the gifts of tongues, miracles, or various other gifts. No one can dispute the baptism with the Spirit in the case of men like the brothers Wesley, and Whitefield and many others, but none of these things happened in connection with them.
Joy Unspeakable, 180

All these matters are governed by this rule: every gift of the Holy Spirit is under the sovereignty and the Lordship of the Holy Spirit. Therefore, when a man says, 'I am going to be healed miraculously at such and such a time', he is denying scriptural doctrine and he has no right to say it. The Spirit dispenses the gifts; he decides to heal one miraculously, and the other not; some are even allowed to

die. God forbid that we should say that anyone who is not miraculously healed is therefore lacking in faith, or that if a man dies as a result of illness, it is because he is lacking in faith. It is all under the sovereignty of the Lord Jesus Christ; what he decides is that which is to take place.
The Life of Joy, 231

It is interesting to observe that when we read the history of the Christian Church, and especially in terms of this doctrine of the sealing with the Holy Ghost, we find that many of these gifts given at the beginning do not seem to have been given in subsequent ages of the Christian Church. This becomes quite clear as we recall the experiences of the great men to whom we have referred, and who lived in different centuries and places and who were so varied in their natural gifts. Not one of them ever 'spoke with tongues'; but they had other striking gifts. Some had the gift of understanding, others the gift of teaching. Wesley had his amazing gift of 'administration', and organization. But none of them seems to have had the gift of miracles. But they clearly had the sealing with the Spirit.
God's Ultimate Purpose, 281

I am not denying that the Spirit can speak to us directly; but I am saying that that is exceptional. And I go further; I say that anything that we may think is the work of the Spirit within us must always be tested by the Word. The Holy Spirit will never do anything contradictory to His own Word.
Life in the Spirit in Marriage Home and Work, 161

You and I, it is true, do not know much about visions, and I do not say that we should seek them, but there are such things. This old world of ours is a visible, a seen, a material world, but there is another world, a spiritual world. Say what you like against the spiritists, and I do say that they are wrong, but they are right in this respect – they know that there is another realm.
God's Way Not Ours, 8

Take the passage from Ephesians 5:19. What are those 'spiritual songs'? I have no doubt whatsoever but that it means singing under the direct inspiration of the Spirit, exactly as you have it in 1 Corinthians 14:15.
Christian Conduct, 88

CHILDREN (Infants)
What really makes us children of God is that God has put His own life into us. God's nature is love, and he has put His nature into us so that we have the love of God. We cannot be children of God if we are not like God; the child is like the parent, the offspring proclaims the parentage, and God in that way makes us His children.
Children of God, 17

We know that we are children of God when we are deeply aware of sin within. I emphasise that deliberately. It is only the children of God who realise that they have a sinful nature.
Children of God, 28

Don't you believe in the universal Fatherhood of God and the universal brotherhood of man; isn't that something which is taught in Scripture?' The reply is, of course, that there is a sense in which all men and women are children of God, in the sense of being the offspring of God; by which we mean that they have been created by God and derived from Him. But at the same time, Scripture is very careful to differentiate that from those who come into this special relationship of sonship to God as the result of the work of the Lord Jesus Christ.
Children of God, 14

The prodigal son was as much the son of his father as was the elder brother. Behaviour, conduct and appearance – all these things do not determine relationship, thank God!
Children of God, 27

CHOIRS
When the Church is not in revival there is an emphasis upon choirs, and not merely choirs, but paid choirs, and paid quartets and soloists in the choirs. And the congregation just sits, or stands and listens, and the choir even does the singing for them. This is quenching the Spirit. There is no need to say to such people, 'Let everything be done decently and in order.' That is their one concern.
Revival, 77

CHRISTIAN
The definition of the New Testament is that a Christian is a man who possesses eternal life.
Saved in Eternity, 125

The Christian is not a good man. He is a vile wretch who has been saved by the grace of God.
Banner of Truth, Issue 275

There was a time when the designation applied to the Christian was that he was a 'God-fearing' man. I do not think you can ever improve on that.
Studies in the Sermon on the Mount (1), 30

By definition a Christian should be a problem and an enigma to every person who is not a Christian.
Banner of Truth, Issue 275

A Christian is the result of the operation of God, nothing less, nothing else. No man can make himself a Christian; God alone makes Christians.
God's Ultimate Purpose, 395

There is a new race of men!
Assurance, 180

The Christian is the greatest thinker in the universe.
Banner of Truth, Issue 275

The Christian is one who has become a sharer in the life of God.
Fellowship with God, 80

I like to think that Christians, in a sense, are men and women who have a label on them; their destination is booked, they are marked. They are 'of God,' and they are for God. They are going to God; they have a new name written upon them, and it is *God*. They are God's property . . .
Life in God, 172–73

The Christian is sorrowful, but not morose; serious, but not solemn; sober-minded, but not sullen; grave, but never cold or prohibitive; his joy is a holy joy; his happiness a serious happiness.
Banner of Truth, Issue 275

What a happy people Christian people are!
Singing to the Lord, 67

We are aware that we cannot explain ourselves to ourselves except in terms of Christ, and we know when we see it in another; nobody else does, but we know one another. This is one of the most mysterious aspects of Christian life and experience. Those who have the life of God always know one another, and they feel an affinity and an attraction which no one else can understand. Other people may mix with them, they may know people very well, and yet there is something those others have not got. There is a barrier; ours is a life which does not show itself in external affairs, it does not show itself even in the mode and manner of living, but it is a life which recognises itself in the other, and this is a great mystery.
Children of God, 18–19

The Christian . . . is a man who can be certain about the ultimate even when he is most uncertain about the immediate.
The Final Perseverance of the Saints, 177

The Christian should know why he is a Christian.
Spiritual Depression, 61

difference

The difference between the non-Christian and the Christian is the difference between a Christmas tree on which people hang presents, and a living tree that bears fruit. They have to put them on the Christmas tree; it does not and cannot produce anything. But in the case of the growing tree it produces fruit. The fruit is no longer imposed from outside; it is something produced from the life, the sap and the power that are in the living tree.
The Sons of God, 36

A Christian *is* something before he does anything; and we have to *be* Christian before we can act as Christians.
Studies on the Sermon on the Mount (1), 96

A journeyman, a stranger, a pilgrim, obviously keeps in the forefront of his thinking the place to which he is going. He can do certain things *en route*, but if you set out upon a journey, surely your object is to arrive at your destination. You are not interested in travelling as such. Travelling is but a means of bringing you to the goal at which you wish to arrive. It is a perfect picture of the life of the Christian in this world; he is a traveller. It means, therefore, that he does not settle down in this world, and feel anxious to do so, and regret the fact that he has to go out of it. He should be anxious to arrive, and so he constantly reminds himself of the place at which he is going to arrive. He would never have set out for it if he did not desire to get there.
The Christian Soldier, 263

One of the great differences between a Christian and a non-Christian should be that the Christian always puts in an interval between the stimulus and the response. The Christian should always put everything into another context. He should think about it; he should not jump to conclusions; he should work the thing out. In other words, and surely this is very vital and important, one of the hallmarks of the Christian should be the capacity to think, to think logically, clearly and spiritually.
Faith on Trial, 80

local church

True Christians are those who are in vital union with the Church. They are not loosely attached to it; they have not just got their names on the roll. They do not merely recognise a general sort of allegiance once a day or on some special Sunday. No, they are bound by vital bonds of union. In other words, they have life in them; they do not have to force themselves, but rather, they cannot help themselves. It is the difference between a member of the family and a great friend of the family; there is something within that tells them. 'This is my life; I am bound to them; these are my people.'
Walking with God, 112

nominal
You can be good, you can be moral, you can even be religious and still not be a Christian.
Life in God, 167

There are too many languid Christians. Too many of us suffer from what Charles Lamb called 'the mumps and measles of the soul'. We are too sickly, too lethargic; we lounge too much. We must brace ourselves together.
The Christian Soldier, 99

People are not made Christians by believing in God. Christians do believe in God, but that does not make them Christians.
Authentic Christianity (3), 213

It is possible for people to take up certain parts of the teaching of Christ and so praise it. A man like Mahatma Gandhi did that. He was not a Christian, but he praised the teaching of Christ and told people they ought to try to practise it. Merely to praise the teaching of Christ does not make one a Christian.
The Love of God, 28

The miserable Christian is guilty of unbelief.
Assurance, 165

There is nothing in God's universe that is so utterly useless as a merely formal Christian. I mean by that, one would have the name but not the quality of a Christian.
Studies on the Sermon on the Mount (1), 173

[Nominal Christians are] . . . spiritual tadpoles.
The Christian Warfare, 157

privilege
I do feel that this is perhaps the greatest weakness of all in the Christian church, that we fail to realise what we are, or who we are. We spend our time in arguing about the implications of the Christian truth or the application of this, that and the other. But the central thing is to realise what the Christian *is*.
Children of God, 23

Jesus Christ is described as the 'King of kings'. Who are the 'kings' of whom He is the King? You and myself!
Assurance, 265

Oh! the privilege of being a Christian! Oh! the honour of being a Christian! We see great people in the world vying with one another for some mark or title of honour, for some high position, or to be near some notable personality. They are

prepared to pay great sums of money for such honour and to make great sacrifices for it. Yet all Christians, whoever they are, and however unimportant they may be in the world, because they are 'in Christ', are, without exception, sharing our Lord's exalted position in glory.
God's Ultimate Purpose, 442–43

If you are not amazed at yourself you are not a Christian, my friend! All Christians are miracles and they should be amazed at themselves.
God's Sovereign Purpose, 241

No man can truly be a Christian without rejoicing that others also have become Christian.
God's Ultimate Purpose, 313

The greatest need in the world now is for a greater number of Christians, individual Christians. If all nations consisted of individual Christians there would be no need to fear atomic power or anything else
Studies in the Sermon on the Mount (1), 73

There is no such thing as an 'ordinary Christian'.
Life in God, 94

According to the New Testament, it should not be difficult to tell who is a Christian, for Christians are not merely people who are slightly better than others. They are not merely people who have added something to their lives. They belong to a different realm, to a different organisation; they are utterly different. 'We are of God, and the whole world lieth in wickedness.' You cannot imagine a greater contrast.
Life in God, 156

tests
The final proof any man can have of the fact that he is a Christian is that he keeps, and delights in keeping, and goes on keeping, the commandments of the Lord.
Walking with God, 55

It takes a Christian to see the blackness of his own heart.
Banner of Truth, Issue 275

The ultimate test that we should apply to ourselves in order to know whether or not we are Christians. Are you living for this world or are you living for the one to come?
Authentic Christianity (4), 125

A man can easily test whether he is a true Christian or not by asking whether he can say truthfully that his relationship to God is the most important thing in his mind and life.
Old Testament Evangelistic Sermons, 22

Though we are children of God we are not promised an easy time in this world. The Bible does not tell us, as the Cults tell us, that we shall walk in some Elysium and never have any more troubles or problems as long as we live.
Assurance, 350

The life of faith is never a life of ease; faith is always practical.
Studies in the Sermon on the Mount (2), 309

A man finally proclaims whether he is a Christian or not by the view he takes of this world.
Banner of Truth, Issue 275

No man ever became a Christian without stopping to look at himself.
Banner of Truth, Issue 275

One of the best tests of whether we are truly Christian or not is just this: Do I hate my natural self?
Banner of Truth, Issue 275

There is no greater fallacy than to imagine that the moment a man is converted and becomes a Christian, all his problems are solved and all his difficulties vanish. The Christian life is full of difficulties, full of pitfalls and snares. That is why we need the Scriptures.
Studies in the Sermon on the Mount (2), 10

The test of a Christian is not his busyness and his activity, it is his knowledge of God, it is his knowledge of the Lord Jesus Christ. It is not difficult to be busy, but when you try to realise his presence, you will soon discover that you have got to give time to this.
Revival, 86

Be laid aside sick in bed for a week. You will soon know whether you are a Christian or not!
Banner of Truth, Issue 275

Get rid of the notion that Christianity is something magical, that you enter into a magic circle, and never have any more problems. It is not going to be like that, Christ says, but rather a life of trial and trouble and temptation.
The Christian Soldier, 315

Anyone who thinks he can live the Christian life himself is just proclaiming that he is not a Christian.
Banner of Truth, Issue 275

The most vital question to ask about all who claim to be Christian is this: Have they a soul thirst for God? Do they long for this? Is there something about them that tells you that they are always waiting for His next manifestation of Himself? Is their life centred on Him? Can they say with Paul that they forget everything in the past? Do they press forward more and more that they might know Him, and that the knowledge might increase, until eventually beyond death and the grave they may bask eternally in 'the sunshine of His face'?
God's Ultimate Purpose, 349

Let us ask ourselves whether we are as fond of the Name as the Apostle Paul was, whether we like to repeat it as he did. And note, not just 'Jesus', but 'our Lord Jesus Christ'. Do you like repeating it? This is one of the best tests of our whole position as Christians. There is nothing without Him. It is all in Him. He is the Alpha and the Omega, the beginning, the end, the All and in all. Let us give Him the glory – 'our Lord Jesus Christ'.
Assurance, 8

The last people, always, to become Christians are the people who think they are already Christians.
Authentic Christianity (4), 12

value
There is no such thing as an unimportant Christian, an unimportant church member; every one of us counts.
The Christian Warfare, 310–11

The Christian is one who has been 'elected', 'chosen of God' and 'precious' for that reason; God's 'peculiar possession', 'His purchased possession', one of the people whom He has set apart for Himself. If we learn to think of ourselves in these terms, with the dignity and everything else that belongs to the position, it will revolutionise our Christian life and all our thinking.
The Final Perseverance of the Saints, 404

CHRISTIAN SCIENCE (Cults)
Christian Science is rubbish philosophically.
Faith on Trial, 44

Christian Science tells us that there is no such thing as matter, and because that is so, there cannot be such a thing as a disease; and, therefore, when we think we are ill, we are not, and what we have got to do is to tell ourselves that we are not ill because we cannot be. But we know that Mrs. Mary Baker Eddy, at the end of her life, had to take morphia and to use spectacles.
I am not Ashamed, 173

CHRISTIANITY
The world, speaking generally, has never *tried* Christianity. It has talked a lot about it.
Authentic Christianity (1), 1

Christianity is Christ.
Saving Faith, 295

Indeed one of the greatest tragedies and problems in this country is . . . that Christianity is rapidly becoming something that only applies to the middle classes, and the majority of people are right outside and uninterested.
Authentic Christianity (1), 288

If the thing that is offered to you as Christianity is a little thing, it is not Christianity. Christianity is the biggest thing in the universe: it is grand, it is glorious!
The Kingdom of God, 75

There is so much today that passes as gospel which has not got an atom of good news in it! You get the impression from some people that Christianity is nothing but a negative protest. The newspapers give us that impression, do they not? Christians! What are they? They are people who are always protesting against something! And so the world thinks they are a negative, miserable lot of people and it is not interested, and I do not blame them because that is not Christianity; it is a travesty of it. True Christianity is the most positive thing in the world, the most thrilling, the most glorious – it is a gospel!
Love so Amazing, 54

challenge
It is a stern message, it is 'the iron rations for the soul', it is a call to 'be men', to 'run a race', to 'build ourselves up'.
The Christian Soldier, 86

The Christian way is a difficult way of life. It is too glorious to be easy.
Banner of Truth, Issue 275

There is a great deal of so-called Christianity which is quite Christ-less.
Revival, 46

Christianity has nothing to give to anyone who does not believe it.
I am not Ashamed, 73

If you can understand your religion it is a proof it is not Christianity. If you are in control of your religion, it is not Christianity. If you can take it up in a bag on Sunday morning when you go to church and then put it down again, that is not Christianity. Christianity is a miracle. It is a marvel.
Authentic Christianity (1), 31

experiential
. . . [U]nless you feel that you are a Christian there remains a doubt as to whether you are a Christian. Unless something has happened to you experimentally, experientially, unless something has happened to you in the realm of your sensibilities, you are not a Christian.
God's Ultimate Purpose, 73

We are not meant to control our Christianity. Rather our Christianity is meant to control us.
Banner of Truth, Issue 275

There is an important subjective element in the Christian faith and, I repeat, if you and I have no experience – I do not care how slight it is – if we have no experience at all of God dealing with us, then we are not Christians. Christianity is the activity, the power, of God. We must have some experience. It may be inchoate, it may be partial and very small, but it must be there, otherwise our faith is merely some arid, intellectual belief that is of no value.
Authentic Christianity (2), 191

logic
There is nothing – and I delight in this, and therefore often repeat it – there is nothing, once you are inside it, that is so rational, so logical . . . as the Christian faith. But if you are outside it, you do not understand it; there seems to be something mysterious and almost strange about it. Why? Because it is God's work, because it is the direct action of the Eternal. He is no longer acting through the laws of nature.
God's Way of Reconciliation, 468

Non-Christian religions
Christianity is Christ, this One Lord. He makes it. Without Him there is no Christianity. He is essential to it. In this respect it is unlike all other teachings. Other teachings can be divorced from their propagators, for example, Buddhism from Buddha; it would not make any vital difference. But in Christianity our Lord is everything. It all results from this amazing, unique fact of the Incarnation and of what He has done.
Christian Unity, 98–99

Christianity is an exclusive teaching; it is an intolerant teaching. I do not say this because I am intolerant, but because I am concerned about your soul. If you say that Christianity is not exclusive and intolerant, then you must say that one religion is as good as another, and I am here to deny that.
Authentic Christianity (3), 214

uniqueness
The Christian faith does not start with the Lord Jesus Christ, it starts with God the Father.
Authentic Christianity (3), 41

A central message of the New Testament is that there is no possibility of prayer, or of entry into the presence of God, except in and through and by our Lord and Saviour Jesus Christ.
The Unsearchable Riches of Christ, 98

There is an aspect of intolerance in the Christian faith.
Christian Unity, 100

value
The Bible does not hesitate to say that if only every man and woman in the world believed on the Lord Jesus Christ truly, and received from Him the gift He has to give, and practised the life that He indicated, all our other problems would be solved. If only everyone on the earth was a Christian in the New Testament sense, there would be no need to worry about the possibility of war. There would be no more drunkenness, nor would there by any more infidelity and divorce and all the other horrible things that have disgraced the life of mankind in this world of time. If only!
Heart of the Gospel, 55

CHURCH, Local
I do suggest that as you think of these things in the light of the New Testament teaching, forgetting what has happened in history, you must surely come to the conclusion that the local independent conception is the one that is most scriptural.
Great Doctrines of the Bible (3), 23

attendance
What a wonderful place God's house is. Often you will find deliverance by merely coming into it. Many a time have I thanked God for His house. I thank God that He has ordained that His people should meet together in companies, and worship together. The house of God has delivered me from 'the mumps and measles of the soul' a thousand times and more – merely to enter its doors.
Faith on Trial, 39

How much do we think in terms of coming together to meet with God, and to worship him, and to stand before him, and to listen to him? Is there not this appalling danger that we are just content because we have correct beliefs? And we have lost the life, the vital thing, the power, the thing that really makes worship, worship which is in Spirit and truth.
Revival, 72

I fail to understand Christians who stay at home on Sunday nights saying, 'Ah, we need not attend tonight's "service"; we know all about the evangelistic message'. Do you know 'all about' the blood of Christ? Do you feel that you really know so much about it, that you can learn nothing fresh about it? A Christian

who does not receive something in an evangelistic service is, to put it at its very lowest, in a most unhealthy condition. If your heart is not made to beat faster every time you hear about 'the blood of Christ' you are not like the Apostle Paul.
God's Ultimate Purpose, 176

What an utter denial it is of the whole of the New Testament, this foolish suggestion that one service a Sunday is enough, one that takes place at nine o' clock in the morning, to get rid of it, as it were, in order that you can then really go and enjoy yourselves and have real happiness in looking at the television or in rushing to the seaside or in playing golf!
Joy Unspeakable, 110

My experience in the ministry has taught me that those who are least regular in their attendance are the ones who are most troubled by problems and perplexities. There is something in the atmosphere of God's house.
Faith on Trial, 40

Are you able to help others and to teach others? If not, the reason may well be that you only attend a place of worship once on a Sunday or perhaps still more infrequently. You imagine that is enough. But if so, why do you fail, why are you not successful in helping others? You need all the help you can be given, especially 'as you see the day approaching'.
The Christian Soldier, 91

Before that evangelical awakening of two hundred years ago the churches were as empty as they are today, perhaps even more so, and they could not get the people to come to listen to the preaching of the gospel. Why? Because they were interested in other things. 'But', says someone, 'they had not got televisions!' I know. But they greatly enjoyed cock fighting and card playing; they greatly enjoyed gambling and they greatly enjoyed drinking. The world has never been at a loss to find an excuse not to go to Church to listen to the preaching of the gospel.
Revival, 29

[Some] go to God's house, not with the idea of meeting with God, not with the idea of waiting upon him, it never crosses their minds, or enters into their hearts that something may happen in a service. No, we always do this on Sunday morning. It is our custom. It is our habit. It is a right thing to do. But the idea that God may suddenly visit his people, and descend upon them, the whole thrill of being in the presence of God, and sensing his nearness, and his power, never even enters their imaginations. The whole thing is formal, it is this smug contentment. I heard a man once describe such people in this way: he said, 'They give me the impression that as they go to their churches, they are really just paying a morning call on the Almighty.'
Revival, 72

buildings
From an address marking the centenary of Westminster Chapel which is sited about a mile from Westminster Abbey and <u>Westminster Cathedral</u>:

Now to me a 'nonconformist cathedral' is a contradiction in terms, and it is, at the same time an abomination. I am not saying that this building is an abomination to me, but I am saying that the whole concept is. I say that because it is indicative of a carnal spirit coming into Nonconformity, a desire to be respectable, a desire to look big in the sight of the world and so on. There is no doubt whatsoever that the design of this building is the result of this inferiority complex showing in an attempt to produce a 'cathedral' that can stand comparison with Westminster Abbey. Nonconformist Cathedral!
Knowing the Times, 229

The Nonconformist fathers generally referred to their places of worship as meeting houses, and it is a good old term. You see, it is a place, not so much where people meet with one another, though that is included, but the essential meaning is this – the place where they meet with God. God grant that in our minds and in our thinking our churches may become more and more meeting houses, that, as we gather there, Sunday by Sunday, we shall say to ourselves, 'We are going to meet with God'. The meeting house, the place of meeting.
Revival, 162–63

discipline
When did you last hear of a person being excommunicated? When did you last hear of a person being kept back from the Communion Table? Go back to the history of Protestantism and you will find that the Protestant definition of the Church is, 'that the Church is a place in which the Word is preached, the Sacraments are administered, and discipline is exercised'.
Studies in the Sermon on the Mount (2), 163–64

'What are the three essential marks of the Church?' I wonder how many would have mentioned the exercise of discipline? There is no doubt at all but that this doctrine is grievously neglected. Indeed, if I were asked to explain why it is that things are as they are in the Church; if I were asked to explain why statistics show the dwindling numbers, the lack of power and the lack of influence upon men and women; if I were asked to explain why it is that so many churches seem to be incapable of sustaining the cause without resorting to whist drives and dances and things like that; if I were asked to explain why it is that the Church is in such a parlous condition, I should have to say that the ultimate cause is the failure to exercise discipline.
Great Doctrines of the Bible (3), 14

You may have to 'deliver him to Satan', a phrase which is used by Paul, 'for the destruction of the flesh, that the spirit may be saved in the day of the Lord Jesus' (1 Cor. 5:15). I do not know exactly what that means, but it probably means something like this – you not only put him out of the membership but stop praying for him. You hand him over to Satan, as it were, and Satan will cause him to suffer, perhaps in his body. He will become wretched and miserable, and that may bring him to his senses and his soul may be saved.
Great Doctrines of the Bible (3), 17

government

As we do so let us be careful to observe that the Apostle does not lay down a rigid system of church order. Indeed it is questionable whether any such thing is to be found anywhere in the Scriptures.
Christian Unity, 168–69

growth

There is all the difference in the world between just adding to the numbers on the roll of a church and the growth of the holy temple of the Lord. We are living in an age which is statistically minded, and you can read reports of countries and places where almost everybody seems to be a church member. But, alas, it does not follow that they are all being built into this holy temple of the Lord. It does not follow of necessity that they are 'lively' stones, that they are a part of this growth. The increase of the church is vital, not mechanical. Men can add to the membership of a church, but God alone, can build, through the Holy Spirit, into the building of the church. This growing unto an holy temple is a vital process.
God's Way of Reconciliation, 430

membership

When I was personally received as a full member of the Christian church in which I was brought up, I was asked one question only. I was asked to name the brook which our Lord and the disciples had to cross while going from the Upper Room to the place of trial. I could not remember the answer to that question; nevertheless I was received into the full membership of the church. That literally is what happened to me at the age of fourteen.
Christian Unity, 61

I never ask anybody to join the Church. I never will. I have never done so. To me it is grievously wrong to plead with people, almost to implore them, to join the Church.
God's Way of Reconciliation, 431

There is no independence in the body. Each part derives its meaning, its essence, from its relationship to the rest. That is the truth about the body; and it

is equally true, says the Apostle, about the Church. Each organ needs the others, and each one benefits by the functions of the others.
Christian Unity, 55

services
The church is not a place where people are to be entertained, or where people come to sit and listen either to singing or to the accounts of other people's experiences, coupled with a brief, light, comfortable message.
God's Ultimate Purpose, 424

The church is not meant to be a place in which one man does everything and nobody else does anything. The church is not a place in which one man alone speaks and the others just sit and listen.
The Gospel of God, 238–39

Do not misunderstand me, but I have a feeling that the Christian Church today is dying of dignity, dying of decorum. Services are beautiful, and perfect, but where is the breath of the Spirit?
The Christian Warfare, 284

A dead church is a contradiction in terms.
Christian Conduct, 199

The church should be the most exciting and thrilling place in the world, and if she is not we are somehow or other 'quenching the Spirit'.
The Christian Warfare, 280

CHURCH, Universal
The Church has only one source of strength, and that is the power of God, the power of his Holy Spirit.
Revival, 287

One of the most dangerous places for a man to be in is the church of the living God.
Evangelistic Sermons, 259

The Christian church replaces the old Temple in Jerusalem.
Spiritual Blessing, 232

abuse
Lloyd-Jones lamented the concept of the State Church and the fashion in which the State uses the Church for its own convenience.

. . . [T]he church is the servant of the state. Her main function is to perform certain things for us. She is useful for a christening, or a marriage, or a funeral. The

other agencies cannot do that kind of thing quite as well. A civil clerk's office may be all right for legal purposes, but there is something about a church service which, after all, adds dignity to the occasion. So the church remains very useful at such times as a marriage, a christening and, of course, a death. Further, if there happens to be a war and things are not going very well for the nation, then, of course, the church can organise a national day of prayer.
Healing and the Scriptures, 56

One of the greatest dangers, perhaps, confronting us as Christians today is to think in terms of 'movements' instead of 'churches'. In the New Testament it is always churches
The Gospel of God, 241

beginning
You can say that the Day of Pentecost was the day of the public inauguration of the Church as the body of Christ. There was something new there which had never been before. There is a sense in which you can speak of the Church in the Old Testament, yes, but it is not the same as the Church was subsequent to the Day of Pentecost.
Great Doctrines of the Bible (2), 36

You must not say that the people of God, the redeemed, start after Calvary or after our Lord's ascension or after Pentecost. The people of God are in the Old Testament as well as in the New.
To God's Glory, 106

The greatest need of all today is a true and an adequate conception of the nature of the Christian Church. It is because we who belong to her lack this that we fail to attract those who are outside.
God's Way of Reconciliation, 394

There is only one really continuous church, and that is this invisible spiritual continuity of those who are 'born again', of those who are 'led of the Spirit'.
God's Sovereign Purpose, 324–25

decline
If the Church had been left to us, and to people like us, the story would have ended long ago.
Assurance, 333

The condition of the Church is what it is today – and I am including the evangelical section – very largely because of ignorance of the 'wiles of the devil'.
The Christian Warfare, 208

We should be much more concerned about the state of the Church herself than about the state of the world outside the Church. It seems increasingly evident

that the explanation of the present state of Christendom is to be found inside the Church and not outside.
Studies in the Sermon on the Mount (2), 256

Now that is what I say is the principle of separation. You cannot possibly remain in an apostate church. You must separate yourself from unbelief and from explicit denials of the gospel.
To God's Glory, 76

Why do the common people in all countries find the church almost fatuously ridiculous? It is God's judgement. God is ridiculing the church because of the abuse and the misuse of which we have all been so guilty.
Spiritual Blessing, 132

She has been trying to attract people to herself for fifty years and more, putting on popular programmes, dramas, music, this that and the other, trying to entice the people, especially the young people, but they do not come. Of course not! They never will until they know the name of the Lord, and then they will come.
Revival, 309–10

We have passed through one of the most barren periods in the long history of the Church. We have been like the prodigal son in that far country, spending our time in the fields with the swine and living on nothing but husks. Yes, we have been in bondage, we have been in fear, we have suffered persecution and derision and it is still going on. We are still in the wilderness. Do not believe anything that suggests that we are out of it, we are not. The Church is in the wilderness. But thank God it is always after such a period that God acts and does his mighty deeds and shows forth his glory.
Revival, 129

The Church and her own leaders began to criticise this book, to set themselves up as authorities, to deny certain aspects of the teaching. They deny the God of the Old Testament, they do not believe in him, they say. They made a mere man out of the Lord of glory, they denied his virgin birth, they denied his miracles, they denied his atonement, they denied the person of the Holy Spirit, and they reduced this Bible to a book of ethics, and of morals. That is why the Church is as she is. The Church rebelled in her doctrine and in her belief. She set up the wisdom of men in the place of the wisdom of God. She became proud of her learning, and of her knowledge, and what she asked about her preachers and her servants was not any longer, 'Is he filled with the Spirit? Has he a living experience of God?' but, 'Is he cultivated? Is he cultured? What are his degrees?' Now, I am not romancing, am I? This is literal history.
Revival, 286–87

I believe that the state of the church is to be explained by one thing only, and that is that the message of the gospel is not being preached.
Saving Faith, 298

Christian people, are we really satisfied with the state of the Christian Church today? Do we ever stop to think about it? There are towns and villages in this land which were once filled with a praying, and praising, and glorying people, towns and villages which stand out in the annals of Christianity in this country once filled with a sense of the glory of God. But today they are desolate, they are deserted, they are forsaken.
Revival, 253

Until the church is crushed to her knees, and has come to the end of her own power and ability, and looks to God for his power and the might of the Holy Spirit – until then I am certain that the declension will continue and even increase. When the church of God is in a state of eclipse and of apparent defeat, it is always because she has forgotten who she is, has forgotten her reliance upon God and has been trusting, in her folly, to her own ability and her own prowess.
Old Testament Evangelistic Sermons, 64–65

ideal
Paul's whole conception of the Church is that it is a place where God is working in the hearts of men and women.
The Life of Joy, 38

In bringing her into being God has done something as entirely new as was the creation of the universe. He did not simply take a Jew and a Gentile and bring them together somehow in a kind of coalition, and make them sit down together round a table and agree to be friendly. No! The Church is a new creation. She is not a collection of parts.
Christian Unity, 53

But there is nothing that so proclaims the glory of God as the Christian Church, the body of which Christ Himself is the Head.
The Unsearchable Riches of Christ, 314

You may have been a Cinderella, the whole Church was a Cinderella, in her rags, slaving and having a hard and a difficult life, doing all the chores for the other sisters. But Cinderella is married to the Prince; and what happens? Instead of having to slave in that way she now has her servants. Whose servants? His servants! Because she has become the bride of this Prince all his servants are her servants, and they minister to her as they do to him.
Life in the Spirit in Marriage Home and Work, 205

The Church is a kind of prism that is placed in the path of the light to break up the whiteness into the colours of the spectrum. What a conception of the Christian Church! Without this the angels could see the light, could see the wisdom in general, but not the amazing variety. It is through the Church as a

medium, that the angels have received this new conception of the transcendent glory of the wisdom of God.
The Unsearchable Riches of Christ, 85

The Church, far from being an afterthought, is the brightest shining of the wisdom of God. It is equally wrong to say that the Church is only temporary, and that a time will come when she will be removed and the gospel of the kingdom will again be preached to the Jews! There is nothing beyond the Church. She is the highest and the most supreme manifestation of the wisdom of God and to look forward to something beyond the Church is to deny not only this verse but many another verse in the Scripture.
The Unsearchable Riches of Christ, 86

The Church is the new Israel, the spiritual Israel, the true seed of Abraham, and she consists of Jews and Gentiles.
God's Ultimate Purpose, 221

If only we had a true conception of the Christian Church! If we only really saw her as she is in the New Testament, if we had but some dim and vague notion of what she was in the early years, and indeed in the early centuries, if we but really understood what she was like in every period of revival and re-awakening, then we would be heart-broken at the present condition. We would be grieved and filled with a sense of sorrow. Are we all troubled when we see something that once was great and famous going down or ceasing to be? The decline and fall of an Empire is a sad spectacle. It is a sad thing to see a great business going down. It is sad to see a great professional man losing his grip. It is sad to see a man who is great at sport suddenly, because of age, beginning to fail. It is something that always fills us with a sense of sorrow and of sadness. Well, multiply all that by infinity, and then try to conceive of the Church of God as she is in the mind of God, and as she was formed and founded, and contrast that with what she is today. 'Oh,' says this man, 'for Zion's sake, for Jerusalem's sake, I will not hold my peace, I will take no rest.'
Revival, 252–53

maturity

Have you ever watched a mason doing his work? Many times as a boy I did this, and it always fascinated me. He took the stone and then with his various types of hammer he knocked bits off. He trimmed it, he shaped it, he fashioned it, he chipped bits off it. He tried it. Then he took it back again because it was not quite right. He would knock off another piece, perhaps with the chisel and the hammer. And so he went on dealing with it until it was just right. Then he put it in, and stood back. Satisfied he put the mortar on, then he took his next stone and did the same to that. Now that is what the Apostle means by 'fitly framed together'.
God's Way of Reconciliation, 461

At this point a certain amount of knowledge of anatomy is helpful. In the case of a joint in the body there is a kind of cup on one bone and into that cup there fits a kind of ball at the end of another bone. The surfaces of both are smooth so that there is no friction, and everything works easily and harmoniously and in an effective manner. According to the Apostle's teaching this should be true of the members of the Church. It is the way in which they are to grow up into Him in all things. The ideal condition of the Christian Church is that in which every member is what he is meant to be, fitting in with every other member and so preserving 'the unity of the Spirit in the bond of peace'. There is to be no creaking, as it were, in the joints, no angularities; everything is to be 'fitly joined together'.
Christian Unity, 259

unity

There are those who seem to think that the one problem in the Church today is the problem of unity. So they give all their time and attention to this. That people are going to hell does not seem to matter to them, they are always preaching about unity, and writing books about it. 'The Unity of the Church' is their gospel. But that has never saved anyone. If all the Churches in the world, including the Roman Catholic Church, became amalgamated and you could say that now we had one great world Church, I venture to prophesy that it would not make the slightest difference to the man in the street. He is not outside the Churches because the Churches are disunited, he is outside because he likes his sin, because he is a sinner, because he is ignorant of spiritual realities. He is no more interested in this problem of unity than is the man in the moon! And yet the Church is talking about the problem of unity as if it were the central problem.
The Christian Soldier, 292

There never will be two churches. There will never even be two divisions in the Christian Church. The Christian Church is one and one only. It takes the same grace of God to convert a Jew as a Gentile, and the Gentile as a Jew, and they will share the same blessings, they are all joint heirs of exactly the same promises and of the same blessed hope.
To God's Glory, 109

There are no divisions and distinctions in terms of birth or background or race or social status in the church of God, they are completely irrelevant. At the same time there are no divisions and distinctions or special categories as regards intellect in the house of God. You may be the greatest genius in the world, it does not matter, when you come in here you are like everybody else, you are in the same position as the biggest fool in an intellectual sense. You may be a man of great learning and knowledge, it does not make the slightest difference when you come in through that door, it avails you nothing. You come in, in exactly the same way as if you knew nothing, precisely in the position of the uttermost ignoramus. In the same way there are no distinctions in terms of one's moral

behaviour and conduct in the past. You may be a paragon of all the virtues, it will not help you here, you will be annoyed if you listen to this gospel, because it will tell you that all your righteousnesses are as filthy rags and that you are in exactly the same position as the most profligate sinner who has come in off the streets.
Old Testament Evangelistic Sermons, 132

History will testify that the most civilising force that the world has ever known has been the Christian Church.
Authentic Christianity (1), 156

CITIZENSHIP
If you write to me, write to me like this: at Westminster, London. Temporary address: Westminster; permanent address: heaven in Christ. I am but a stranger here, heaven is my home.
Love so Amazing, 139

COMFORT
We must remember that we are not only to live in the fear of the Lord, but we are to live in the comfort and the knowledge of God. He not only sees what is happening to you when you are taken ill, He not only knows when you are suffering bereavement and sorrow, He knows every pang of the heart, He knows every heartache; He knows everything; there is nothing outside His omniscience. He knows all about us in every respect and He therefore knows our every need. From that our Lord draws this deduction. You need never be anxious, you must never be worried. God is with you in this state, you are not alone, and He is your Father. Even an earthly father does this in a measure. He is with his child, protecting, doing everything he can for him. Multiply that by infinity, and that is what God is doing with respect to you, whatever your circumstance.
Studies in the Sermon on the Mount (2), 142

There is no comfort except to those who believe that Jesus is the Son of God, that He died to make atonement for our sins, that He was buried, that He literally rose triumphant o'er the grave, having conquered the last enemy, and that He has ascended through the heavens.
The Final Perseverance of the Saints, 26

COMMANDMENTS
In a sense there was nothing new in the Ten Commandments. Why then were they ever given? For this reason, that mankind, the children of Israel included, in its sin and its folly had forgotten and strayed away from these fundamental laws of God pertaining to the whole of life. So God, as it were, said, 'I am going to state them again one by one; I am going to write them and underline them so that people shall see them clearly'.
Life in the Spirit in Marriage Home and Work, 244

The commandments of God to non-Christians are a yoke; they feel they are a task and a burden, and in their heart of hearts they hate God because of this, and they would be very glad to be emancipated out of it all. But not to the Christian; His commandments, says John, are not a task and a terrible duty to the one who really is born again – His commandments are 'not grievous.'
Life in God, 35

COMMUNION
The term *communion*, therefore, represents not only our communion with the Lord but also our communion with one another.
Great Doctrines of the Bible (3), 53

There is no new or additional grace given in the Lord's Supper.
Great Doctrines of the Bible (3), 56

CONDEMNATION
The opposite to condemnation is never sanctification, invariably it is justification.
The Law: Its Functions and Limits, 283

CONFESSION
Is there anything more difficult than to admit that we are wrong?
Authentic Christianity (3), 69

CONGREGATION
Good listeners are produced by good preaching
Preaching and Preachers, 155

Far too often the pew has controlled the pulpit, and great harm has come in the Church. The Apostle warns Timothy that a time is coming when people 'will not endure sound doctrine'.
Christian Unity, 201

I would lay it down as being axiomatic that the pew is never to dictate to, or control, the pulpit. This needs to be emphasised at the present time.
Preaching and Preachers, 143

The preacher never needs to know the individual facts about his congregation . . . Why? Well, because he knows that every single human being is not righteous, and it really does not matter from the standpoint of the preacher whether they have just emerged out of a gutter or whether they have come out of the best appointed drawing room in London; it does not matter whether they have come from the West End or the East End, the North Pole or the South. What does it matter? It does not matter how they are dressed, what they look like, how respectable or disreputable . . . They are souls; they are people; and therefore they are not

righteous and they need this gospel because it is the only thing that can save them. And when they come to see the preacher at the end, and they begin to give a catalogue of their sins, the preacher who really knows his Scriptures should say, 'Stop! I do not mind what you have done or what you have been. You are just a sinner like everybody else and you need the same Saviour'.
The Righteous Judgement of God, 199–200

responsibility

Let me be quite direct and practical. Do you have any expectation when you enter a Christian service? What is your mood, what kind of condition are you in, what is your attitude towards what you are doing? Do you go to a place of worship simply because it is Sunday morning? Is it just an item in the programme? And is it just a matter of singing some hymns, hearing the reading of the Scriptures, listening to a sermon, and so on? Just a matter of habit, repeating what you have done many times before? Is that the way in which you go into God's house? God have mercy upon you if it is!
The Christian Warfare, 283

But the preacher – though he has prepared, and prepared carefully – because of this element of spiritual freedom is still able to receive something from the congregation, and does so. There is an interplay, action and response, and this often makes a very vital difference . . . the responsiveness and eagerness of his congregation lifts him up and enlivens him. But the preacher must be open to this; if he is not, he is going to miss one of the most glorious experiences that ever comes to a preacher.
Preaching and Preachers, 84–85

How many people pray before they go to a service that the Spirit of God might come upon the preacher and use him and his message? The hearers, as well as the preacher must pray for that, otherwise they are looking to him and to his message.
Revival, 124

Do we give the impression when we come to our places of worship that we are doing the most wonderful and thrilling thing in the world? Are we alive, are we rejoicing? How do we compare with these other people? A staid, lifeless Christian is a denial, in many respects, of the gospel at its most glorious point. To be heavy-footed, slow-moving, lethargic, having to be whipped up and roused constantly, and urged to do this and that instead of running to it, and rejoicing in it, is a sad misrepresentation of Christianity.
The Christian Soldier, 285

CONSCIENCE

Every time our conscience accuses us it is a proof that man was originally sinless.
Great Doctrines of the Bible (1), 176

The man who has been justified by faith, and who has peace with God, can answer the accusations of his own conscience.
Assurance, 19

But someone may ask, 'Does not conscience trouble the unregenerate man?' It does, but there is all the difference in the world between an unregenerate man who has trouble with his conscience, and a man who is able to say 'It is no more I that do it, but sin that dwelleth in me.' In the case of the unregenerate man, the total personality of the man is 'aware' of the speaking of conscience, but he is united against his conscience. He loves sin, desires sin, and wills sin, and he wishes that he had not got a conscience. *He* does not 'condemn' what he is doing, he is simply aware that his conscience condemns it. He is worried about something, as it were, outside himself; hence he tries, by means of psychology and everything else he can lay hold of, to get rid of this voice of conscience. As a whole he is against this, but the man the Apostle is describing is a man who is divided in himself – 'It is no more *I* that do it'.
The Law: Its Functions and Limits, 204–5

Conscience is something, in a sense, apart from man. It has been put in him by God; it is a reminder of the voice of God within him, an inward monitor, and a man cannot really manipulate his conscience. He can go against it, but that is not manipulating it. It is possible, as this Apostle says again in writing to Timothy, for the conscience to be seared 'with a hot iron'. But nevertheless it is true to say that the conscience is an independent witness.
God's Sovereign Purpose, 15

Now the conscience is a kind of voice, a faculty, if you like, that is in all human beings. It is an inward monitor which tells us that certain things are wrong and that we should not do them. Whether we like it or not, it is there, and it expresses its opinion and it condemns us when we do wrong . . . The conscience is something that is mainly negative. Its business is not so much to tell us what is right as to tell us what is wrong and to condemn us if we do it. The conscience is not a perfect instrument by any means, and a man's conscience can vary a good deal during his life. The Apostle Paul himself tells us elsewhere that when he persecuted the church of Christ he did it 'in all good conscience'. Indeed, he says that he had lived until that moment 'in all good conscience', but he came to see that some things which he had thought were right were wrong, and so we must not regard the conscience as a perfect instrument. Nevertheless we should always obey it. 'Ah, yes', you may say, 'but your conscience may be unenlightened'. If that is so, then it is my business to subject myself to further teaching. A conscience can be feeble, it can be unenlightened, and I can educate it, I can teach it and train it; but whatever state my conscience may be in, it is never right for me to do anything against it.
The Righteous Judgement of God, 118–19

CONSISTENCY

The first Christians conquered the ancient world just by being Christian. It was their love for one another and their type of life that made such an impact upon that pagan world, and there is no question but that this is the greatest need of the hour – the Christian quality of life being demonstrated among men and women. That is something to which we are all called and something which we can all do.
The Life of Joy, 22

When Hitler walks in and annexes Austria we are horrified. Yes, people are horrified who do the very same thing in their personal lives. They do it in the matter of other men's wives; they do it in the matter of another man's post or position in business. It is the same thing exactly.
God's Way of Reconciliation, 85–86

If you claim to love Christ and yet are living an unholy life, there is only one thing to say about you. You are a bare-faced liar!
Banner of Truth, Issue 275

To divorce forgiveness of sins from the actual living of the Christian life is nothing but rank heresy!
Banner of Truth, Issue 275

CONSUMMATION (Animals; Second Coming)

The perfect harmony that will be restored will be harmony in man, and between men. Harmony on the earth and in the brute creation! Harmony in heaven, and all under this blessed Lord Jesus Christ, who will be the Head of all! Everything will again be united in Him. And wonder of wonders, marvellous beyond compare, when all this happens it will never be undone again.
God's Ultimate Purpose, 206–7

No bomb can be invented, no bacteria can be cultivated and used, no chemicals or gases can be brought into use that can ever make the slightest difference to these things. That is God's plan as revealed in Scripture, and God's plan will be carried out; and if you and I are in Christ we are involved in it. We are destined to be elevated and restored to what man was meant to be. We shall be 'lords of the creation'.
God's Ultimate Purpose, 207

There is to be a regeneration of the whole cosmos; the very physical world itself will be perfect. There will be 'new heavens and a new earth, wherein dwelleth righteousness' (2 Peter 3:13). 'The wolf shall lie down with the lamb . . . and the lion shall eat straw like the ox', and 'a little child shall lead them' (Isaiah. 11:6–7). Absolute perfection! It is coming! It is the ultimate end of God's purpose. There is a new world awaiting us.
The Unsearchable Riches of Christ, 77

At the end there will be a perfect new humanity, complete and entire in Christ. He is the Head, we are the body; He is the first-born among many brethren, something entirely new. He is the second Man, He is the last Adam. That is how God saves, that is God's plan of redemption. Does it not help you to understand the incarnation as you have never done before? It is not taking out of the old mass of humanity and doing something to it; it is the production of something entirely new.
God's Sovereign Purpose, 137

The Lutherans have always taught a new creation of heavens and earth, whereas the Reformers have generally taught that the present earth and heavens will be so delivered from evil and sin that they are virtually completely new. It does not matter, of course, which it is, and we cannot finally decide. The important thing to realise is that we shall dwell in the kind of condition that is described in Revelation 21 – no sorrow, no sighing, a perfect state of affairs.
Great Doctrines of the Bible (3), 247

What we call heaven is life in this perfect world as God intended humanity to live it. When He put Adam in Paradise at the beginning Adam fell, and all fell with him, but men and women are meant to live in the body, and will live in a glorified body in a glorified world, and God will be with them.
Great Doctrines of the Bible (3), 247–48

Will there be another war? I do not know but of this I am certain, a day is coming when evil men will wax worse and worse, and there will be wars and rumour of wars, and pestilence and foulness, and the whole world will be seen to be violent against God in a way that it has never been before. Then, suddenly, there will be a sign in the heavens and the Son of man, the Lord of glory, the King of kings and Lord of lords, will appear on the clouds of heaven surrounded by his holy angels. Then he will judge the world in righteousness, he will destroy all his enemies and set up his glorious kingdom of righteousness and peace.
Authentic Christianity (4), 157

CONTENTIOUSNESS
[Contentiousness] is of the Devil.
Revival, 66

CONVERSION
All teaching which says that *we* can decide for Christ is automatically false.
Spiritual Blessing, 198

Do not try to live on your conversion. You will be done before you know where you are. You cannot live on one climatic experience; you must keep on looking to him every day.
Spiritual Depression, 158

affects
Try to imagine that persecuting, foolish, Saul of Tarsus – that very clever, good and religious man. Just think of him 'breathing out threatenings and slaughter'; think of the spirit of hatred that animated him, and contrast it with the man who wrote this letter (Philippians), and there you will see what the gospel can do.
The Life of Joy, 12

It is a change in nature, a *translation*.
Children of God, 90

The first sign of spiritual life is to feel that you are dead!
The Law: Its Functions and Limits, 145

A man's temperament is not changed when he is converted. If you imagine that when the Apostle Paul says, 'If any man be in Christ, he is a new creature; old things are passed away; behold, all things are become new' (2 Corinthians 5:17) he means that every Christian is identical with every other Christian, you are completely wrong. The fundamental elements in our personality and temperament are not changed by conversion and by re-birth. The 'new man' means the new disposition, the new understanding, the new orientation, but the man himself, psychologically, is essentially what he was before.
The Christian Warfare, 211

What a man is in the matter of abilities and powers and propensities before conversion, he still is after conversion. He is not given natural powers that he did not have before. He has the same powers exactly. Take as a convenient example, the very man who wrote these words, the Apostle Paul. As a personality he was the same when he was Paul the Apostle as he was as Saul of Tarsus. As Saul of Tarsus, as a persecutor, and an injurious person, and a blasphemer, he was a man who did things very thoroughly, with great vigour and with great feeling. Saul of Tarsus never did a thing by halves. Whatever he believed in, and whatever he did, he did with all his might. He was a vehement persecutor, and when he was converted and became the Apostle Paul, those precise qualities stand out still. He did not suddenly become a quiet man, or a quiet preacher! We are aware of the passion and the power and the vehemence as we read his epistles. In other words, 'the members', the total way in which a man expresses himself, are the same after conversion as before conversion.
The New Man, 256

basis
[Conversion] is always an intensely personal experience.
Old Testament Evangelistic Sermons, 14

If I am in Christ at all, He is not only my justification, not only my righteousness, but also my sanctification, and also my final redemption. I cannot take

parts of Christ. He is a whole Christ, and if I am in Him all His benefits come to me.
Assurance, 277

There is no 'of course' about being a Christian. It is something entirely new. It is by no means inevitable or something which is bound to happen. Indeed, becoming a Christian is a crisis, a critical event, a great upheaval which in the New Testament is described in such terms as a new birth, or a new creation, or a new beginning. More than that, it is there described as being a supernatural act wrought by God Himself, something which is comparable to a dead soul being made alive. It means the direct intervention of God in a human life by His infinite grace in and through Jesus Christ His Son.
Evangelistic Sermons, 166

You cannot receive Christ in bits and pieces.
Banner of Truth, Issue 275

Are you relying on anything in yourself at this moment? If you are, you are not a Christian. Are you relying on the fact that you have been brought up in a Christian country? God have mercy upon you! If you still think this is a Christian country I am afraid we are not speaking the same language. Are you relying upon the fact that you were christened when you were a child, or that you were baptised when you were older – is that what you are relying on? Are you relying upon the fact that you are a member of a Church and that your name is on a roll – is that it? God have mercy upon you! Anyone can do that, especially today, when there is no longer strictness in these matters. Are you relying upon the good you have done? Are you relying upon the fact that you have never got drunk, that you have never committed adultery, that you are not a murderer – are these the things on which you are relying? Then, I say, you are outside! I do not care how respectable you are, you are outside. 'Not by works of righteousness which we have done' – 'not according to our works'.
I am not Ashamed, 137

The very fact that a man believes is proof he has been born again; it is the first fruit that is manifested in the life of one who has been born of God.
Life in God, 17

crisis
We have neglected the law-work, we have been too anxious to hurry people into some kind of 'decision'. It is when you have suffered a great deal of pain that you most appreciate the relief. It is the man who has been healed at the very door of death who is most grateful for his cure. It is the sinner who has had a glimpse into hell who is most appreciative of the glories of heaven.
Assurance, 305

There is no such thing as 'coming to Jesus'. In one sense, a man cannot even come to Christ. He can only come to the Lord Jesus. If this doctrine is true a man cannot accept Him as Saviour only, and then perhaps later decide to accept Him as Lord, for He is always the Lord. The One who died for our sins is the Lord. And He died for our sins because sin is under the wrath of God; it is transgression against the law, it is enmity against God, so it must be punished. If I say that I need a Saviour it is because I need a Saviour from sin, including deliverance from the power of sin and everything connected with sin. If I have a true conception of sin I cannot only ask to be forgiven. I must desire to be delivered from its power and pollution as well. We cannot believe in 'Jesus' and leave out 'the Lord'. We believe in one indivisible Person. In Him there are two natures in one Person; and when we believe in Him we believe in Him as the Lord of glory and the Lord of our life. When we believe in Him we believe that He died for our sins, that He has bought us, purchased us, ransomed us. When we believe that, we give ourselves to Him, We do not 'come to Jesus', and we do not believe in Jesus: we come to the Lord Jesus, we believe in Him as He is.
God's Ultimate Purpose, 321

Holy Spirit
If you expect a natural man to believe the gospel simply because you are putting it to him, you are denying the gospel; you have not understood it yourself. He cannot do it. It is no use your getting excited or bringing pressure to bear upon him; it is all of no value. The man cannot help himself! He needs the enlightenment that the Holy Spirit alone can give. You needed it; he still needs it.
God's Sovereign Purpose, 34–35

Merely to put the gospel before a man is not enough, something must be done in the man. The Spirit is in the Word; but the Spirit must be in the man also, and without this he cannot see the truth
God's Ultimate Purpose, 407

There are no shades of difference between being 'not Christian' and being 'Christian'. It is not that you go from black to white through various shades of grey, and you cannot quite tell where you are – the black is beginning to be affected by a little white, and then there is a little more, and a little more, and at last, you say: Ah! This is white! It is not that. That is thoroughly false; that is a complete contrast to what the apostle is teaching here. It is either black or white, he says, and there are no intermediate almost imperceptible stages. It is not like those subtle changes in the colour of the spectrum where you cannot quite tell at any given point where one colour ends and another begins. Not at all! This contrast is clear and definite.
God's Way of Reconciliation, 230

It is a miracle that there is a single Christian in the world or ever has been.
God's Ultimate Purpose, 414

tests

If you feel you have any right to forgiveness you are not, as I understand it, a Christian.
Faith on Trial, 89

There is no more thorough test of our profession of Christianity than just this: are we enjoying this peace with God?
Assurance, 17

You cannot become a Christian without being made humble.
Authentic Christianity (1), 114

There is no better test than this: to look at the place of prayer in their lives.
Authentic Christianity (1), 173

Has our natural state of fearfulness with respect to God, our enmity with respect to God, been removed?
Assurance, 17

CONVICTION

John Bunyan tells us in *Grace Abounding* that he was in that condition and in an agony of soul for eighteen months. The time element does not matter, but any man who is awakened and convicted of sin must be in trouble about this. How can he die and face God?
Assurance, 18

There is no peace between man and God until a man grasps this doctrine of justification. It is the only way of peace.
Assurance, 18

I lay down this proposition, that 'the spirit of bondage and fear' always precedes the 'Spirit of adoption'.
The Sons of God, 207

Take for instance the great event at Kirk-of-Shotts in Scotland in 1630. As the result of the sermon preached by John Livingstone on that notable Monday morning there were many people who were in an agony of conviction as described perfectly in the second section of Romans chapter 7. Some remained in that state for hours, some for days, and some for weeks. They felt utterly lost. They saw the spirituality of the Law, they saw their own utter failure and the uselessness of all their own efforts. They could not find release and relief. There they were, groaning, some literally lying under the hedgerows, others knocking at the door of the minister in the early hours of the morning, crying for the relief which they could not find. That, it seems to me, is the position described so perfectly by the Apostle Paul in Romans 7:13–25. It is a very early

manifestation of spiritual life; but it is no more than that – conviction but not conversion.
The Law: Its Functions and Limits, 262

At some time or other the Spirit of God visits each one of us and moves us and disturbs us. It may be in a meeting such as this, or while singing some hymn, or perhaps at the death or funeral of someone who is very dear to us. Perhaps, again, in some accident face to face with our own death, or in one of many other possible circumstances and positions, the Spirit of God deals with us. We become conscious of a power and a presence that we have never felt before. We become melted and softened for the time being. It suddenly dawns upon us that we have not been what we ought to have been, that our lives have been sinful and selfish, that all along we have been worldly and have forgotten God and His eternal love in Jesus Christ.
Evangelistic Sermons, 26

The Holy Spirit always convicts – always. But he does not always convince and in this book of Acts you will find many instances of people convicted without being convinced.
Authentic Christianity (2), 211

And the Holy Spirit convinces by enabling men and women to believe – as we have seen. I want to impress upon you that it is he alone who can do that. Nobody alone can convince anybody about the truth of these things apart from the Holy Spirit.
Authentic Christianity (2), 212–13

COUNSELLING
'What is the greatest essential in a counsellor?' I would say that it is a quiet mind and that he is at rest in himself. You will remember how our Lord put this on one occasion – 'Can the blind lead the blind? Shall they not both fall into the ditch?' (Lk. 6:39). In other words, if a man is in trouble with himself, and is restless, he is really in need of counselling himself. How can he give useful counsel to another?'
Healing and the Scriptures, 71

When someone tells you that he or she has told you all his or her secrets you can always be sure that that is never the case. However frank and open a person may be there is always something which is held back and reserved.
Old Testament Evangelistic Sermons, 238

Do not allow particulars to interfere with the whole. Or, to use a medical analogy, do not be too upset by the appearance of particular symptoms if you know that the patient as a whole is getting better and making progress. He is a very poor doctor who gets too alarmed and excited about particulars; he must keep his eye on the patient as a whole.
The Final Perseverance of the Saints, 178

'Pull yourself together'. There is nothing more idiotic to say to a poor person who is in the grip of the spirit of fear than 'pull yourself together'. That is the one thing he cannot do. If he could he would. And yet, that is what the world says, not the clever world but the stupid world, which believes in a sort of muscular outlook upon life: 'Pull yourself together'!
I am not Ashamed, 173

If he is a Christian I at once know the line on which I can deal with him and help him; if he is not, I really cannot help that man until he becomes one. I cannot medicate his symptoms until the disease has been dealt with. I cannot answer him his particular question unless he accepts the total view of life, death and eternity which the gospel provides.
I am not Ashamed, 56

preaching
True preaching does deal with personal problems, so much so that true preaching saves a great deal of time for the pastor. I am speaking out of forty years of experience. What do I mean? Let me explain. The Puritans are justly famous for their pastoral preaching. They would take up what they called 'cases of conscience' and deal with them in their sermons; and as they dealt with these problems they were solving the personal individual problems of those who were listening to them. That has constantly been my experience. The preaching of the gospel from the pulpit, applied by the Holy Spirit to the individuals who are listening, has been the means of dealing with personal problems of which I as the preacher knew nothing until people came to me and at the end of the service saying, 'I want to thank you for that sermon because if you had known I was there and the exact nature of my problem, you could not have answered my various questions more perfectly. I have often thought of bringing them to you but you have now answered them without my doing so'. The preaching had already dealt with their personal problems. Do not misunderstand me, I am not saying that the preacher should never do any personal work; far from it. But I do contend that preaching must always come first, and that it must not be replaced by anything else.
Preaching and Preachers, 37

As preaching goes down personal counselling goes up.
Preaching and Preachers, 17

I maintain that ultimately the only true basis for personal work, unless it is to degenerate into purely psychological treatment, is the true and sound preaching of the gospel,
Preaching and Preachers, 40

COVENANT
Covenant in the Bible is always something that is entirely and solely and only from God's side. God, moved by nothing in us at all, but entirely by His own

grace and His own eternal love comes to the people and He says, 'I am going to do so and so and I pledge Myself that I will do it.'
God's Sovereign Purpose, 54

There is only one covenant of grace and it all centres around the Lord Jesus Christ. The old points forward to Him; the new reveals Him and holds Him forth to us in person. He alone is the fulfilment of everything that is promised from Genesis 3:15 onwards. It is all in Him. The original covenant with regard to redemption was fully and clearly made with Him.
Great Doctrines of the Bible (1), 242

The covenant of grace is that arrangement between the triune God and His people, whereby God carries out His eternal purpose and decree of redemption by promising His friendship. The promise is full and free salvation to His people upon the basis of the vicarious atonement of the Lord Jesus Christ, who is the mediator of the covenant, and His people accept this salvation by faith. It is the promise of God's friendship, of His being our God, of entry into intimate relationship with Him, and knowing Him, and it is all made possible by Jesus Christ.
Great Doctrines of the Bible (1), 227–28

CREATION (Consummation)
The universe, the cosmos, every star in its orbit, the sun and moon, every power, every atom with its magnetic force and power, all are under his power. Everything in nature and creation, man and all his powers, his devices, his machinations, everything that he is capable of doing, it is all under the power of God, under the power of Christ.
Saved in Eternity, 185

There are no rejects out of His factory. God's work is always perfect, and it is always complete.
God's Way of Reconciliation, 196

I cannot see how we are entitled to interpret this term 'day' in any other sense than by saying that it means twenty-four hours. The difficulties of the other suppositions make it, to me at any rate, quite impossible.
Great Doctrines of the Bible (1), 132

As you have already seen, if you begin to play fast and loose with the scriptural teaching at any one point, you will find that your whole system will be shaken. And therefore, though – again one has to say it – there are certain things one does not understand, yet for myself I have no difficulty whatsoever in accepting this third chapter of Genesis as being literal, actual history.
Great Doctrines of the Bible (1), 182

Read your modern scientists on the origin of life and you will find that they cannot explain it. They cannot bridge the gulf from the inorganic to the organic.
Studies in the Sermon on the Mount (2), 114

How ready men are to believe any theory that claims to explain away the act of Creation; they accept avidly a mere theory such as that of evolution, which is becoming increasingly discredited on scientific and philosophical grounds.
God's Ultimate Purpose, 410–11

We do believe that whatever is asserted in the Scripture about creation, about the whole cosmos, is true because God has said it, and though Scripture may appear to conflict with certain discoveries of science at the present time, we exhort people to be patient, assuring them that ultimately the scientists will discover that they have been in error at some point or other, and will eventually come to see that the statements of Scripture are true.
Knowing the Times, 346

anti-creationists

What do they believe then? Go and ask them how the world has come into being – the Cosmos – and they will say, 'Well, this is it: there were once two great planets'. You say, 'Where did they come from?' They answer, 'We don't know, but there were two planets, and one day, nobody knows why, one of these passed a little bit too near the other, and in so doing it knocked a piece off the second that fell into space, hence our world!' That is in accord with the gigantic brain of the modern man who cannot believe in God! You show him the order – spring, summer, autumn, winter – the perfection of a flower which you have dissected – the perfection of the human frame or the frame of any animal: you show him the whole order of creation, and he says, 'It is all accident, all a matter of chance. No reason, no end, no purpose at all!' I am literally quoting such a man as Professor Julian Huxley. This is what they believe. It is not surprising that the Apostle called it 'vain reasonings, foolish and wicked'. Rejecting the perfect biblical explanation for the sake of a philosophy – what man thinks about it all! There is only one word to use; it is vain; it is nothing; it is confusion; it is chaos, and the whole future is equally uncertain. That is their position.
The Gospel of God, 378

future

If God is God, the great Creator, and if God is all-powerful with all rule and authority at His command, then the very character of God makes it quite impossible that He should leave creation as it is at the present time.
The Final Perseverance of the Saints, 57

As creation is tied to man, that which happens to man is inevitably bound to happen to creation.
The Final Perseverance of the Saints, 61

The fall of man has affected creation, and creation is not today as it was at the beginning, nor as it will be again when evil and sin are removed out of the world.
Great Doctrines of the Bible (1), 19

Man had no part whatsoever in the first creation, and he has no part whatsoever in the new creation.
To God's Glory, 288

CREED
Christianity is not a vague feeling; it is something very definite. You can know whether you believe it or whether you do not. The creeds and confessions came into being because if you do not believe them you have nothing but chaos. If you do not believe in a body of doctrine, then what have you got? What is the message?
Love so Amazing, 62

CRITICISM
'Speaking the truth in love' has come to mean that you more or less praise everything, but above all, that you never criticise any view strongly, because, after all, there is a certain amount of right and truth in everything.
Christian Unity, 243

Criticism in a true sense is never merely destructive; it is constructive, it is appreciation.
Studies in the Sermon on the Mount (2), 167

THE CROSS (Atonement, Blood of Christ)
We cannot afford to be vague and uncertain as to the meaning of the death on the Cross.
The Final Perseverance of the Saints, 383

The incarnation is not a show. The death on the Cross is not a tableau. No, no!
Assurance, 238

The cross is the supreme and the sublimest declaration and revelation of the holiness of God.
Great Doctrines of the Bible (1), 71

Look at the cross my friend. Have you ever really looked at it?
The Cross, 29

The Cross is the greatest display and exposition of the character of the everlasting God . . . you do not see that glorious person alone; you look again and see that it is not only the Son that is involved in this Cross. The Father is involved, he is there. Have you ever seen him there?
The Cross, 72

necessity
The hour that produced the cross is the central, pivotal point, of history and God always knew about it, the Lord came for that hour.
Saved in Eternity, 111

'That hour' – His hour – what an hour!
Saved in Eternity, 117

Is it conceivable that God would have sent His only begotten beloved Son to the shame and the suffering and the ignominy of the Cross if it were not absolutely essential? If teaching could have saved us, the necessary teaching would have been given.
Assurance, 148

penal substitution
At Calvary God was laying your iniquity on his Son. God was taking your sins and punishing them in him. His blood was shed that your sins might be blotted out. That is the only answer and the only explanation for Christ's death.
Authentic Christianity (1), 267

There is a sense in which it can be said that the Lord Jesus Christ is the only one who has ever tasted death in all its bitterness and horror. That is why we see Him there sweating blood in the Garden. That is why we hear Him crying out upon the cross. That is why He died so soon and the authorities were surprised that He was already dead. That is why His heart literally broke, it actually ruptured. It was because he *tasted*. And my argument is this: Would God the eternal Father ever allow His only begotten, beloved Son to endure that if it were not absolutely essential? But take another statement which says the same thing – Romans 8:32: 'He that spared not his own Son, but delivered him up for us all, how shall he not with him also freely give us all things?' Notice especially the first part: The full wrath of God against sin, the full blast of it, descended upon Him.
Great Doctrines of the Bible (1), 331

The offering of Isaac by Abraham is a type of what God Himself did on Calvary's hill.
The Final Perseverance of the Saints, 389

reaction
The Cross therefore condemns us before it sets us free.
God's Ultimate Purpose, 167

The offence of the cross is this – that I am so condemned and so lost and so hopeless that if He, Jesus Christ, had not died for me, I would never know God, and I could never be forgiven. And that hurts; that annoys; that tells me I am hopeless, that I am vile, that I am useless; and as a natural man I do not like it.
The Gospel of God, 266

I only know that my rags and tatters have really gone when I see them on the Person of Jesus Christ the Son of God who wore them in my stead and became a curse in my place. The Father commanded Him to take my filthy rags off me and He has done so. He bore my iniquity; He clothed and covered Himself with my sin. He has taken it away and has drowned it in the sea of God's forgetfulness. And when I see and believe that God in Christ has not only forgiven but also forgotten my past, who am I to try to look for it and to find it? My only consolation when I consider the past is that God has blotted it out. No other could do so. But He has done so. It is the first essential step in a new beginning. The past must be erased, and in Christ and His atoning death, it is!
Evangelistic Sermons, 238

If you see the meaning of the cross, you will thank him for the remainder of your life and throughout eternity in the glory. Have you seen it?
Love so Amazing, 244

Then suddenly they, like Jacob of old, became conscious of the fact that there was a ladder hanging in front of them, not erected from the earth but suspended from heaven, there waiting for them, constructed without their knowing it – the cross of Jesus Christ – and they began to sing:

> As to the holy patriarch
> That wondrous dream was given,
> So seems my Saviour's cross to me,
> A ladder up to heaven.

Evangelistic Sermons, 198

CULTS (Christian Science, Experience)
The cults generally betray their spurious character at the very outset by promising far too much.
Assurance, 61

It is one of the characteristics of cults that they tend to make an assault upon a man's essential personality.
The New Man, 257

You will find that it is always wise to test the cults on the matter of prayer; because they do not really believe in prayer. This is not surprising in view of their wrongness about sin and salvation, and the blessed Persons of the Holy Trinity, and our whole relationship to them. They do not know anything about prayer. What they know is their own formula. They know nothing about a soul agonising in prayer before God. They regard that as terrible! They know nothing about 'waiting upon God', struggling in prayer, striving to lay hold upon God!
The Christian Warfare, 131

The cults are a striking criticism of the Christian Church, for if the Christian Church were functioning as she should be, the cults would never have an opportunity at all. Hence the appearance of cults is a condemnation of the Christian Church and a mark of her failure.
The Christian Warfare, 133

– D –

DEATH (Afterlife)

We must prepare for death, because it may come at any moment, and because we can do nothing afterwards about it, but, having settled that, we then face how to live until we get there.
Authentic Christianity (1), 170

Let the bombs fall, let war come, let disease and pestilence ravage the lands, let me die – what is it? Translation! To be with him! This old body of mine, the body of my humiliation, the body of infirmity, the body of disease, the body of death, transfigured, changed, glorified, made like the body of Christ's resurrection, and I, in this new, glorified body, ushered into his blessed presence to spend my eternity with him. It is because they knew things like that that these people were filled with gladness.
Authentic Christianity (1), 198

Then, beyond it all, we see our inability in our inability to die well. Every one has got to die but there is a way of dying that is glorious, that is magnificent, that is wonderful; and we cannot achieve that. Death is an awful spectre. Death to most people – to all people outside Christ – is hateful and ugly, something that they do not like to think about and they object to being reminded of it. And when they meet death, they do not know what to do. They are left, helpless, paralysed, unable to say with the apostle Paul, 'To me to live is Christ, and to die is gain' (Phil.1:21).
Authentic Christianity (1) 229

The disposal of your body is not the great question; the great question is the destiny of your soul.
Authentic Christianity (1), 294

It is a terrible thing when a man reaches that point when he knows that he must die, and the Gospel that he has argued about and reasoned about and even 'defended' does not seem to help him, because it has never gripped him. It was just an intellectual hobby.
Spiritual Depression, 57

affects

When you die, you go out of your body; your naked spirit goes on and it stands before God in judgement. And it gives an account of itself, for God gave us this

spirit and he meant us to use it to his glory. So he will challenge us and examine us as to what we have done with it; and we will be judged in terms of that.
Love so Amazing, 80

The Bible teaches quite plainly a conscious existence after death and before the resurrection.
Great Doctrines of the Bible (3), 70

When a man has a true grasp of the doctrine of justification by faith he no longer has a fear of death, no longer a fear of the judgement.
Assurance, 21

When the Christian believer dies he goes in spirit to be with Christ.
*The Final Perseverance of the Saint*s, 85

. . . [T]he Lord Jesus Christ does manifest Himself, in moments of extreme agony and crisis, to help us. Many have testified to this immediately before their death – the greatest crisis of all. Suddenly He has appeared to them, and the people standing by the bedside have seen a smile upon their faces. I remember being at the bedside of an old saint, aged 78, who had once been a terrible sinner. I shall never forget it. Suddenly he must have seen the Lord, for he held out his hands and said, 'I am coming, Lord!
The Christian Soldier, 123

If a philosophy of life cannot help me to die, then in a sense it cannot help me to live.
Banner of Truth, Issue 275

When I come to be an old man, and when I come to die, if I am truly Christian, death to me will be but an entrance, an entrance into a glorious life. I can put that best by contrasting it with what Tennyson said:

> Sunset and evening star
> And one clear call for me!
> And may there be no moaning of the bar,
> When I put out to sea.

No! – with the greatest possible respect to the great poet – that is not Christian. The Christian when he dies, does not cross the bar and set out to sea. No: it is rather, as Charles Wesley put it:

> Safe into the haven guide,
> O receive my soul at last.

That is the Christian view of death. It is going home, it is entering into harbour, 'An entrance will be ministered unto you'. Not a setting out on to an uncharted

ocean, not going vaguely into some dim, uncharted world. Not at all, but an entrance into the haven, going home. What does it all mean? It means that the Christian dies like that because he knows God. He has striven diligently to know Him better and better. He knows Christ. He knows where he is going. He does not feel lonely as he is dying because Christ is with him . . . So the fear of death is gone – he does not object to going because he knows exactly where he is going, and to whom he is going. He thinks also of the 'abundant' entrance.
Sermons on 2 Peter, 50–51

believer

The moment you come to the New Testament, and especially when you read the Gospels, you find an entirely new outlook upon death, something new and strange which the world has never known before.
The Life of Joy, 99

Have you noticed that in the New Testament we are not told that Christians 'die'? Christians 'fall asleep'.
The New Man, 123–24

If you and I are in Christ when the last act comes, the final crossing, we shall be carried by angels. That is death to the Christian.
The Life of Joy, 105

Anyone who realises the truth of salvation, anyone who realises what the Lord Jesus has actually done, will have been delivered, not only from the power of death, but even from the fear of death; not only from the devil, but from all the fear the devil can raise, and has raised, in the mind of all of us.
Liberty and Conscience, 123

I remember reading of the death of a Christian, I cannot even recall his name . . . to the doctor who was attending him he said, 'It is of more consequence that you should repent than that I should recover. For if I die I shall go to God, but if you do not repent you will perish.
Liberty and Conscience, 127

The Christian is one who should be able to face death as Paul faced it, and he should be able to say: 'To me to live is Christ, and to die is gain', and: 'having a desire to depart, and to be with Christ; which is far better.' He is entering into his eternal home, going into the presence of God. Even more, the Christian not only dies gloriously and triumphantly; he knows where he is going. He is not only not afraid; there is a sense of anticipation. There is always something special about him.
Studies in the Sermon on the Mount (1), 318

fear
The world today is as terrified of death as it has ever been.
Assurance, 260

Death is so devastating apart from Christ; it seems to be the end of every-thing.
Assurance, 259

Death is non-productive.
Assurance, 233

inevitability
We are all struggling to keep ourselves young and to fight off death. You can postpone it for a year or two but you cannot evade it. There he is with his scythe, advancing nearer and nearer and nearer the day and we all know it must inevitably come when he will hammer at your door and say to you, 'Move on' and you will have to go.
Authentic Christianity (2), 184

There was no need for man to die. If he had obeyed God, and had continued liv-ing his life in correspondence with God, he would never have undergone phys-ical death. It was possible for him, therefore, not to die. But the result of the fall was that now it was not possible for him not to die. It is put like this in Latin; the original condition was *posse non mori*; now it is *non posse non mori*. Now he must die. It is impossible for him not to unless there is some special interven-tion.
Great Doctrines of the Bible (1), 186–87

preparation
Do you know how to die?
Old Testament Evangelistic Sermons, 189

To me there is nothing more fatuous about mankind than the statement that to think about death is morbid. The man who refuses to face facts is a fool.
Banner of Truth, Issue 275

Of course we do not want to be unhappy on our deathbed. We want to enjoy the blessings of this glorious salvation. Yes; but if we want to die like the righteous we must also want to live like the righteous. These two things go together.
Studies in the Sermon on the Mount (1), 89

We never get annoyed with the man who persuades us to take out a health or a life insurance policy – that is admitted to be the height of wisdom. 'Surely,' one man says, 'you are not going to take these risks, your house may be burnt down'. Or another says, 'Can't you see how wise it is to make provision for

these possibilities?' The thing on which modern man prides himself so much is that he is making provision, and he covers himself in every respect. And yet, when it comes to this, the most certain and the most vital and the most important fact and event of all, he completely reverses the process and even becomes annoyed with anyone who impresses upon him the duty and the importance of facing it and of making some provision for it.
The Life of Joy, 98

A modern man makes preparation and arrangements for practically everything, except his dying; he even makes arrangements for his funeral, but not for his dying. He takes an insurance to look after his burial, he will insure everything, make arrangements for everything except the most important thing of all, the very act of dying, and he never faces that; and that is the whole cause of the modern tragedy and the modern failure.
I am not Ashamed, 188–89

You must not begin to think of how you will die. You must not lay down your postulates and your desires and your demands. Leave it all to him, He is in charge, and you will be carried on angels' wings into the presence of God.
Liberty and Conscience, 109

sin
Death has resulted directly from sin. It is the punishment of sin, it is penal. It is not just a part of man's constitution.
Assurance, 195

unbeliever
I always feel one of the most difficult tasks that we ever have to do is write a letter of sympathy when a dear one has been taken from a family which we know is not Christian.
The Life of Joy, 90

There is nothing more tragic than for a man to find at the end of his life that he has been entirely wrong all the time.
Studies in the Sermon on the Mount (2), 106

The intellectual critic is soon answered. We have but to ask him to explain the meaning of life and death.
Banner of Truth, Issue 275

DEBATE
Lloyd-Jones was critical of those who used the pulpit as a platform for discussion. This was an abuse of its function – the pulpit is to declare and to reason out the implications of the gospel.

The Christian Church was never meant to be a cockpit in which men argue and fight and debate and wrangle about the vital matters of Christ and His work.
God's Way of Reconciliation, 476

If only at the beginning of their argument, debates and discussions someone could get up and say: 'Gentlemen, remember that though we cannot see him, God can see us and that though we cannot hear him with the natural ear, he can and does hear us. Remember, further, that his eye is upon us here and now and his ear open to our words. And then recollect that we are but creatures of time and that he is eternal. Above all, bear in mind as you speak; his return, and the fact that at any moment, we know not when, we may find ourselves standing before him as our judge. You may now begin!'
Old Testament Evangelistic Sermons, 73

'And the house when it was in building was built of stone made ready before it was brought thither.' Then – 'So that there was neither hammer nor axe nor any tool of iron heard in the house, while it was in building' (1 Kings 6v7). What a vital principle this is! Being interpreted and put into its modern dress it is this. There should be no discussion and no debate and no disagreement in the Church about vital truths. There is to be none of this noise of chiselling and hammering and forming and preparation in the Church. That happens before you come into the Church. There should be no discussion in the Christian Church about the Person of the Lord Jesus Christ. There should be no discussion in the Church about the position and condition of man in sin. There should be no discussion in the Church about the substitutionary atonement, and regeneration, and the Person of the Spirit, and all the doctrines of grace. There must be no noise of discussion about these things. All that should have happened beforehand.
God's Way of Reconciliation, 474

The gospel of Jesus Christ is not something which offers itself to us for debate or discussion, but for our definite acceptance and belief. It desires not our approval but demands our obedience. It does not court discussion but rather commands diligence.
Evangelistic Sermons, 24

But the Christian message is not like all these philosophies and views of life. Not only that, it is not a matter of theory, just something to argue about, a good subject for a debating society. How wonderful! Let's have an argument about religion!
Love so Amazing, 93

DECEIT
Deceit is the central and most essential trouble with the human race.
The Kingdom of God, 141

DENOMINATION

There, is a multiplicity of denominations, and men do not hesitate to set themselves up and to start denominations – not in terms of vital truth but in terms of matters which are not even secondary, but of third-rate fourth-rate, even perhaps twentieth – of hundredth-rate importance.
Knowing the Times, 309

DEPRAVITY

The truth we are reluctant to face is that there is no depravity and no cruelty that is beyond the ingenuity of quite ordinary people who are otherwise amiable and even conventional!
Love so Amazing, 169

DEPRESSION

I do not hesitate to say that the devil turns men and women in upon themselves, knowing that when they are looking at themselves they are not looking at God, and so he produces all these moods and depressions within us.
Great Doctrines of the Bible (1), 124–25

You cannot isolate the spiritual from the physical for we are body, mind and spirit. The greatest and the best Christians when they are physically weak are more prone to an attack of spiritual depression than at any other time and there are great illustrations of this in the Scriptures
Spiritual Depression, 19

The kind of person who thinks that once you believe on the Lord Jesus Christ all your problems are left behind and the story will be 'they all lived happily ever after' is certain sooner or later to suffer from this spiritual depression.
Spiritual Depression, 51

Spiritual depression or unhappiness in the Christian life is very often due to our failure to realize the greatness of the Gospel.
Spiritual Depression, 34

DEVIL (Demonism, Evil)

A prominent note in Lloyd-Jones' ministry was his acknowledgement of evil and the person of the devil. At a time when C.S. Lewis was warning about malevolent spirit forces Lloyd-Jones, in pursuit of faithful biblical exposition, called the Church back to a recognition of the reality of Spiritual Warfare. He commented on a piece in the London Times *when sixty eight prominent clerics had identified themselves with a letter denying a literal devil. His most extended treatment is to be found in* The Christian Warfare Sermons on Ephesians 6. *In value, in my opinion, this easily surpasses* The Screwtape Letters. *Alongside it, as the next in the series, is* The Christian Soldier. *Arguably this is one of the greatest treatments covering the nature and reality of spiritual warfare.*

attacks

So often I have to deal with people who have been sent to a psychologist, a psychoanalyst, or somebody like that, and whose problem very frequently is simply that they have without realising it been besieged and attacked by the devil.
Great Doctrines (1), 115–16

The devil is not so much against us as against God. We are nothing in his sight except that we are God's people. The devil's one consuming passion and ambition is to spoil and destroy the work of God.
The Christian Warfare, 94

What are the works of the devil; what has he been trying to do? Well, his great endeavour is to separate men and women from God.
Children of God, 63

Do we not know something of what it is, perhaps, to wake up in the morning and to find that before we have had time to do any thinking, thoughts come to us, evil thoughts; perhaps even blasphemous thoughts? You were not thinking, you were doing nothing, you had just awakened; but suddenly the darts reach you. That is what the Apostle means by 'the fiery darts of the wicked one'.
The Christian Soldier, 301

There are other spirits, and these other spirits are very powerful, and can give wonderful gifts. Satan can counterfeit most of the gifts of the Holy Spirit. For example, there are spirits who can heal. There are strong phenomena in this world in which we live and the test of the gifts of the Spirit is this: Do they testify to the fact that Jesus is God in the flesh? Do they glorify the Son of God? As that is the supreme work of the Holy Spirit, so every spirit must be tested by that particular test.
Saved in Eternity, 87–88

Some of the greatest saints have had a terrible conflict with the devil on their death beds . . . reminding them of their past sins, reminding them of all they have not done . . . of their work and their service . . . In the time of their physical weakness, and with death staring them in the face, the devil has tried to shake them. The only answer to give him is still the same; it is [put on] 'the breastplate of righteousness'.
The Christian Soldier, 256

The greatest saints, the patriarchs of the Old Testament, and prophets, had all been defeated by the wiles of the devil; so he does not hesitate to approach our Lord and to speak as he did, offering to give Him all the kingdoms of the earth if He would but bow down to him and worship him. That is indicative of the great power of the devil.
The Christian Warfare, 81

You may know that an attack comes from the devil and not from yourself: (a) if it appears to come from outside; (b) if you hate the suggestion made; (c) if it leads to anxiety, depression, doubts and over-concentration on self.
Banner of Truth, Issue 275

counselling
One clear diagnostic point is that one becomes aware of a dual personality. There is another person. You see it in the face, hear it in the voice. It is an unnatural and quite different voice and can very often be accompanied by horrifying facial expressions. There is also – a most important point – an alteration between what we may call a normal and abnormal element. These persons can be one moment quite normal and can discuss things quite readily for a time; then suddenly they change. The 'other person' seems to take charge. They will tell you they are conscious of suggestions and voices; and frequently that they have come to have abnormal powers. In my experience there was a woman who was able to hold a complete conversation with a man in Swedish, a language of which she had never learned a word.
Healing and the Scriptures, 165–66

A still more significant pointer is their reaction to the name of our Lord. I always tell ministers who are confronted by the duty of treating such cases to use the phrase – 'Jesus Christ is come in the flesh' and to note the reaction. Talk to them of 'the blood of Christ' and you will generally find that they will react quite violently to this . . .
Healing and the Scriptures, 165–66

demonism
I know perfectly well that the humanist, the 'modern man', laughs with scorn when he hears a man saying something like that. 'What', he says, 'do you still believe in the devil in this day and age? Do you still believe in evil spirits?' Of course I do! I have no explanation of the human tragedy, the human problem, except in terms of the devil.
Authentic Christianity (4), 214

I would divide the contemporary phenomena of the demonic kind into two groups. There is first what may be called demon 'oppression'. It is oppression – not depression (or 'possession'], although there may seem little difference between oppression and depression. I would prefer to call such cases 'satanic attacks'. There is an immense literature concerning the lives of the saints in church history which gives what seem to be authenticated examples of oppression from satanic sources. I believe that examples are becoming increasingly common today.
Healing and the Scriptures, 161

We have been told recently by a popular writer on counselling that we need not consider the possibility of demon possession in our pastoral work, as that ended with the apostolic era.
God's Ultimate Purpose, 6

There is no scriptural evidence for saying that the manifestations of demon activity – the activity of evil spirits – ended at that (the apostolic] time.
Healing and the Scriptures, 159

Demonic activity is on the increase. What is the reason? Well, I would say that primarily it is due to the lowered spirituality, and the godlessness of the whole country. There is always a kind of hangover after a great period of spiritual revival. The influence continues for several generations. This country has been living on the capital of the Evangelical Awakening of the eighteenth century for nearly two centuries. I believe we have come to the end of it . . . But the influence has now gone. As godlessness increases, and the whole concept of God in the public mind diminishes, you would expect a corresponding increase in manifestations of the evil forces.
Healing and the Scriptures, 159–60

There is a plurality of evil spirits. There are thousands, perhaps millions, of evil spirits.
Christian Unity, 58

Christians in certain circumstances may become possessed . . . If we open the doors to evil powers we can be possessed by them.
Healing and the Scriptures, 166

There are cases where this condition is undoubtedly the result of the work of evil spirits; we can see clearly that there is another personality at work. But even short of direct possession we must recognise the fact that our adversary, the devil, does in various ways, through using a lowered physical condition or taking advantage of a natural tendency to over-anxiety, thus exercise a tyranny and power over many. We have to understand that we are fighting for our lives against some tremendous power. We are up against a powerful adversary.
Studies on the Sermon on the Mount (2), 148

limitations
The devil is under the control of Christ, because he has absolute power and even the devil is subject to it. Christ has conquered, and what the devil does is under the sufferance of God, for God's inscrutable reason and purpose.
Saved in Eternity, 185–86

The devil is very clever and very subtle, but not quite as clever as he thinks he is. When the devil brought about, through men, the crucifixion and the death of the Lord Jesus Christ, he thought he was producing his final masterpiece; but ultimately that is what destroys him.
The Law: Its Functions and Limits, 166

The devil is not omnipresent.
The Christian Warfare, 80

The devil is not eternal – he was made by God.
Great Doctrines of the Bible (1), 119

The devil, as we see clearly, not only in the book of Job but everywhere else in Scripture, only has power as God allows him to have it. He has no absolute power. He has no authority in and of himself, but God allows him to exercise certain powers, and undoubtedly one of them is this power over the realm of death.
Great Doctrines of the Bible (1), 343

strategy

I am certain that one of the main causes of the ill state of the Church today is the fact that the devil is being forgotten. All is attributed to us; we have all become so psychological in our attitude and thinking. We are ignorant of this great objective fact: the being, the existence of the devil, the adversary, the accuser, and his 'fiery darts'. And, of course, because we are not aware of this we attribute all temptation to ourselves. So the devil in his wiliness will have succeeded admirably.
The Christian Warfare, 292

We should never speak loosely or flippantly about the devil. I am often appalled as I hear good Christian people referring jocularly to the devil. The Bible never refers to him in that light and flippant manner; it emphasises his power, his status.
Great Doctrines of the Bible (1), 122

There are times when the enemy concentrates on individual Christians, on Christian churches, or sections of the Christian Church, almost upon countries at times, and in this malign manner he does his utmost to destroy the work of God by hurling these 'fiery darts' at us.
The Christian Soldier, 302

The devil is at his very cleverest when he persuades people that there is no devil. Concealment is the whole art of angling. One of the first rules in fishing is to keep yourself out of sight, to camouflage yourself. Throw out your line and let it be a long one so that the fish does not see you sitting or standing by. Hide yourself! It is one of the first rules in angling; and the devil is a past master at this. So when he can persuade the Church, especially, that there are no such beings as the devil and principalities and powers and demons, everything is going perfectly well from his standpoint. The Church is drugged and is deluded; she is asleep, and is not aware of the conflict at all.
The Christian Warfare, 106

unbeliever

I emphasise that the devil does not use his 'wiles' against the unbeliever, the non-Christian. There is no need for him to do so. There is nothing at all

difficult from the devil's standpoint in keeping the person who is not interested in Christ, and who does not believe in Him, in a state of sin. Our Lord
Himself has reminded us that 'the strong man armed kept his goods in
peace'.
The Christian Warfare, 97

DEVOTIONS
If you really believe that just to read a few verses and a short comment on them
in a matter of five minutes, and to have a brief word of prayer, is adequate for
your day, then I say that you do not know anything about the wiles of the
devil.
The Christian Warfare, 153

On whom do you use that box of ointment which you have? To whom and to
what do you give yourself utterly and entirely? Who attracts your interest, who
calls forth your praise and your thanksgiving?
Evangelistic Sermons, 211

If you would know the love of Jesus 'what it is', give Him opportunities of
telling you. He will meet you in the Scriptures, and He will tell you. Give time,
give place, give opportunity. Set other things aside, and say to other people, 'I
cannot do what you ask me to do; I have another appointment, I know He is
coming and I am waiting for Him'. Do you look for Him, are you expecting
Him, do you allow Him, do you give Him opportunities to speak to you, and
to let you know His love to you?
The Law: Its Functions and Limits, 62

DISCIPLESHIP
*Dr Lloyd-Jones personally and consistently disabused people of the notion that he had
sacrificed his career as a doctor in order to become a preacher. His sentiments are reflec-
ted in this general statement*
_____

Do not think of what you have to leave; there is nothing in that. Do not think of
the losses, do not think of the sacrifices and sufferings. These terms should not
be used; you lose nothing, but you gain everything. Look at Him, follow Him,
and realise that ultimately you are going to be with Him, and to look into His
blessed face and enjoy Him to all eternity
Studies in the Sermon on the Mount (2), 236

You and I would probably never have called most of the Apostles who were
fishermen and unlearned men. We would have called a series of men noted as
philosophers. But our Lord, as the Head of the Church, chose some very ordinary men as well as this unusual and remarkable man Paul. It was He who
chose them all. He knew how to lay the foundation.
Christian Unity, 194

DISCIPLINE

It is a terrible thing not to know the chastening of the Lord.
Spiritual Blessing, 151

You know the people I am really alarmed about, those I am most sorry for, are the people in whose lives nothing ever goes wrong. That is a terrible thing. I look back across my little life, I thank God more than anything else for the way in which he has frustrated my plans and purposes 'O love that wilt not let me go!' The 'Hound of Heaven' that will not let me go, that brings me into difficulties, makes me unhappy, knocks me down, makes me cry in agony! Thank God he has done it all, He has done it for my good.
Authentic Christianity (4), 251–52

Many seem to think that Christianity means that you book your ticket, and take your seat in some kind of celestial railway, and thereafter you are wafted passively to heaven without any further troubles. But that is not Christianity! It is a fairy-tale; it is the teaching of the cults. In God's Word you are told to 'mortify the deeds of the body', to 'make no provision for the flesh'. Thank God for a virile gospel; thank God for a gospel that tells us that we are now responsible beings in Christ, and which calls upon us to act in a way that glorifies the Saviour.
The Sons of God, 142

I venture on this assertion, this prophecy: If the West goes down and is defeated, it will be for one reason only, internal rot. There is no problem of discipline on the other side because there is a dictatorship there, and therefore they will have efficiency.
Life in the Spirit in Marriage Home and Work, 259

If ever men needed to make covenants with their eyes it is now.
The Sons of God, 142

It is not a bad thing to say to ourselves before we go any further: 'Throughout the whole of this day, everything I do, and say, and attempt, and think, and imagine, is going to be done under the eye of God. He is going to be with me; He sees everything; He knows everything. There is nothing I can do or attempt but God is fully aware of it all. "Thou God seest me".' It would revolutionise our lives if we always did that.
Studies in the Sermon on the Mount (2), 15

We all probably eat and drink too much.
Banner of Truth, Issue 275

The great need in the Christian life is for self-discipline. This is not something that happens to you in a meeting; you have got to do it!
Banner of Truth, Issue 275

Do not resist Him therefore, do not resist the ointments, the emollients, the gentle teaching which He gives in His instruction in the Word in various other ways. Because, believe me, if you become deeply stained with sin, He has some very powerful acids that He can use, and which He does use, in order to rid you of the sin!
Life in the Spirit in Marriage Home and Work, 178

Child of God, I warn you to be careful. If you try to live a life of sin, then be prepared for the application of the words, 'Whom the Lord loveth he chasteneth'. He will not allow you to continue in sin, He will pull you up. He may strike you with illness, He may rob you of a loved one, He may smash your business, He may ruin some bright hopes and prospects you may have. He may level you to the dust, He will not let you go. He has set His mark upon you; you belong to Him, and He is going to perfect you; and nothing is going to stop Him.
The New Man, 146

God is preparing you for holiness. He is not an indulgent father who hands out sweets indiscriminately and does not care what happens to us. God is holy, and He is preparing us for Himself and for glory; and because we are what we are, and because sin is in us, and because the world is what it is, we must needs be disciplined. So He sends us trials and tribulations in order to pull us up, and to conform us to 'the image of his Son'.
Faith on Trial, 82–83

There is nothing so good for the promotion of humility as chastisement, and we need it if we are to be humble and meek and lowly.
Spiritual Depression, 247

DISCIPLES (the Twelve)
I never cease to be grateful to these disciples. I am grateful for the record of every mistake they ever made, and for every blunder they ever committed, because I see myself in them.
Spiritual Depression, 137

DISCOURAGEMENT
If I were asked to hazard an opinion as to what is the most prevailing disease in the Church today I would suggest that it is discouragement.
The Christian Warfare, 302

DIVORCE (Marriage)
We should make it our business in life to list certain things that must never be done. We must never even consider them. I do not hesitate to assert that the appalling increase in divorce cases at the present time is simply due to the failure to realise this principle. I mean that when two people marry and take their solemn vows and pledges before God and before men they ought to be locking a certain back door that they should never even look at again. But that is not the

way today. People seem to get married and to leave the back door, which leads to separate lives, open. They are looking backwards over their shoulder, and they often allow themselves to think of the possibility of breaking up the marriage before they have even made their vows. That is why life is as it is at the present time. People no longer have their absolutes.
Faith on Trial, 29

DOCTRINE

Unfortunately there are still large numbers of Christians who . . . say, 'I cannot stand doctrine; it is too much for me. I find it difficult and boring. Give me the sort of Bible lecture which will do the whole of Hebrews in one evening and I will be very happy.'
Great Doctrines of the Bible (1), 298

If God has chosen to use such terms as righteousness, justification, sanctification, redemption, atonement, reconciliation, propitiation, then it is our duty to face those terms and to consider their meaning; it is dishonouring to God not to do so. Someone may say, for instance, 'I am not interested in all those terms; I believe in God, and I believe in living as good a life as I can in order to please Him.' But how can you please God if you refuse to consider the very terms that He Himself has revealed to the men who wrote the record?
Walking with God, 23

It is important that we take the doctrines of Scripture in their right order. If you take the doctrine of regeneration before the doctrine of the atonement you will be in trouble if you are interested in the rebirth and having new life, before you are clear about your standing with God, you will go wrong and you will eventually be miserable.
Spiritual Depression, 46

balance

. . . [T]he true position is never at one extreme or the other, but always in the middle.
Evangelistic Sermons, 175

Every doctrine is dangerous, and can be, and has been, abused.
Assurance, 22

The man whose doctrine is shaky will be shaky in his whole life. One almost invariably finds that if a man is wrong on the great central truths of the faith, he is wrong at every other point.
Banner of Truth, Issue 275

I spend half my time telling Christians to study doctrine and the other half telling them that doctrine is not enough.
Banner of Truth, Issue 275

experience

There is nothing which I know of which is more unscriptural, and which is more dangerous to the soul, than to divide doctrine from life. There are certain superficial people who say, 'Ah, I cannot be bothered with doctrine; I haven't the time. I am a busy man, and I have not the time to read books, and have not, perhaps, the aptitude. I am a practical man. I believe in *living* the Christian life. Let others who are interested in doctrine be interested!' Now there is nothing that every New Testament epistle condemns more than just that very attitude.
The Gospel of God, 169

If your knowledge of doctrine does not make you a great man of prayer, you had better examine yourself again.
Banner of Truth, Issue 275

The end of all doctrine is to lead to the knowledge of God, and the worship of God.
Christian Unity, 142

. . . [T]he way to a rich subjective experience is, in the first instance, a clearer objective understanding of truth. People who neglect doctrine rarely have great experiences. The high road to experience is truth, and to concentrate on experience alone is generally to live a Christian life which is 'bound in shallows and in miseries'.
God's Ultimate Purpose, 436

. . . [M]en cannot pray without doctrine; they cannot go into the presence of God except 'by the blood of Jesus'. There is no other way of getting there, there is no entry into 'the Holiest of all' . . .
The Final Perseverance of the Saints, 148

The knowledge of God is ultimately the sum of all other doctrines; there is no sense, there is no meaning or purpose, in any other doctrine apart from this great central, all-inclusive, doctrine of God Himself.
Great Doctrines of the Bible (1), 47

The New Testament always lays down its doctrine first, and then, having done so, says, 'If you believe that, cannot you see that this is inevitable?'
The Life of Joy, 174

The man who isn't interested in doctrine will never have a big experience.
Banner of Truth, Issue 275

false

False doctrine makes joy in the Lord impossible.
The Life of Joy, 19

If 'speaking the truth in love', 'holding the truth in love', means that we are to smile upon all views and doctrinal standpoints, and never criticise and condemn and reject any views at all, how do we avoid being 'children, tossed to and fro and carried about by every wind of doctrine'? This supposed 'loving spirit' makes it impossible to use terms such as 'sleight of men' and 'cunning craftiness' and 'lying in wait to deceive'. The very text itself, and especially the context, make that interpretation completely impossible; indeed it is a denial of the Apostle's statement.
Christian Unity, 244

. . . [W]rong teachings are subtle and attractive and you feel that this is what you need, that it must be right . . . You remind yourself, for instance, of men like George Whitefield and John Wesley who were undoubtedly filled with the Spirit in an astounding, amazing, mighty manner by God, outstanding saints of God and among God's greatest servants; yet you find that they observed the first day of the week and not the seventh, you find that they were not baptised in a particular manner, you find that they never spoke with tongues, you find that they did not hold healing meetings, and so on . . . Cannot you see that these new teachings which claim so much are denying some of the greatest Christian experience throughout the ages and the centuries? They are virtually saying that truth has only come by them and that for 1,900 years the Church has dwelt in ignorance and in darkness. The thing is monstrous.
Spiritual Depression, 188

necessity

. . . [I]f we go astray in our doctrine, eventually our life will go astray as well. You cannot separate what a man believes from what he is. For this reason doctrine is vitally important. Certain people say ignorantly, 'I do not believe in doctrine; I believe in the Lord Jesus Christ; I am saved, I am a Christian, and nothing else matters.' To speak in that way is to court disaster, and for this reason, the New Testament itself warns us against this very danger. We are to guard ourselves against being 'tossed to and fro and carried about with every wind of doctrine', for if your doctrine goes astray your life will soon suffer as well.
God's Ultimate Purpose, 118

My observation over the years is that it is the people who have not been taught the truth negatively as well as positively who always get carried away by the heresies and cults, because they have not been forewarned and forearmed against them.
Banner of Truth, Issue 275

The whole purpose of doctrine is not merely to give us intellectual understanding or satisfaction, but to establish us, to make us firm, to make us solid Christians, to make us unmovable, to give us such a foundation that nothing can shake us.
God's Ultimate Purpose, 302

Take away the apostolic doctrine and you take away my motives for holy living.
Authentic Christianity (1), 136

DOGMATISM
The fact that we have become Christians does not mean that we shall be automatically right in all we think and in all we do.
Life in the Spirit in Marriage Home and Work, 87

DOUBT
Do not conclude, then, that because you are assailed by doubts you are not a Christian. It is the devil that is at work. He will hurl doubts at you. The Apostle describes them as 'the fiery darts of the wicked one'. They come at you from every direction. He will suggest all sorts of difficulties and doubts, anything to stop men believing in God. There is nothing more important than that we should differentiate between the temptation to doubt and the act of doubting itself.
The Christian Warfare, 86

– E –

ECCLESIASTES
Have you ever read the book of Ecclesiastes? It ought to be compulsory reading at a time like this when men and women boast so much of their knowledge and understanding.
Authentic Christianity (1), 230

ECUMENISM
I cannot have fellowship with a man who tells me that because I was christened as a baby I am therefore a Christian.
Christian Unity, 269

If we united all the denominations and added all the powers of each together even that would not create spiritual life. The burial of many bodies in the same cemetery does not lead to resurrection. Life is more important than unity.
Knowing the Times, 24

EDUCATION
I think it is the right of every child that is born into this world.
Old Testament Evangelistic Sermons, 68

ELECTION (Calvinism)
I am not saying that the understanding of this truth is essential to salvation.
God's Sovereign Purpose, 153

A young man like George Whitefield, brought up in the Bell Tavern in Gloucester – who would ever have thought of it? And it is so true in all ages and generations. This is how God does His work, always full of surprises and astonishment and amazement. So let us be ready for this.
God's Sovereign Purpose, 327

. . . [I]t is His desire that all should come to repentance, He has ordained that the gospel should be preached to all, and that all men everywhere should be commanded to repent and to believe the gospel. The free offer of salvation is to be made to everybody. That is the expression of God's 'desire' . . . God's desire that men should be saved does not save anybody. It is God's will and determination

that saves, and what we are told about that is that God has willed and determined to save only some.
God's Sovereign Purpose, 216

The call of the gospel, which has been given to all, is *effectual* only in some.
Great Doctrines of the Bible (2), 65

People often argue that this doctrine of divine election and choice leaves no place for evangelism, for preaching the gospel, for urging people to repent and to believe, and for the use of arguments and persuasions in doing so. But there is no contradiction here any more than there is in saying that since it is God that gives us the crops of corn in the autumn, therefore the farmer need not plough and harrow and sow; the answer to which is that God has ordained both.
God's Ultimate Purpose, 90

Election alone accounts for the saved, but non-election does not account for the lost. That is worth repeating!
God's Sovereign Purpose, 285

The doctrine of election must never be supposed to teach that man is not responsible.
To God's Glory, 163

All who are saved are saved because God has foreknown them, chosen them, predestinated and called them. Yes, but those who hear the gospel and who do not believe it are responsible for their unbelief.
Saving Faith, 341

Man in sin has always had a desire to know what he is not meant to know, so people ask the question, 'Why are only some saved; on what principle and on what grounds does God do that?' Let us be clear about this. I do not know! I will go further, I am not meant to know! I will go further still; I should not even desire to know! Sufficient for me is that any one individual is ever saved. It is the riches of God's glory alone that can ever do that. And, having seen that, I have seen more than enough.
God's Sovereign Purpose, 244–45

The real mystery is not that everybody is *not* saved, but that anybody *is* saved – that is the mystery! God owes nothing to anybody, but if He chooses to do something with what is His own, should our eye be evil because He is good? God has a right to show mercy to whom He will; He has a right to have compassion upon whom He will; there is no ground of complaint whatsoever.
God's Sovereign Purpose, 164

Do you want to ask, 'But why are only some saved?' The answer to that is that none deserve it; all should be damned, and therefore God is free to show and manifest His mercy when He wills, when He chooses, and where and when and in whom He pleases and He chooses.
God's Sovereign Purpose, 244

Many people will find themselves in hell eventually who have heard the general call. There are men who are living in sin and gloating in it who can tell you exactly what the gospel says. They can describe what the call to repentance means, and what the offer of the gospel means. They have a general intellectual knowledge of it. They have heard the general call, but they have not responded to it; it has not been 'effectual' in their cases.
God's Ultimate Purpose, 370

ELOQUENCE
There is scarcely a more dangerous gift to possess than the gift of speech, and the ability to put things plainly and clearly, thereby influencing the hearers. How many a minister, a preacher, has been ruined because of his ready gift of speech!
The Christian Warfare, 334

EMOTION AND EMOTIONALISM
Can a man see himself as a damned sinner without emotion? Can a man look into hell without emotion? Can a man listen to the thunderings of the Law and feel nothing? Or conversely, can a man really contemplate the love of God in Christ Jesus and feel no emotion? The whole position is utterly ridiculous.
Preaching and Preachers, 95

Emotion is a vital part of Christian faith; but emotionalism is not.
The Christian Warfare, 157

What is true emotion as contrasted with both emotionalism and sentimentalism? It is never artificially or lightly produced. Man cannot create emotion; it is too deep for that. It is always the result of an understanding of truth itself. True emotion always results from a recognition of the truth; and the result is that it is characterised by depth. There is also an element of nobility in it, and of wonder and amazement. You never find that in emotionalism, which is all excitement, frothy, voluble, on the surface. Neither does emotion have the politeness of the mere sentimentalist.
The Christian Warfare, 204

If you think you have felt something in a service now and again, and you desire to know whether it is true emotion or not, the time for testing it is not while you are still in the building; it is the day after . . . It will move you to action. It will master you, guide you, direct you; it will be with you; it will have energized

you, it will have been productive. It is comparable to what the Apostle in writing to the Galatians calls 'the fruit of the Spirit'; and it is glorious abiding fruit.
The Christian Warfare, 204–5

Some people live on emotionalism or on sentimentalism. As they believe that nothing matters except this kind of riot or excitement of the emotions, they will, of course, do everything they can to encourage it; and quite often it is deliberately worked up. There are services in which people clap their hands and shout and sing and repeat certain types of choruses – it is done deliberately to work up excitement. And the more excited they get, and the more emotional they become, the more wonderful, they think, the blessing of the Spirit has been. It is mere emotionalism.
The Christian Warfare, 198–99

Emotionalism is a state and a condition in which the emotions have run riot. The emotions are in control. They are in a kind of ecstasy. And if emotionalism is bad, how much worse is a deliberate attempt to produce it. So any effort which deliberately tries to work up the emotions, whether by singing, or incantation, or anything else, or, as you get it in primitive people, in various dances and things like that, all this, of course, is just condemned by the New Testament. The mere playing on the emotions is never right.
Revival, 75

ENTHUSIASM
John Wesley was constantly charged in the same way, even by his own mother, Susannah Wesley. Why could he not preach like everybody else? What was he so excited about? Why all this disturbance? Susannah Wesley was a very godly woman, but she could not understand this son of hers, who suddenly had become an enthusiast.
Revival, 73

There is no problem of discipline in a graveyard; there is no problem very much in a formal church. The problems arise when there is life. A poor sickly child is not difficult to handle, but when that child is well and full of life and of vigour, well, then you have your problems. Problems are created by life and by vigour, and the problems of the early church were spiritual problems, problems arising because of the danger of going to excess in the spiritual realm.
Joy Unspeakable, 19

ESCHATOLOGY
The whole period from the coming of our Lord, and especially from His death and resurrection and ascension and the descent of the Holy Spirit on the day of Pentecost – the whole of the period from that until His final return is 'the last time.'
Walking with God, 97

These matters of prophecy are very difficult, and the people who speak dogmatically about them are just displaying their own ignorance.
Walking with God, 98

ETERNAL LIFE
is ultimately a question of knowing God.
Saved in Eternity, 138

Eternal life must be conceived of in terms of quality rather than mere quantity, or duration. That does not mean that the element of length and duration does not enter in, because it does. But over and above that, is this question of the quality – the thing that is always emphasised in the Scriptures. Our Lord puts it like this: 'I am come that they might have life, and that they might have it *more abundantly*' (John 10:10).
Saved in Eternity, 148

Now 'eternal' not only concerns duration; it does mean that, but it means something else also. Eternal life means life of a certain quality. Life in this world is not only a temporary limited life; actually, as far as death is concerned, it is always, in a sense, a living death. Life outside God is not life, it is existence, for there is a difference between the two. You remember how our Lord put it in that great high priestly prayer recorded in John 17:3: 'And this is life eternal, that they might know thee the only true God, and Jesus Christ, whom thou has sent.' Eternal life always carried that suggestion. Apart from God, life, as we call it, is really death
Saved in Eternity, 148

ETERNAL PUNISHMENT (Hell, Wrath)
God's punishment of sin is eternal. If you believe in wrath you must believe in eternal destruction. The parallels are used everywhere in the Scripture. There is nothing in the Scripture about another chance, another hope, another opportunity beyond death. There is nothing about 'conditional mortality'. It is 'everlasting destruction from the presence of the Lord'. People have tried to say that you can get out of this by means of varying translations. You cannot! The terms are parallel everywhere, and the whole sense and meaning of the Scripture makes it quite plain and unmistakeable. It is everlasting. And God's wrath against sin reveals and manifests itself as death, not only physical death, but still more terrible, spiritual death.
The Gospel of God, 351

ETERNAL SECURITY
Oh, the unutterable folly of men and women who try by philosophy to understand the inscrutable, the eternal, and reject such a doctrine! Some people believe that you can receive eternal life from the blessed Son of God and then lose it, then regain it, and then lose it again, and go on thus uncertainly in this

world until you come to die. My friends, it is an insult to God! It is an insult to God's glorious plan of redemption, it is an insult to God's eternal way of doing things – 'that he should give eternal life to as many as thou hast given him'.
Saved in Eternity, 179–80

What grand security we have because we are 'in Christ'! The Christian is not one who is redeemed and saved today but who may fall from it tomorrow and be lost. There is no 'in and out' in salvation. You are either 'in Adam' or you are 'in Christ', and if you are 'in Christ' you have eternal security, you are in Him for ever.
Assurance, 182

. . . [Eternal security] is a doctrine for believers only.
The Final Perseverance of the Saints, 199

Would you like to face eternity on a novel by H.G. Wells and Co?
Old Testament Evangelistic Sermons, 97

We are now in the life of Christ, and because we are in the life of Christ we are eternally safe, we are eternally secure.
Assurance, 153

I cannot understand people who say that a man can be born again today but that tomorrow he may cease to be born again. It is impossible, it is monstrous, it is almost blasphemy to suggest it. You can have emotional experiences that come and go; you can take decisions and then renounce them. But the Bible teaches the activity and the action of God. And when God does a work it is done effectually; and if you are in Christ you are in Christ. If you are a partaker of the divine nature and joined to, and made a part of, Christ in spiritual union, there can be no severance.
Faith on Trial, 103

ETERNITY
It will be ushered in by our Lord's Second Coming, by the Last Judgment, by the casting to final perdition of everything that belongs to sin and evil, and by the introduction of 'the new heavens and the new earth wherein dwelleth right-eousness'. It cannot have any other meaning. The whole creation is going to be delivered, not temporarily, but absolutely, from the bondage of corruption into 'the liberty of the glory of the children of God'.
The Final Perseverance of the Saints, 85

. . . [Y]ou will spend eternity exactly along the very same lines upon which you have proceeded in this world.
Old Testament Evangelistic Sermons, 239

Oh blessed day! May God grant us grace to see these things so clearly that we shall ever live in their light, and ever, therefore, live lightly and loosely to this passing, condemned world which is to be destroyed. May we live as children of the light and children of the day, as children of God, as those who are going to see Him, to be with Him and share His eternal glory with Him,
Great Doctrines of the Bible (3), 248

We are in time, we are limited in our conception, and we cannot understand eternity; so, because of the limitation of time, when we try to describe eternity we have to say, 'in the beginning'; by which we mean there was no beginning. It sounds paradoxical but there is no better expression of it.
Fellowship with God, 50

ETHICS

It is no part of the Christian Church's business to be exhorting the world to practise Christian ethics, for it cannot do it. It is difficult for the Christian, it is impossible for the world, so there is no single ethical exhortation in the Bible to a person who is not standing on the Christian position.
Walking with God, 71

EVANGELISM

Dr Lloyd-Jones had strong views on evangelism and campaigns. Sometimes these have been misunderstood. Though affirming his belief that the office *of evangelist like that of the original apostles had ceased* (Christian Unity, 192) *the evangelistic ministry continues. Indeed in a frequently quoted remark his wife once commented that her husband would never be understood unless it was realised that first of all he was a man of prayer and then an evangelistic. He believed that the weekly programme of the church should be evangelical and throughout the years of his Welsh and London ministries his Sunday evening sermon (as were many of his expository ones) was invariably evangelistic. Though he distanced himself from the appeal system his evangelistic passion was intense and sustained throughout* the whole sermon.

doctrine
True evangelism I would maintain is highly doctrinal
Knowing the Times, 58

Do not argue with unbelievers about election and predestination; argue with them about this: Why do they not believe the gospel? That is the problem for them. Why do they continue in sin? Why do they not know that their sins are forgiven? Why have they not been born again? Why not? Here is the answer, hold them face to face with that, render them inexcusable.
God's Sovereign Purpose, 218

Evangelism does not consist in telling stories and playing on people's emotions, and then pressing them to a decision at the end without any true knowledge on

their part of what they are doing. No, but it is the outlining of this 'form of doctrine', this message, this truth. Then you go on to tell them that from this complete hopelessness and helplessness and despair God has provided a way of escape.
The New Man, 214

The gospel of God's Son starts with the evangelistic message, but it does not stop there. It goes on to teach – and, indeed, teaching is a part of the evangelizing if it be true evangelism. Indeed, let me put it like this – all the profound doctrines of the Epistle to the Romans come under the heading of 'the gospel of his Son'. All is the good news from beginning to end; and nothing must be left out.
The Gospel of God, 219–20

personal witness
If you and I and all the other Christians walked through this world as men and women who are experiencing the 'abundance of grace' and this 'much more', we should find that people would stop us at work, and in the business or the profession, and on the street, and they would say, 'Tell me, what is this? I want to know about it, I want it for myself'.
Assurance, 239

Our first duty towards an unbeliever is to make him face himself.
The Final Perseverance of the Saints, 199

We must always start with holiness, as the Scripture does; and therefore the preaching of holiness is an essential part of evangelism.
God's Ultimate Purpose, 102

There is no better test of our spiritual state and condition than our missionary zeal, our concern for lost souls.
God's Sovereign Purpose, 31

As you talk to other people whose whole position you may feel to be questionable, the first thing to do with them is to make them talk. Get them to talk about what they conceive a Christian to be; and if they regard themselves as Christians get them to state why they regard themselves as Christians. Encourage them to talk along those lines, and as they do so concentrate on one thing only – does the name of the Lord Jesus Christ come into it at all or not, or how much? You will find quite frequently that people will talk at great length without even mentioning His name. The test which I have always found to be crucial is to ask such a person this question, 'If you had to die tonight and to stand before God, what would you say? On what would you rely? What would your position be?'
The Law: Its Functions and Limits, 35

If every member of the Christian Church were adult, were strong, were able to take strong meat, and to teach others, you would find that the world would be evangelised in a way we have never known.
The Christian Soldier, 89

Christianity spread by 'cellular infiltration' as Communism has since spread. A man speaks to his neighbour or to his workmate. That is one chief method by which evangelism must take place today. We all have the opportunity wherever we are, whatever we are . . .
Life in the Spirit in Marriage Home and Work, 356

Once a man has the love of Christ in his heart you need not train him to witness; he will do it.
The Unsearchable Riches of Christ, 253

urgency
If you and I only realized fully the state and the condition of men and women by the thousand round and about us, I think we would sometimes be unable to sleep. Do you really believe and know that the unbeliever, the person who dies an unbeliever and in his sin, goes to *hell*? Well, if we really believe that, there will be a sense of constraint in our lives. You will not care what people will think of you. You will not be so punctilious about these matters; you will say, Whoever they are and whatever they are, they are dying in sin; they are wretched as they are – there is worse to come! I *must*. I must speak.
The Gospel of God, 254

The business of evangelism is not just to solve people's problems; psychology does that, the cults do that, many things do that. The thing that separates the gospel from every other teaching is that it is primarily a proclamation of God and our relationship to God. Not our *particular* problems, but the same problem that has come to all of us, that we are condemned sinners before a holy God and a holy law. That is evangelism.
The Gospel of God, 95

EVIL (Devil)
The Bible gives us no explanation as to the ultimate origin of evil, and I suggest to you, therefore, that if you waste a second of your time in trying to speculate about that you are guilty of a lack of faith, because faith means to be content with the revelation given.
Great Doctrines of the Bible (1), 121

All we know is that God has permitted evil, and though evil is very powerful and works much havoc, it is still under the almighty hand of God. However this is not to say that God created evil. God permits it and then overrules it.
To God's Glory, 239

So why are things as they are now? And the Bible has its answer. It tells us that there was a rebellion in the angelic places, than an unusually bright angelic spirit, in his pride, rebelled against God. The Bible calls that spirit 'the devil', and tells us that when he fell, a number of angels fell with him. That angelic spirit is now God's great antagonist: he hates God with all his being. He came to God's perfect creation and he tempted the highest being there. It was Eve who was first tempted by the devil, and she led Adam to agree with her. The temptation was to defy God. And they did. Adam and Even listened, they rebelled, they sinned against God and in doing so they fell.
Authentic Christianity (4), 42

So then, the teaching is this: God does not create evil or put it there, but He aggravates what is there for His own great purpose. God never made Pharaoh an unbeliever, but because he was an unbeliever God aggravated his unbelief in order to bring to pass His own great purpose of showing His power and His glory. He did not create the evil disposition in Pharaoh. We are not told that. All we are told is that Pharaoh being the man he was, God used him for His own purpose. And not only that: God saw to it that he was there at that particular point and juncture in order that He might do this through him.
God's Sovereign Purpose, 175

God is the eternal antithesis to evil
To God's Glory, 215

EVOLUTION (Creation, Anti-Creationism)
The biggest hoax in the world for the last 150 years has been the theory of evolution.
Banner of Truth, Issue 275

For the past thirty-seven years or so I have had to read, for various reasons, this argument about evolution, and I am more than tired of it.
Great Doctrines of the Bible (1), 136

I always say that one very good reason for rejecting the theory of evolution is that the moment I accept it I am in trouble and difficulty with the doctrine of sin, and the doctrine of faith, and the doctrine of the atonement. Truth is interrelated: one thing affects another. Do not be too ready to form opinions on one fact or one set of facts. Remember that it will affect other facts and other positions. Look at the subject from every conceivable aspect, bearing in mind not only the thing itself but also its consequences and implications.
Faith on Trial, 28

If you believe in the doctrine and theory of evolution, which says that man is a creature that has evolved out of the animal, and is still evolving and has not yet

'arrived', well, you really cannot have a doctrine of salvation – you will not know what Paul is speaking about in this Epistle to the Romans. In a sense, if the theory of evolution is true, a man does not need salvation.
The Gospel of God, 272

If you are discussing these matters with one of these people who believe in the theory of Evolution, the thing to ask him is this: If this theory is right, why is the world as it is? Why have we had our two world wars? Why has this twentieth century been such a miserable and appalling century?
The Gospel of God, 317

Scientists have often fallen into error concerning this matter. A hundred years ago, and later, there were those who, believing in the theory of Evolution, were saying quite dogmatically that the thyroid gland had no function, but that it was one of a number of vestigial remains. They spoke similarly concerning various other ductless glands. But today we know that these glands perform vital functions. Such people are still saying that the appendix has no function, but what they really mean is that they do not know what it is, and they will probably discover that it has a most important function. The point I am stressing is that there is nothing in the body, nothing even in a single smallest cell, not a hair, but has a function, a purpose. It may appear to be very insignificant in and of itself; but it is in the body and it works with the other elements, and has its part to play.
Christian Unity, 170

The difficulties I am left with, if I accept the theory of evolution, are altogether greater than the few residual difficulties I am left with when I accept the biblical record.
Great Doctrines of the Bible (1), 138

Does an original bang explain everything satisfactorily? Is it all accident? Where did that matter come from that was exploded and dispersed in the 'big bang' that scientists talk about? That leaves so much unexplained, and as you look at all the order and the design and the arrangement and the perfection in nature, and at providence and history and all these things, I ask you: Are you comfortable with your neat little theories? Can you really explain the whole cosmos without God?
Authentic Christianity (1), 321

The real trouble in the world today is that man does not know who he is and what he is; he does not realise his own greatness. For instance, the theory of evolution is an utter insult to man from the standpoint of the biblical account – man is great and glorious and wonderful in the mind and conception of God.
Great Doctrines of the Bible (1), 169

If man had evolved out of the animals, then there would not be this pause between the creation of the animals and the account of the creation of man; the account would have gone on directly from one to the other.
Great Doctrines of the Bible (1), 155

The theory of evolution is an utter insult to man from the standpoint of the biblical account – man is great and glorious and wonderful in the mind and conception of God.
Great Doctrines of the Bible (1), 169

EXAMINATIONS and Theological Training

Lloyd-Jones had very firm views on theological education. He believed in the training of the mind and the benefit of academic study which should be subject to rigorous testing. He was however distrustful of secular universities and their divinity departments. Here theology is viewed as just another discipline and the Bible just another text book. He believed the Bible to be unique. It reveals its secrets to the searching soul by the illumination of the Holy Spirit. Cramming for examinations and intensive study at a purely intellectual level may lead to an abuse of Scripture. Spirituality often suffers in the world of academia. The university is not the best place to train for the ministry.

A man does not understand the Bible simply by knowing Greek or Hebrew. He knows the Bible because he has the Spirit of God in him.
Knowing the Times, 369

. . . [S]ome of us have always had a feeling that it is dangerous to have examinations on scriptural knowledge. Some of the Reformers held that view, Martin Luther especially. Some of the Puritans also held it. There should never be such a thing as a 'Degree in Scripture Knowledge'. This is so, not only because it is wrong in and of itself, but also because it tends to encourage this tendency to stop at truths and to miss the Person. We should never study the Bible or anything concerning biblical truth without realizing that we are in His presence, and that it is truth about Him.
The Unsearchable Riches of Christ, 208

I personally have never believed in having examinations in connection with biblical knowledge. I believe it is a false thing to do in and of itself. We tend to lose this idea that the Bible is given to us in order that it may build us up in our faith, in order that it may do something to us spiritually. There is nothing more dangerous than to have our heads packed with knowledge concerning the contents of the Bible, if that stops in the head and does not move our hearts and does not influence our wills.
God's Sovereign Purpose, 26

The moment you begin to approach the Bible as a 'subject', you are already in trouble. We should never approach the Bible theoretically; the Bible should

always preach to us, and we must never allow ourselves to come to it in any way but that. Nothing is more dangerous than the expert's or preacher's approach to the Bible.
Studies in the Sermon on the Mount (2), 290

I have come to the view that the teaching of theology should never be separated from the Bible. If I were pressed hard I would be prepared to say that theology should never be taught except through sermons! The great danger is to turn theology into an abstract theoretical, academic subject. It can never be such because it is knowledge of God.
Knowing the Times, 371

There is a sense in which it is almost blasphemous that there should be examinations in connection with this knowledge with which we are concerned.
Knowing the Times, 366

EXPERIENCE

Every conceivable experience which the Christian may have to face has already been met and dealt with somewhere in the Scriptures. There is no such thing as a new experience in the realm of the Spirit; you will find everything catered for here.
The Life of Joy, 10

I am getting very tired of evangelicals attacking pietism. I maintain that the true evangelical is always pietistic and it is the thing that differentiates him from a dead orthodoxy.
Knowing the Times, 333

The essence of the Christian position is experience – experience of God! It is not a mere intellectual awareness or apprehension of truth. That can be of the devil. If it does not bring me to the knowledge of the Father, and of His Son, it is of no value to me. But let me remember, on the other side, that it is equally important that my experience should be an experience of the Father and of His Son. There are cults that can change your life, cults that can deliver you from things that defeat you, cults that can give you happiness. Psychotherapy also can do so, and many other agencies, even an operation on your brain. We must have a test. If the experience is not an experience of the living God through His Son who has come to live and to die and rise again in order to give it; if it is not through the Holy Spirit, it is not a true Christian experience.
The Christian Warfare, 197

A little child can paddle at the edge of the ocean, but out in the centre in the depths, the mightiest Atlantic liner is but like a cork or a bottle. It is illimitable. We enter into the Christian life as children, and begin to paddle; but we must go on and out into the depths.
The Unsearchable Riches of Christ, 154

Christians are so much afraid of excesses and enthusiasm that they are only satisfied that they are Christians when they are really miserable. What a tragedy! What blindness, what misunderstanding of Christian doctrine!
The Christian Warfare, 281–82

Experience is not primarily something subjective; it is, rather, the result of something which is based upon the belief of an objective truth.
Fellowship with God, 62

Actually another belief that is very common today is the tendency to dismiss these high experiences as just ecstasy. People try to explain them psychologically as the enthusiasm of youth, or people being carried away by emotionalism. But that is to limit 'the Holy One of Israel' that is to quench the Spirit. That is to put a barrier between that which God has made possible for us and ourselves.
Enjoying the Presence of God, 89–90

If my experience does not tally with the New Testament, it is not the Christian experience. It may be wonderful, it may be thrilling, I may have seen visions. But, I say, it matters not at all; if my experience does not tally with this, it is not the Christian experience. How vital it is, therefore, to grasp this central truth.
Fellowship with God, 64

– F –

FACTS
Facts are not enough.
Love so Amazing, 134

FAILURE
Go back, and read the story of the children of Israel, and you will find invariably that when they were defeated, it was never due to the strength of the enemy, it was always due to their own internal weakness.
Old Testament Evangelistic Sermons, 63

If you feel that you are empty, if you feel you are nothing, if you feel you are poor and wretched and blind, if you hate your inclination to sin and have any suspicion of a feeling of self-loathing and hatred, you can take it from me that you have eternal life, for no one ever experiences such things until the life of God comes into his or her soul.
Life in God, 109

FAITH
Our faith in the Lord Jesus Christ is not our righteousness; our faith does not constitute our righteousness. Faith is simply the instrument by which we receive the righteousness. Or, again, take it like this: our faith does not justify us. If you begin to speak like that, you see, you turn faith at once into works. You say, Ah, I am justified because of my faith; it was my faith that did it; and immediately you have got something to boast of. The other man had not got faith, and I had faith, my faith has saved me. At once you are contradicting Romans 1:17. Our faith does not justify us. It is the righteousness of Jesus Christ that justifies – and nothing else!
The Gospel of God, 306

. . . [T]here is always an element of assurance of faith, but I do not mean by that, that there is always 'full' assurance of faith.
Assurance, 24

There are these three essential elements in faith – believing, being persuaded, and acting. To put it another way, the mind is involved, the heart is involved, and the will is involved.
The Gospel of God, 313

True faith involves feeling and the will as well as the intellect.
The Sons of God, 270

Faith means that I should be content with the revelation that is given me, that I should be content not to ask questions, that I should not even desire to know more, that I should say, 'I am satisfied with what you have given me to understand.'
The Life of Joy, 194

Faith is an activity, it is something that has to be exercised. It does not come into operation itself, you and I have to put it into operation.
Spiritual Depression, 143

Faith is unbelief kept quiet
Spiritual Depression, 143

doubts
Let me use another illustration. Faith in this matter is remarkably like the needle of a compass, always there pointing to the magnetic north. But if you introduce a very powerful magnet at some other point of the compass it will draw the needle over to it and cause it to swing backwards and forwards and be most unstable. But it is certain that the true compass needle will get back to its true centre, it will find its place of rest in the north. It may know agitation, it may know a lot of violence, but it will go back to its centre, it always finds the place of rest, and the same thing is always true of faith. So the mere fact that we may be tempted to doubt, the mere fact that we may have to struggle and bring out all arguments, and go over the whole question again, does not mean that we have not got faith. In a sense it is a proof of faith, as long as we always arrive back at the position of rest.
Assurance, 23–24

It seems to me that to interpret faith as a kind of constant uncertainty is to deny the teaching of the Word of God that we are His children. Indeed, 'the Spirit itself beareth witness with our spirit, that we are the children of God' (Romans 8:16). Such knowledge is possible to us. We ought to be in a position of knowing that we have eternal life, that we know God, and that we know Christ.
Life in God, 93

effort
I still say that faith at times may have to fight. But I hasten to add that faith not only may have to fight, faith does fight, faith can fight; and faith always fights victoriously in this matter of justification.
Assurance, 23

Faith is never bare. Faith is not just a matter of saying 'Yes, I believe, I accept that teaching.'
The Sons of God, 270

Faith, according to our Lord's teaching . . . is primarily thinking; and the whole trouble with a man of little faith is that he does not think. He allows circumstances to bludgeon him. That is the real difficulty in life. Life comes to us with a club in its hand and strikes us upon the head, and we become incapable of thought, helpless and defeated. The way to avoid that, according to our Lord, is to think.
Studies in the Sermon on the Mount (2), 129

tests
It is not a mere believism; and it is important to realise that, because trials and tribulations test mere believism.
Assurance, 62

It is a poor type of Christianity that has this wonderful faith with respect to salvation and then whimpers and cries when confronted by the daily trials of life. We must apply our faith. 'Little faith' does not do this.
Studies in the Sermon on the Mount (2), 134

A faith that does not help us when we need it most of all is not the Christian faith; for this never fails.
Assurance, 61

Faith is always practical.
The Christian Soldier, 305

FALL, THE (Adam, Animals, Consummation, Creation)
The background to the Bible is something that happened before human history began – the great question of the devil and the origin of the devil and of evil. We do not know everything about it – it has not pleased God to reveal everything – but he has revealed this much, that quite apart from our history there was a kind of cosmic fall. As we have seen, one of the greatest of God's angelic beings rebelled against him. He is the devil, called Satan, and his one object is to defeat God. And what is unfolded in this great drama in the Bible is the attempt of the devil to destroy God's works, and to defeat God. God made his world perfect – Paradise – but the devil came in and started a fight. He persuaded man that an injustice had been done against him, and the whole of humanity, and the whole universe.
Saved in Eternity, 113

You cannot really hold the biblical doctrine of salvation without accepting its history, and part of that history is, as this passage shows so plainly, that creation is as it is because at a given point in history, as Genesis 3 tells us, God cursed the earth.
The Final Perseverance of the Saints, 56

The most brilliant plan that has ever been executed in this world of time was that of the Devil in respect to Adam and Eve in the Garden of Eden. What a

perfect plot! What a perfect scheme! How well the Devil knew how to approach them and how plausible and insinuating was his method! Such has been the great characteristic of his followers ever since.
Christian Unity, 238

There were no thorns and thistles in nature before the fall.
Love so Amazing, 270

When the lord of creation fell, creation fell.
Love so Amazing, 270

'Do you believe things like that today?' My dear friend, today's world is what drives me to believe in it. I do not see a world going upwards, but a world going downwards. I do not understand life apart from the doctrine of the fall, the doctrine of evil, the doctrine of hell, the doctrine of the devil. It is all here in this book. The Bible explains it. It is not accident and chance. God made the world in that perfect manner and it is as it is because of the devil and evil and his influence upon this world of ours
I am not Ashamed, 66

Once there was some great palace which has now fallen to ruins, and there is a sign outside which says. 'Centuries ago, such and such a king once dwelt here.' Now, as a result of the fall, it is written over man, 'Here God once dwelt.'
Great Doctrines of the Bible (1), 188

When man fell, he did not cease to be man. His essential manhood remained, and that retains that part of the divine image in which he was originally created.
Great Doctrines of the Bible (1), 175

When man fell, not only was he separated from God, his spiritual faculty itself was paralysed. His mind is dark and dim, his whole understanding is darkened, he lacks the ability and the capacity.
God's Ultimate Purpose, 407–8

Man is fallen; he has become the slave of sin. The highest pinnacle of God's creation, the 'lord of creation', he fell and everything fell with him; the ground was cursed and chaos entered.
The Final Perseverance of the Saints, 360

When man fell he lost something, he lost an aspect of the image, but he did not lose the entire image; something essential to the image still remains. And that at once suggests that there are certain elements in this image of God which are to be found in each person.
Great Doctrines of the Bible (1), 170

FAMILY (Marriage)

Whether we like it or not, a breakdown in home-life will eventually lead to a breakdown everywhere. This is, surely, the most menacing and dangerous aspect of the state of society at this present time. Once the family idea, the family unit, the family life is broken up – once that goes, soon you will have no other allegiance. It is the most serious thing of all.
Life in the Spirit in Marriage Home and Work, 245

In the Old Testament it is quite clear that the father was a kind of priest in his household and family; he represented God. He was responsible not only for the morals and the behaviour but for the instruction of his children.
Life in the Spirit in Marriage Home and Work, 294

There is no greater recommendation to . . . the power of the Christian faith than a Christian husband and wife, a Christian marriage and a Christian home.
Life in the Spirit in Marriage Home and Work, 227

FASTING

I wonder whether we have ever fasted? I wonder whether it has even occurred to us that we ought to be considering the question of fasting? The fact is, is it not, that this whole subject seems to have dropped right out of our lives, and right out of our whole Christian thinking.
Studies in the Sermon on the Mount (2), 34

There are some people who fast because they expect direct and immediate results from it. In other words they have a kind of mechanical view of fasting; they have what I have sometimes called, for lack of a better illustration, the 'penny in the slot' view of it. You put your penny in the slot, then you pull out the drawer, and there you have your result. That is their view of fasting. If you want certain benefits, they say, fast; if you fast you will get the results.
Studies in the Sermon on the Mount (2), 39

Fasting is to be turned into feasting and misery into joy.
Old Testament Evangelistic Sermons, 259

FEAR

The fear of men is taken away immediately when we realize that the living God is among us.
Revival, 126

When you respect a person you do not fear that person. What you fear is that you may do something to displease him, and that, not because you fear that he may punish you, but sometimes even because you may feel that, because he is who and what he is, he will not punish you! Reverence is ultimately based upon

love; it is the recognition of the greatness of the privilege of being allowed to approach God. There is nothing craven about that; there is no torment in it; there is no bondage in it.
The Sons of God, 224

There is a right fear of God and we neglect and ignore that at our peril, and there is a craven fear 'a fear that hath torment'
Spiritual Depression, 168

FEELINGS (Experience)
If we have never felt anything in connection with our faith, then we do not have a true faith. You cannot really believe in this great salvation without feeling something. A man who has a real knowledge of the truth we have been describing is a man who is deeply moved by it. It must be so. You cannot truly realize the presence of God and remain unmoved.
The Christian Soldier, 235

We must be clear about the position of feelings. We must not rest too much on them, but neither must we exclude them.
Assurance, 163

If we are going to base our position solely upon what we feel, and what we are at this moment, then we have nothing to say to the attack thus made upon the Christian faith, especially by psychology. If we base our position entirely upon experience, we will convince nobody. The answer to the good psychology argument is that we are dealing with certain historical events and facts which we must never allow ourselves to forget.
Saved in Eternity, 82–83

How often, in dealing with enquirers after salvation, does one have to point out that the New Testament never says, 'Whosoever feeleth shall be saved,' but 'whosoever believeth.' People often say, 'In a sense I do accept that teaching; but, you know, I cannot say that I have felt anything.' To which the simple reply is that the New Testament does not insist upon feeling. It says, 'do you believe; are you prepared to venture your all upon this?' So it is sufficient for you to say, 'I live by this; whether I feel or whether I do not does not matter; we are not saved by feeling but by believing.'
Life in God, 105

FEMINISM
The protagonists of feminism think that they are exalting women, but actually they are not doing so. Man and woman are different, and are meant to be different, and a truly Christian woman always recognises this.
The Law: Its Functions and Limits, 19

FORGIVENESS

It is part of my duty and my commission as a preacher to say that God, in his justice, cannot forgive men and women by simply saying, 'I forgive you'. I have ample grounds for making that statement. If God could so easily have forgiven people he would have done it.
Authentic Christianity (3), 62

If God could have forgiven sin just by saying, 'I forgive', He would have done so, and Christ would never have been sent into this world. The work that was given to Him to do, this work, this assignment, this task, was given to the Lord Jesus Christ because, I say again, without it, God cannot forgive sin. He must not only justify the ungodly, He must remain just. The way of salvation must be consistent with the character of God. He cannot deny himself, He cannot change Himself, He is unchangeable.
Saved in Eternity, 99

Indeed forgiveness in a sense makes me feel even more hopeless. If God in his grace and compassion has forgiven the guilt of my sins because he has laid them on his own son and punished him instead of me, then that makes me feel more like a worm than I have ever felt before.
Authentic Christianity (3), 83

The trouble with many of us is that we heal ourselves too quickly.
Faith on Trial, 85

Do you think that you deserve forgiveness? If you do, you are not a Christian.
Banner of Truth, Issue 275

The Christian is a man who believes he is going to look into the face of Christ. And when that great morning comes, when he looks into the face of One who endured the cruel cross for him in spite of his vileness, he does not want to remember, as he looks into those eyes, that he refused to forgive someone while he was here on earth, or that he did not love that other person, but despised and hated him and did everything he could against him. He does not want to be reminded of things like that.
Studies in the Sermon on the Mount (1), 318

Unforgiving people have not been forgiven themselves; those who are forgiven are so broken by it that they cannot but forgive others.
Children of God, 115

FREE WILL

The only man who has ever had free will was Adam, and we know what he did with it.
God's Sovereign Purpose, 208

Do not talk to me about 'free will'; there is no such thing. There is no such thing as free will in fallen man.
God's Sovereign Purpose, 207

Man's will has been bound ever since the fall of Adam. By nature man is not free to choose God. The 'god of this world' makes it impossible for him to do so. We are 'dead' in trespasses and sins.
Assurance, 310

There are so many who say: If God is God, and if God has the power, and if God is merciful and gracious, why did He not destroy a man like Hitler at the beginning of his regime; why did He not wipe him out, and all his forces, and thereby save suffering; why did He not intervene earlier; why did He not assert Himself? . . . When such people are thinking about others they expect God to control them; but when they think of themselves they say, 'It is very wrong of God to control me. I am a free man; I must be allowed to do whatever I like; I am a free person, I must have my liberty.' Yes, they must have liberty, but the other man must not!
Faith on Trial, 59–60

FREEMASONARY (Cults)
The term 'mystery' as used in the New Testament does not mean a kind of mystic secret which is only revealed to a few initiates and which is deliberately kept from and guarded from everyone else, as was characteristic of the 'mystery religions' so common in Paul's day . . . It was a closely-guarded secret that was confined to certain philosophers and exceptional people; it was never given to the common people. There are certain cults and secret societies at the present time which are clearly based upon such ideas. Their meetings are held behind closed doors, and the candidate has to pledge himself never to divulge the secret and is taught a secret sign by which he may recognise his fellow devotees. That is the very antithesis of Christianity, which proclaims, preaches, expounds, heralds its message and desires everyone to know it.
God's Ultimate Purpose, 188

GENESIS
It claims to be history. It claims to be giving facts, and the history that follows immediately and directly out of it is certainly true history and not allegory.
Great Doctrines of the Bible (1), 134

GLORY
Do not allow thoughts about the coming visible manifestation of the kingdom to rob you of the realisation of the fact that the Lord Jesus Christ is reigning *now*. He is glorified, the crown is upon His brow; He is the King at this moment. He will come in visible manner; but He is King now, as certainly as He will be then.
God's Ultimate Purpose, 440

'Whom he did predestinate, them he also called: and whom he called, them he also justified: and whom he justified, them he also glorified.' This has already happened. There are foolish people who say you can be justified and then lose that status. But that is impossible; these are links in an unbreakable chain. If you have been justified you have been glorified – your final glorification has already happened in the purpose of God. These are all past tenses to give us absolute proof of the certainty. In certain ways the most daring statement in the whole of Scripture is this statement that we are already glorified.
The Final Perseverance of the Saints, 212

I like repeating this; I like to talk about this glory to which we are going – don't you? Can you ever hear of this too frequently? That you and I are going to be glorified in our very bodies! We shall see Christ and be like Him and we shall reign with Him. We shall reign over angels; we shall reign over the world; we shall be partakers of the inheritance with Him. We are 'joint-heirs' with Him now, and we are going to be joint-sharers in the inheritance with Him. That is the glory! – Perfectly redeemed – body, mind and spirit – with not a trace of evil or sin anywhere near us, but without spot, or wrinkle, or any such thing – whole, entire, glorified, even as He is glorified!
God's Sovereign Purpose, 243

To use an obvious comparison, it is exactly as if you were sitting in a theatre and you see nothing but curtains. You have no idea as to what is behind the curtains.

But there is something there; and suddenly the curtain goes up, or is drawn aside, and you find yourself looking at a great sight. That is the idea. It is not to be created, it is not something that is yet to be produced; the glory is there. What will happen is that this glory will be 'revealed', it will be 'made manifest', it will be 'shown'.
The Final Perseverance of the Saints, 37–38

Our bodies are weak and subject to illness and infections and coughs and colds and aches and pains and all these things. It is all the result of the Fall. And there is no real beauty. All the beauty of man, the most handsome man or woman, is only relative beauty, and there are seeds of decay in it. But when we are glorified our very bodies shall be perfect, every vestige of sin will be taken out of them, and all the results and consequences of sin will be entirely removed. There will be no trace of sin left, and every one of us will be glorious in beauty.
Assurance, 51

The Church will have renewed her youth. Dare I put it like this? The Beauty-Specialist will have put his final touch to the church; the massaging will have been so perfect that there will not be a single wrinkle left. She will look young, and in the bloom of youth, with colour in her cheeks, with her skin perfect, without any spots or wrinkles. And she will remain like that for ever and for ever. The body of her humiliation will have gone; it will have been transformed and transfigured by the body of her glorification.
Life in the Spirit in Marriage Home and Work, 175–76

We never become God-men. We still remain man, but glorified man, perfect man. We are not transfigured or transformed into God.
Saved in Eternity, 152

We are concerned about getting the reluctant outsiders into the Church, but when you and I know something of the glory of God, and when those others see that we are being 'changed from glory into glory', they will come to us of their own accord as they have always come to such people.
Assurance, 57

GOD
The Christian gospel does not start with the Lord Jesus Christ, it starts with God the Father. The Bible starts with God the Father always, everywhere and we must do the same – because that is the order in the blessed Trinity: God the Father, God the Son, God the Holy Spirit.
Saved in Eternity, 42

awe
I can remember a group of us young men, all smoking cigarettes or pipes, laughing and joking, being clever and talking about God! If we had known

anything about God we would have put our cigarettes out and thrown away our pipes; we would have taken the shoes from off our feet; we would have realised we were on holy ground and we would have got down on our knees.
Love So Amazing, 197

There is nothing that so alarms and frightens me as I listen to people discussing these matters, as the glib way in which they talk about God. God, they say, ought to do this or that and they express their opinions. Do you realise what you are saying, my friend, do you realise that this God is a consuming fire, a holy God, 'the Father of lights, with whom is no variableness neither shadow of turning.' I beseech you be careful how you use the very name of God. I can understand the ancient Jews and their fear of using the Name.
Old Testament Evangelistic Sermons, 41

Perhaps something has been going wrong – we may find ourselves like that man in the seventy-third Psalm, who had been having a hard time while the ungodly were very prosperous, and we begin to say, 'Why does God . . .?' Oh, my dear friends, the next time that thought or feeling arises in your breast, stop for a moment and remember that you are thinking and speaking about the uncorruptible God, this glorious Being; glorious in His holiness, infinity, and majesty! Let us put our hands upon our mouths and be content to wait until He reveals His purpose to us. How dangerous it is to speak, without thinking, about God, the Creator 'who is blessed for ever, Amen'. Let us stop for a moment! God forbid that we should ever be guilty of speaking about God in a manner that is unworthy!
The Gospel of God, 387

The very Name of God should be an object of Reverence. You know that the Jews did not use the Name Jehovah; they felt it was too sacred. Somehow or other we have lost that sense of Reverence, but the Apostle calls us back to it here. The very thought of God in His transcendence, in His majesty and infinity, and in His glory should humble us. We should speak of Him with reverence and with godly fear.
The Gospel of God, 386

existence

I have always argued that the human eye alone is more than enough for me to prove that there is a God, a creator. This delicate, sensitive organ, so refined, able to discriminate as it does, this little organ which so governs the whole of our life in almost every respect. Is this accident? No, the whole thing is so perfect; it is such a perfect instrument, beyond anything that man could possibly make, that it postulates a great Mind, a great Designer, a great Artist.
I am not Ashamed, 60

forgiveness

God, being God, cannot just forgive sin.
Saved in Eternity, 99

The forgiveness of sins, I dare to say, taxed even the wisdom of God.
The Unsearchable Riches of Christ, 87

holy
My friends, is not this the thing we need to preach to the world, that God is holy, that God is righteous, that he hates sin with an eternal hatred, and will punish sin. That is his own revelation of himself.
Revival, 232

immutability
God's will is an unchanging will, and it is an unchangeable will because God is God. What God wills, God does; what God purposes, God executes. The unchangeable will of God is the bed-rock of everything. If I do not believe that, I have no faith at all. It is an absolute truth that God is.
Faith on Trial, 100

God's character never changes, but His dealings with people change.
Great Doctrines of the Bible (1), 61

God does not change. As someone put it, 'Time writes no wrinkle on the brow of the Eternal.' And man does not change; he is exactly what he has always been ever since he fell and has the same problems.
Preaching and Preachers, 41

How can you at one and the same time say that God is immutable and unchangeable, and still tell us that the Bible talks about God repenting, because repentance means to change one's mind? And clearly the answer is this: God's character never changes, but His dealings with people change.
Great Doctrines of the Bible (1), 61

We cannot grasp the ultimate working of God's mind. It is no use asking, Why this? and, Why that? Why did God raise up Pharaoh? Why did He choose Jacob and not Esau? Why does He punish us if all things are determined and decreed? The answer is, 'Nay, but, O man, who art thou? You are pitting yourself against the mind of God. You are forgetting how small you are, how finite you are, how sinful as a result of the fall. You have to leave the ultimate understanding until you arrive in glory. All you have to do here in time is to believe that God is always consistent with Himself, and to accept what He has plainly and clearly told us about His eternal decrees, about what He has determined and decided before He ever created the world.
Great Doctrines of the Bible (1), 102

justice
If ever you feel tempted to say that God is not fair, I advise you to put your hand, with Job, on your mouth, and to try to realize of whom you are speaking.
God's Ultimate Purpose, 16

God is one, and God is indivisible, and God always acts as Himself. You must not set the love of God against the justice of God. God always acts in the fullness of His being, He always acts in love; at the same time He always acts in justice, and you must never say that God's love acts apart from His justice or apart from His righteousness. Neither must you say that His justice and His righteousness act apart from His love. God acts as God and you must never drive a wedge between these attributes.
Assurance, 148

love
God delights in His love even more than He delights in His justice.
Assurance, 231

The love of God is seen in its fullness in Christ's death.
Assurance, 111

Whatever one may say about the love of God in Christ Jesus there is always something more to be said. This is the theme of the angels in glory, it is the anthem, the song of all the redeemed. It is the theme that will occupy us throughout eternity.
Assurance, 140

To know something of the love of God one must have some understanding of what has happened in and to the Son of God, 'the beloved'. It is in Him that we measure the love of God truly.
God's Ultimate Purpose, 141

Such is the love of God. He sees men reviling His Son, He sees men laughing at Him, He sees men taking up stones to throw at Him, His Beloved. The God who made the world out of nothing, and who could bring it to an end in a moment, the God with whom nothing is impossible looks on and watches the world refusing His 'beloved', persecuting Him and wounding Him. There we have some measure of the love of God. As you read the story in the four Gospels remember that it is 'the Beloved' you are reading about, and that the Father is ever looking at His Beloved and at the world's treatment of Him.
God's Ultimate Purpose, 142–43

If we are going to attribute our sentimental, loose, unjust and unrighteous notions of love to the everlasting Godhead, then we place ourselves in the most precarious position.
Great Doctrines of the Bible (1), 333

mercy
He has no pleasure in what unbelievers are, and no pleasure in destroying them. He is allowing them to go on, as it were, in order that they might listen

to the gospel. That is God's desire and pleasure, but it does not save them. His long-suffering and patience with Pharaoh did not change him. Our Lord's patience and long-suffering with Judas did not change him. God's long-suffering with this world in which we live with the whole human race is not bringing it to belief in the Lord Jesus Christ. But what a demonstration it is of the long-suffering and the patience of God! We would never know anything about them if He did not withhold His wrath.
God's Sovereign Purpose, 216

name

That the name of God stands for the character of God is seen again in Psalm 22:22, 'I will declare thy name unto my brethren . . .' And, in the New Testament, you will find that our Lord's great claim just before His death upon the cross was, 'I have manifested thy name unto the men which thou gavest me' (John 17:6). Later He said, 'I have declared unto them thy name' (v. 26). To declare the name of God is to tell the truth about God. It is to put this great truth about God's being in a form that men and women can grasp and apprehend.
Great Doctrines of the Bible (1), 80

You should never say 'Dear God'. Our Lord did not speak thus; He said 'Holy Father'.
The Sons of God, 224

More and more, as I consider these things, and spend ever-increasing time in reading my Bible, I understand why the ancient Jews never mentioned the name Jehovah. They were filled with such a sense of awe and reverence, they had such a conception of the majesty of God, that in a sense they dared not even utter the name. I much prefer that, to hearing people saying, 'Dear God'. I do not find such an expression in the Bible. I do find 'Holy Father', but never 'Dear God'.
Great Doctrines of the Bible (1), 53

omnipotence

God's power not only surpasses our power of expression, it surpasses our power of comprehension! Take all the dictionaries of the world, exhaust all the vocabularies, and when you have added them all together you have still not begun to describe the greatness of God's power.
God's Ultimate Purpose, 397

omnipresence

God's infinity suggests to us that He is the cause of everything else; all existence, all being, derives from Him. His infinity also reminds us that He is free from all restrictions and all bounds; there is no limitation whatsoever where God is concerned, He is everything, everywhere, unlimited. Or perhaps the best way of thinking of it is this: the exaltedness of God, the sublimity of God, the

ineffable majesty of God, or the transcendence of God, above and beyond everything.
Great Doctrines of the Bible (1), 53

omniscience
You cannot move but that God sees you, you cannot act but that he is watching you, no thought enters into your mind but that he is aware of it. He not only sees you but sees through you, to the very depths of your being. We are as an open book before him.
Old Testament Evangelistic Sermons, 239

If I could understand God I should be greater than God, and if he is only to do what I can understand, and what I think he ought to do, he will no longer be God but my servant.
Old Testament Evangelistic Sermons, 173

sovereignty
You will find that the will of God expresses itself in two main ways. He declares certain things which He Himself is going to do: that is called the decretive will of God. He also prescribes certain things for us to do: that is the prescriptive will of God.
Great Doctrines of the Bible (1), 67

When God begins God continues.
God's Way of Reconciliation, 196

God is incapable of leaving anything half done.
Faith on Trial, 101

The Bible does not deal with trivialities, with mere incidents of time. Nations may rise and fall, but God's plan goes steadily on. Furthermore, the plan will not be modified to suit the whims and fancies, the likes and the dislikes of any individual or of any nation.
The Unsearchable Riches of Christ, 78

wrath
Before there can be peace between God and man, and man and God, something has to happen with respect to the wrath of God, which is a revealed fact.
Assurance, 15

The fact that we proclaim and preach the doctrine of the wrath of God, as the Apostle does, does not mean that we teach any division in the blessed Trinity. The Apostle has told us that the wrath of God is against all ungodliness and unrighteousness of men, but then he goes on to say that the same God has sent forth the Son as a propitiation for our sins.
Assurance, 105

There is no teaching in the Scripture about the universal Fatherhood of God, and the universal brotherhood of man.
God's Sovereign Purpose, 257

Belief in a supreme God is an instinct that all people have in common. Everyone who is born into this world has this instinct.
Great Doctrines of the Bible (3), 73

GODLINESS
I wonder why it is that the whole idea of the godly man has somehow or other got lost amongst us? Why is it that Christian people are not described as 'god-fearing' people?
The Life of Joy, 179

The truly godly man is never a showman. He knows enough about the plague of his own heart never to be guilty of that.
The Righteous Judgement of God, 146

The Church has been trying to preach morality and ethics without the gospel as a basis; it has been preaching morality without godliness; and it simply does not work. It never has done, and it never will. And the result is that the Church, having abandoned her real task, has left humanity more or less to its own devices.
Preaching and Preachers, 35

GOOD WORKS
You may have spent the whole of your life in doing good works, but I say that you have no more right to eternal life than the most dissolute vagrant in the world today.
Saved in Eternity, 131–32

This century has suffered more as the result of the teaching of 'good pagans' than, perhaps, of anyone else. Because of their very excellencies and because of their natural abilities, these people are the most convinced of all unbelievers, the most fervent of all the opponents of the Christian faith.
Authentic Christianity (3), 199

GOODNESS
If you are to say that everybody who lives a good life is a Christian, then you must scrap the New Testament and do away with the Christian church since it is not necessary.
Christian Conduct, 19

GOSPEL (Society, Unevangelised)
The primary business of the Christian gospel is not to give us blessings. Its primary function is to reconcile us to God.
Assurance, 10

affects

The gospel comes to us and makes us see that by living a life apart from God and apart from Christ we are living a life which is a travesty of human nature and we are doing something that is utterly insulting to God. Man is meant to be a living soul in communion with God – the gospel makes us see that.
Old Testament Evangelistic Sermons, 29

If the gospel is not bearing fruit in you, then you are outside Christ and you are not ready to die and face God in the judgement.
Love so Amazing, 96

The gospel always gets rid of complications.
Authentic Christianity (1), 202

The paradoxical character of the gospel was first stated by that ancient man, Simeon, when he had the Infant Jesus in his arms. He said, 'This child is set for the fall and rising again of many in Israel.' There is the paradox. At one and the same time He is set for the fall and for the rising again. The gospel always does these two things, and unless our view of it contains these two elements, it is not a true one.
Studies in the Sermon on the Mount (1), 310

When you know that to take a certain course is the only cure for a disease, that it is specific, that it cures it to a certainty, and that nothing else can do so, you do not regard it as being narrow-minded to use that remedy and to refuse to waste time with other remedies. That is not being narrow-minded, it is just being sensible and sane and rational.
The Christian Soldier, 25

This gospel which leads men to sing, always first of all saddens them. If, therefore we have never been saddened by the gospel that is the reason why the gospel has never made us sing. To put it in more theological language: The gospel is bound to convict us before it can convert us.
Westminster Record Dec 47, 91

Does the gospel really wrong you when it tells you the truth about yourself, when it exposes all the hidden things of your heart and all the inmost recesses of your soul?
Old Testament Evangelistic Sermons, 154

The gospel tells all men at the very beginning that it does not matter how able a man may be, that alone will never make him a Christian. It puts the able man on exactly the same level as those who are most lacking in intellect. It reduces all, as we have already seen, to a common level. It deliberately says that intellectual pride is probably the last citadel to give way when the Holy Spirit is

dealing with a man's soul. The gospel does not glory in intellect. It does not glory in moral effort and striving. It tells you at the very beginning that you can do all you like and it will avail you nothing; that all your righteousness will be as 'filthy rags', that all your wonderful works will be 'dung' and 'refuse' – of no use at all to you!
The Gospel of God, 263

Take a lump of clay, which you can mould and fashion almost as you like. Put it out in the blazing sunshine and it will become as hard as a brick. I think there is something of that idea here, and I look at it like this: the goodness and the forbearance and the long-suffering of God are shining down upon mankind like the sun, and they are meant to soften and to melt us, but what they do to these people is to harden them. The sun does both things – it melts butter, but it hardens clay. And, according to the Apostle here, it is always one or the other. That is why the preaching of the gospel and listening to the gospel both carry such a tremendous responsibility – they either soften or they harden. They are bound to do one or the other. And what Paul says here is that these people, because of their completely wrong attitude, are hardened by the very thing that was meant to melt them, and to soften them.
The Righteous Judgement of God, 68

I say, therefore, that every time you and I hear the gospel our responsibility is increased. The more we have heard the gospel, the clearer our understanding of it, the greater is our responsibility.
The Righteous Judgement of God, 109

definition
The Christian gospel is unique. It tells us: Be what you are; realise what you are; and proceed to show that you are what you are. Nowhere else in the world do we find such a message.
Christian Conduct, 113

The gospel, by definition, is supernatural, miraculous and divine.
Authentic Christianity (4), 224

Have you ever followed the gospel to its logical conclusion? If not, do so now. Here is the argument. How simple and how logical it is. There is God, the Judge eternal. Here am I, the sinner. God demands certain things of me and has made them quite plain and clear in His law, which is also attested by my own conscience. I *have* to appear before Him.
Evangelistic Sermons, 157

The narrowness of the gospel – I speak with reverence – is the narrowness that is in God Himself.
Evangelistic Sermons, 275

The gospel is not something that invites us to join in a great search or a great quest. It is an announcement. It is a revelation. It is an unfolding, an unveiling of something. It means, 'making manifest' or 'making plain and clear'.
The Gospel of God, 295

modernity
I am sorry Mr Modern Man, even your great brain cannot understand miracles, and the sooner you realize that the better. If the gospel were something that you and I could understand it would not be the 'glorious gospel of the blessed God'; it would be a philosophy that we dissect and apprehend. But it is not.
Authentic Christianity (2), 193

Old and New Testament
The great message of the gospel of God is essentially the same in the Old Testament and in the New. The real difference between the two is simply in the mode of expression – faint and indistinct in the Old Testament, and clear and loud in the New.
Old Testament Evangelistic Sermons, 257

origin
If we fail to realise that the gospel and all it professes is primarily an activity on the part of God, and not on the part of man, we have entirely failed to understand it.
Old Testament Evangelistic Sermons, 243

As the gospel is purely a matter of revelation given to the apostles by God, we cannot add to it, or subtract from it. So anything that may have happened in the world since the writing of the New Testament makes not the slightest difference. We are dealing here with things about God and eternity, and we know nothing about them. On this subject there has been no additional knowledge during the last two thousand years. None at all.
Love so Amazing, 64

social consequences
People do not understand the message of Christianity. They think that Christianity teaches world reform and urges us to make the world a better place, pass acts of Parliament, do social and political good, gradually transform society until the whole world is changed . . . the gospel has never promised to bring the new Jerusalem to 'England's green and pleasant land'. You can call for your swords, you can call for your spears, you can talk about your mental flight, and you will die a complete failure.
Authentic Christianity (4), 98

All the greatest benefits that humanity has ever known have come through this gospel. Good deeds! Where did hospitals come from? The Christian Church.

Where did education come from . . . Where did relief for the poor and suffering come from . . . Look at the missionary activities. Look at the light that has been taken to the dark places of the earth. What is the basis of liberty in England? The Magna Carta. Yes, but that did not do very much according to the best historians of today. Do you know where our modern liberty has really come from? I can tell you. It came through the Puritans of the seventeenth century . . . And did you know the trade unions are a direct outcome of the evangelical revival of two hundred years ago?
Authentic Christianity (2), 17

unevangelised

A man who has never heard the gospel and has never had an opportunity of hearing it, will not be judged as if he had heard it.
The Righteous Judgement of God, 105

What, then, is the position of pagan people who have never heard the gospel at all? How are they saved? By what are they saved? . . . We cannot answer the question. All I can say is this: I know that they were all condemned by their moral consciousness, and I can say equally that no one can be saved outside the Lord Jesus Christ. And I know no more. But I will go further: I am not meant to know anymore. There would be something about it in the Bible if I were meant to know more, and there is not a word. You cannot raise it on the basis of Scripture – Scripture does not deal with the question at all, and we cannot go beyond that. The moment you do, you are beginning to speculate, and the moment you begin to speculate you are doing something very dangerous . . . There is only one thing to do – we bow our heads before Him. We are content with the absence of clear teaching, with the absence of revelation. We submit to it.
The Righteous Judgement of God, 134–36

urgency

The greatest need in the world tonight is the authoritative proclamation of this one and only gospel.
To God's Glory, 270

Ah! It is always madness that rejects Christ.
Evangelistic Sermons, 112

We *must* – we *must* fight for the faith in these momentous times.
Knowing the Times, 59

There is no 'love of God' for you unless you have repented or unless you do repent. Make no mistake about this. Do not rely or bank on God's love. It is only given to the penitent; there is no entry into the kingdom of God except by repentance.
Evangelistic Sermons, 122

And I ask you to consider it again prayerfully in the presence of God as you value your own immortal soul and its eternal destiny.
Studies in the Sermon on the Mount (2), 250

'What' you say. 'Is it part of the gospel of Christ to tell people to be afraid, to fear?' It is.
To God's Glory, 122

GRACE
What is grace? It is a term notoriously difficult to define. Grace essentially means 'unmerited favour', favour you do not deserve, favour you receive but to which you have no right or title in any shape or form, and of which you are entirely unworthy and undeserving. We may call it condescending love – love coming down.
God's Ultimate Purpose, 37

abundant
Grace always abounds. Grace must never be thought of in static, mechanical, mercenary terms. No, no! There is no measure to grace, no limit – it is illimitable.
Assurance, 234

The 'gift by grace' always leads to superabundance.
Assurance, 248

We do not shuffle into this grace; we are introduced and presented, standing erect upon our feet. 'Ah but', you say, 'I have been a vile sinner, I have been a terrible sinner, how can I possibly go into the presence of God with boldness?' My reply to that is that if you do not go in with boldness you do not enter by faith. Realize that you go in Christ's hand, that His righteousness is upon you and that He leads you in.
Assurance, 41

O Christian friends, do not make bargains with God. If you do you will get only your bargain; but if you leave it to his grace, you will probably get more than you ever thought of . . . do not keep a record or an account of your work. Give up being book-keepers,
Spiritual Depression, 130

common
There is a light in the world apart from the gospel. Take all human glimmers of moral and intelligent enlightenment, take everything in the world that limits the darkness of Satan, where does it come from? The Bible says that the light in all people, whether unregenerate or regenerate, comes from God, from Christ, any light has come from Him.
Great Doctrines of the Bible (1), 294

irresistible

There should be no trouble or difficulty about this; not only is grace irresistible, it must be irresistible. For if grace were not irresistible no one would ever have been saved. That follows of necessity from the fact that we were dead spiritually, and were at enmity to God, hating His Truth. How can we be saved therefore? There is only one answer – the power of grace is irresistible.
Assurance, 344

The idea that grace presents itself to us, but that the final choice remains with us as to whether we are going to take advantage of it or not . . . is a contradiction of the entire biblical teaching concerning the way of salvation. If that idea were true then no one would ever be saved.
Assurance, 344

Grace is the fount and the source which leads to this ocean of peace.
The Gospel of God, 172

motivating

The 'grace' that made him [Paul] a preacher drove him across continents, and across seas; it made him preach day and night with tears and pleading; it was the most vital force in his life. This was the thing that 'constrained' him, and made him say, 'Woe is me if I preach not the gospel'! He was driven by the thought of these riches of God's grace, and the ignorance of men and women concerning them. It was his chief reason for writing this Epistle to the Ephesians.
God's Ultimate Purpose, 174

saving

First, 'saving grace'. This is the original way in which grace comes to us, bringing forgiveness of sins. Then 'restraining grace'. We noticed that it was God who held this man back (Ps. 73). His feet were almost gone. Why did he not slip? He thought it was the recollection of the harm he would be doing to the weaker brother. But the question is, Who put that into his mind? It was God. God restrains us. God allows His children to wander very far, so far at times that some people say, 'That man has never been a child of God.' But that, as we have seen, is to fail to understand the doctrine of back-sliding. God seems to allow us to go a long way, but He never allows us to go all the way. He holds us by our right hand, He restrains us. Then we saw the working of 'restoring grace'. God brought this man back and took him to the sanctuary.
Faith on Trial, 96

You remember that saintly man John Bradford, one of the Marian martyrs, who four hundred years ago was put to death at Smithfield Market. You remember how he put it as he was walking along with a friend and saw a poor fellow

being taken to be put to death because of some crime that he had committed. The saintly John Bradford looked at him and said, 'There, but for the grace of God, goes John Bradford!' And that should be the feeling of every Christian. We are what we are, not because of our goodness, not because of our lives, not because of *anything* in us. It all comes from the love of God – that everlasting, inscrutable love.
The Gospel of God, 167

The ultimate test of our spirituality is the measure of our amazement at the grace of God.
Banner of Truth, Issue 275

sovereign
Grace reigns, and it does not share the Throne with anybody or anything else. You must not put your good works there, or the Church, or priests, or saints or the Virgin Mary or anything else. Grace occupies the Throne alone; and if you try to put anything alongside it, it means that you have not understood 'the reign of grace'.
Assurance, 319

Grace is the only power that is big enough to take the field against sin.
Assurance, 316

Grace is not sentimental; holiness is not an experience.
Studies in the Sermon on the Mount (1), 197

We are what we are by the grace of God, and by that alone. And as that is true of us now, so it will be true of us on our deathbeds. We will have nothing that we can rely upon save the purpose of God, and that we are included in it by His grace.
God's Sovereign Purpose, 319

Grace is the alternative to sin, and the only alternative to sin. Or to put it another way, grace is the only antagonist of sin, the only antithesis of sin.
Assurance, 316

Grace is not simply offered to us; grace acts . . . Grace acts, and acts as a king.
Assurance, 318

There is nothing that can withstand the power of the reign of grace.
Assurance, 339

unchanging
You cannot go in and out of grace; you cannot be saved one day and not be saved the next, and go back and forth. You are either under the dominion of sin and Satan, or else you are under the dominion of grace and of God.
The New Man, 143

If you are biblical you must take the same ground as the Apostle Paul. Paul says that we must boast of this, we must exult and glory in it. But how can you do so if you are uncertain about it? That is also the reason why any doctrine that teaches a possibility of falling away from grace is unscriptural. You cannot boast and exult and glory in the ultimate of salvation if you may suddenly lose it all.
Assurance, 55

unmerited

There was nothing in mankind to recommend it to God, nothing in human nature, nothing in any one of us to recommend us in anyway to God and to His love. Indeed the truth about us was, and is, that there was everything in us that was wrong and vile and hateful, everything calculated to antagonise God towards us – enemies, hateful, vile, ungodly, sinners as we were. We must realize that our salvation is entirely gratuitous, and arises only and altogether from the love of God in His infinite grace.
Assurance, 124

If a man delights in free grace, and in the 'free gift', you can be sure he is a man who has seen his utter sinfulness and hopelessness and helplessness.
Assurance, 256

Do we delight to talk about 'free grace' and 'free gift'? Pharisees never do so because they realise that these terms make them out to be paupers as all others. They like to feel that they have earned salvation or at least that they have made a contribution towards it. They do not like to emphasise the 'freeness' of salvation.
Assurance, 256

GUIDANCE

I have always laid this down as a principle in the matter of guidance. I have not hesitated to say to people, 'When you have worked it all out; if you have decided on a certain course and if you consult other people and they agree with you and everybody seems to be on that side, unless you have got absolute freedom in your spirit do not do it – wait.
God's Sovereign Purpose, 38

A man seeking guidance and trying to carry out God's will in this world is like a train in Paddington Station or some other London railway terminus. There it is, everything is ready, the passengers are all in their seats, the power to begin the journey is present, but the train is not moving. Why not? The signal has not dropped! And the train does not move, though everything is ready, until that final signal has dropped. To me, the final signal is this deep consciousness within. Never act against it.
The Christian Warfare, 330

God's normal way of guidance, and of healing, and of all these other matters, is through means. We are meant to get our guidance through the Scriptures, through an enlightened spiritual mind and understanding, through an enlightened reason, through an enlightened conscience. That is how God normally guides us. Thank God that He does so; and He gives us certainty through these methods.
The Christian Warfare, 329

GUILT
To expiate means to extinguish guilt.
Great Doctrines of the Bible (1), 302

– H –

HABIT

All evil habits do not suddenly fall away out of your life. God in His grace may, and often does remove some of them, but He leaves others. The force of habit is a terrible power, so great that there is nothing but the power of God that can keep us and preserve us against it. Though we have a new mind, and a new outlook, and desire to live the new life, certain habits tend to hinder us. It is the power of God alone that can enable us to conquer them.
God's Ultimate Purpose, 419

What could more clearly illustrate the tyranny and enslaving power of evil thoughts, vicious habits and bad company, than powers that correspond to the iron bands on the body, the iron bars at the window and the brass gates outside all? Is anyone so foolish as to deny the truth of this picture? Is it an easy thing to break with bad company? Can you without much effort break yourself of a long continued evil habit and practice? Above all, do you find it an easy thing to control your mind and rid it of all its impure thoughts, all its evil imaginings, all its unkind and bitter judgments and envyings? Tell me, are you free? Free from the control of friends and associates, free from the influence of others which you know is wrong, free from the grip of every evil habit and practice, free from all these sins of the mind which reduce us to despair and shame? Are you free? Have you ever tried to free yourself? Can you achieve moral and spiritual freedom? Can you break all the bars of iron and the fetters and the gates of brass? Has anyone ever done so unaided? Has it ever been achieved except in Christ Jesus our Lord and in the new life and power which he alone can give?
Old Testament Evangelistic Sermons, 187

HAPPINESS

The happiest people the world has ever known have always been those who have had the glorious view of salvation, and who have seen that they are 'in him' – that is the great New Testament phrase, 'in Christ' – and that they are lost in him. And so they live as more than conquerors in this world and are immune to most of the things that are finally responsible for all our unhappinesses and our miseries.
Saved In Eternity, 96

The last person to be really happy is the person who is living for happiness. If you set out to look for happiness you will never find it; happiness will never be

sought directly and if you do not realise that, you will go wrong about happiness and about peace. Set up happiness or peace as the goal and you will never get there.
Authentic Christianity (2), 227

Whenever you put happiness before righteousness, you will be doomed to misery.
Studies in the Sermon on the Mount (1), 75

I am not suggesting we should perpetually have that inane grin upon our faces which some people think is essential to the true manifestation of Christian joy. You need not put anything on, it will be there; it cannot help expressing itself.
Spiritual Depression, 14

HATRED
Now let us examine the terms: 'Jacob have I loved, but Esau have I hated.' It seems perfectly clear that these words must not be taken in their absolute sense, but people have often stumbled at this term 'hated'. This is surely a term that must be interpreted here in the light of what we read, for instance, in a statement made by our Lord, recorded in Luke 14:26. We are told there that our Lord 'turned, and said unto them' – the great multitudes that followed Him – 'If any man come to me, and hate not his father, and mother, and wife, and children, and brethren, and sisters, yea, and his own life also, he cannot be my disciple.' That is the same word, and obviously that is not meant to be taken in its literal and absolute sense of hatred. What our Lord is indicating is a relative attitude. He means that if you put anybody before Him, you cannot be His disciple. You have, as it were, to regard even your nearest and dearest in a lesser light, and even as a hindrance and an obstacle to you, if they would insinuate themselves between you and Christ. You hate what they are doing, you hate what they are in that respect only; you do not hate them as persons.
God's Sovereign Purpose, 121

Every natural person hates God.
Love so Amazing, 196–97

HEALING (Charismatic Gifts)
These are the friends who say that a Christian should never be ill, that sickness and illness are the result of the Fall and that the Atonement has dealt with the Fall in every respect. They teach that healing is in the Atonement and that you can and should claim it with the consequence that the Christian should never be ill. The Apostle's answer is, 'We groan being burdened, waiting for the adoption, to wait, the redemption of our body'. The body is not fully and finally redeemed here in this life; and to say that it is, is to claim far too much.
The Final Perseverance of the Saints, 102

Nothing tends to bring the gospel more into disrepute than extravagant claims, or claims which can be dismissed on natural or other grounds. I would not hesitate to say that we should be careful to attribute to the direct intervention of God only that which we have entirely failed to account for by any other hypothesis. Failure to do this will inevitably lead, eventually, to muddled thinking, which in its turn will lead to disappointment and sorrow.
Why Does God Allow Suffering? 23

People say, 'Claim this gift; claim healing.' You cannot claim healing. The Apostle himself claimed healing three times and did not get it. Never claim; never even use the word. We are to submit ourselves – it is the Spirit who gives.
Joy Unspeakable, 175

There is such a thing as a natural gift of healing; there is a kind of natural, almost magical power in certain people. For instance the whole question of electricity in the human frame is most interesting. We are merely beginning to understand it. There are people such as water-diviners who possess certain curious gifts. Then there is the whole question of telepathy, transference of thought and extra-sensory perception. These things are just coming into our ken. As the result of such gifts and powers many can do marvellous and wondrous things, and yet not be Christian. The natural power of man can simulate the gifts of the Holy Spirit, up to a point. And, of course, we are reminded by Scripture that God, in His own inscrutable will, sometimes decides to give these powers to men who do not belong to Him in order to bring to pass His own purposes.
Studies in the Sermon on the Mount (2), 270

The atonement of Christ, say the faith healers, covers all the evil effects and consequences of sin. Not only my guilt and the punishment I deserved; it goes beyond that, and urges that all that the body has suffered as the result of sin is dealt with in the atonement. So a Christian should never be sick, should never be in ill-health; he should always enjoy perfect health, he should never die from any disease whatsoever. But the argument is incomplete. If you argue that all the effects of sin are dealt with directly by the atonement, then you should also say that a Christian should never die, because physical death is one of the consequences of the Fall and of sin.
The Sons of God, 81

God has so made the universe that normally things happen according to what we call 'the laws of nature'. So if you are ill, you are given treatment, and in time you gradually get better. That is all right, but it is always God who heals. If it is not God's will that you should be healed, you can have the best treatment in the world and you will not get well. God normally heals indirectly, by means of doctors and medicine, but he sometimes heals without them. He heals directly.

God is not confined by his own laws. He has made them and if he chooses at times to act independently of them, why should he not?
Authentic Christianity (1), 227

HEART
In Scripture the word 'heart' generally means the very centre of the personality. It does not mean the seat of the affections only; it also includes the mind, the understanding and the will. It is therefore the very citadel of the soul.
The Unsearchable Riches of Christ, 147

We cannot read one another's hearts. There are things inside our hearts that no one else knows.
The Final Perseverance of the Saints, 139

HEAVEN (After Life)
The only reason for wanting to go to heaven is that I may be with Christ, that I may see him.
The Life of Joy, 108

anticipation
Unmixed joy, and glory, and holiness, and purity and wonder! That is what is awaiting us. That is your destiny and mine in Christ as certainly as we are alive at this moment. How foolish we are that we do not spend our time in thinking about that.
Studies in the Sermon on the Mount (1), 147

Not to be interested in heaven and hell is to be unlike the Lord Jesus Christ; it is to be unlike all the Apostles; it is to be unlike the greatest saints, the best people this world has ever known. How much time do you spend in thinking about heaven? How often do you set your gaze there?
God's Ultimate Purpose, 386

This is a wonderful thing to contemplate. These bodies of ours individually, yours and mine are going to be glorified. No infirmities will remain, no vestige of disease or failure or sign of age; there will be a grand renewal of our youth. And we shall go on living in that eternity of perpetual youth, with neither decay nor disease, nor any diminishing of the glory which belongs to us. That is what the church is going to look like externally.
The Christian Warfare, 176

Spiritually I am in heaven at this moment 'in Christ', in one sense as much as I shall ever be; but my body is still living on earth, I am still in this world of time. My spirit has been redeemed in Christ as much as it will ever be redeemed; but my body is not yet redeemed, and I am, with all other Christians, 'waiting for the adoption, to wit, the redemption of our body'

(Romans 8:23). Or, as Paul expresses it in writing to the Philippians, our position in this world of time is that 'our conversation is in heaven; from whence also we look for the Saviour, the Lord Jesus Christ: who shall change our vile body, that it may be fashioned like unto the body of his glorification, according to the working whereby he is able even to subdue all things unto himself' (3:21). In my spirit, I am already there, but I am still on earth in the flesh and in the body.
God's Ultimate Purpose, 76

Do you ever look forward to being in heaven? That is not being morbid, I like the way in which Matthew Henry put it, 'We are never told in the Scriptures that we should look forward to death; but we are told very frequently that we should look forward to heaven'. The man who looks forward to death simply wants to get out of life because of his troubles. That is not Christian; that is pagan. The Christian has a positive desire for heaven, and therefore I ask: Do we look forward to being in heaven? But, more than this, what do we look forward to when we get to heaven? What is it we are desiring? Is it the rest of heaven? Is it to be free from trouble and tribulations? Is it the peace of heaven? Is it the joy of heaven? All these things are to be found there, thank God; but that is not the thing to look forward to in heaven. It is the face of God. 'Blessed are the pure in heart; for they shall see God.' The Vision Splendid, the *Summum Bonum*, to stand in the very presence of God – 'To gaze and gaze on Thee'. Do we long for that? Is that heaven to us?
Faith on Trial, 111

We are to enjoy foretastes of heaven here in this world.
Revival, 222

assurance
Of this 'family' of the redeemed some are in heaven already, and some are still on earth; but they all belong to the same family, the whole family.
The Unsearchable Riches of Christ, 116

description
People sometimes ask, Why are we told so little about heaven, why are we told so little in detail about the eternal state? The answer is quite simple. Because we are sinful, because we are fallen, our language is fallen also, and any attempt to describe the glory of heaven would be a misrepresentation of it.
God's Way of Reconciliation, 418

The New Testament does not tell us much more than that, because we could not stand it; our language is inadequate, and if it were adequate, the description would be so baffling we could not tolerate it, the thing is so glorious and wonderful.
Children of God, 34

Human language is totally inadequate to describe happenings in heaven. That is why we are told so little about heaven in the Bible.
The Final Perseverance of the Saints, 135

destination

The young Philip Henry fell in love with a young lady who belonged to a higher class of society than his own; and she fell in love with him. They wanted to get married, so she began to speak to her parents about this. They did not like the proposal. They did not know this man Philip Henry, they did not know his family. The father turned on her at last and asked, 'Where has he come from?' And the daughter, good Christian that she was, gave her immortal answer saying, 'I do not know where he has come from, but I do know where he is going'. What else really matters?
Christian Unity, 86

Someone once described Christians as 'a colony of heaven, waiting for the homeland'. We have been sent here to colonise this particular place but we really belong there; there is the homeland; that is the place to which we belong.
The Life of Joy, 106

intermediate

. . . What is generally described as 'heaven' in the Scripture is the condition described by Paul in Philippians 1:23, where he talks about being 'with Christ, which is far better'. That is the intermediate state for this good reason, that in the eternal and final state, the body is involved. But when he talks about 'being with Christ, which is far better', the body is not involved. The body may be in a grave, it may be in the depths of the sea somewhere, it may have been blown to atoms. He is not referring there to the body. That is the intermediate state, the state and condition of the redeemed while they are waiting for the resurrection of the body and its final glorification.
The Final Perseverance of the Saints, 86

preparation

We are in a preparatory school at the moment. This is not the life, it is only the preparation. It is the glory that awaits us that is really the life, and for that we are being prepared. That glory is pure, it is holy. There is no sin in heaven; there is no evil there. Do you think that, as you are, you are fit to go to heaven? Of course you are not!
The Christian Warfare, 253–54

qualification

Any man who thinks he deserves heaven is not a Christian. But for any man who knows he deserves hell there is hope.
The Cross, 75

reality

Our eternal state is not going to be lived in the heavens, in the air, in some vague, nebulous spiritual condition. We are taught here that we shall spend our eternity on the glorified earth under the new heavens – 'the new heavens, and the new earth, wherein dwelleth righteousness'. In other words, we can say that heaven in an eternal sense is going to be 'heaven on earth'. Heaven on earth – that is where we shall spend our eternity, and not as disembodied spirits, for the whole man will be redeemed, the body included. A concrete body must have a concrete world in which to live; and we are told that that will be the case. The whole creation is going to be delivered. All that we know now of the evil in creation will be done away with when the 'elements will melt with fervent heat', and the heavens will be on fire. That will mean the dissolution of the present, and the exclusion from the cosmos of all evil and sin.

The Final Perseverance of the Saints, 88–89

HELL (Devil and Demonism, Eternal Punishment, Unevangelised)

Throughout his ministry Lloyd-Jones warned of the reality and argued for its eternal duration over against annihilationism and universalism.

I'd rather hobble into heaven than walk into hell!

Banner of Truth, Issue 275

division

The Bible clearly divides mankind into the saved and the lost, those who are going to be with God and those who are going to be shut out from His presence eternally, those who are going to heaven and those who are going to hell. It is in the Old Testament and it is here in the New. Our Lord Himself taught it. It is everywhere.

God's Sovereign Purpose, 159

duration

Hell is a condition in which life is lived away from God and all the restraints of God's holiness. [. . . is described in this passage (Romans 1 v 21–14) exaggerated still more, and going on endlessly!] In other words, hell is people living to all eternity the kind of life they are living now, only much worse! That is hell. Can you imagine anything worse! It is men and women without any control at all, finally abandoned by God. He 'gave them over'. He gives them over eternally, and they are just left to themselves and to manifest all that is in them, all this foulness and vileness.

The Gospel of God, 392–93

Constantly in the Scripture the fates of the believer and the unbeliever are contrasted in that way and each time exactly the same word is used in both cases – eternal on the one hand and eternal on the other. So if there is no such thing as everlasting destruction, there is no such thing as everlasting life, and all that is promised to the believer will only last for a while and then come to an end.

Great Doctrines of the Bible (3), 73–74

Neither does the Apostle say here that it is only going to be for a limited period of time – that they are going on to have tribulation and anguish perhaps for a year or two, or perhaps for a century or two, perhaps for a millennium or two, and then they will be annihilated – there is no conditional immortality in the New Testament. He just says that as the one group go to eternal and everlasting life, these others go to tribulation and anguish – they will exist in that condition. And he does not suggest any end to it, neither does the Scripture anywhere else.
The Righteous Judgement of God, 89

. . . [A] life of sin will be an everlasting separation from God. There is nothing more terrible and horrible to contemplate than that – eternity outside the life of God, left to ourselves . . . 'everlasting destruction from the presence of the Lord, and from the glory of his power.'
The New Man, 283

Perish means perish; it does not mean go out of existence. It is the opposite to eternal life; it is the same as everlasting destruction. It is the same as that place where their 'worm dieth not and their fire is not quenched'. It is the state of those who are outside the life of God. There is the warning, and we ignore it at our peril.
The Righteous Judgement of God, 107

Jesus Christ
If you do not like the doctrine of hell you are just disagreeing with Jesus Christ. He, the Son of God, believed in hell; and it is in His exposure of the true nature of sin that He teaches that sin ultimately lands men in hell.
Studies in the Sermon on the Mount (1), 235

No one taught this doctrine more clearly than our Lord himself, and that is why he said 'I am come that they might have life'.
Saved in Eternity, 130

reality
I have no interest in a so-called gospel which does away with the fear of hell.
Faith on Trial, 120

There is a hell, whatever the modern man may say. He is only speculating, he does not know.
Love so Amazing, 21

Hell is a place of torment, a place of suffering, a place of misery. It is a place of evil and of spite and malignity. Do you know what it is? I believe it is some sort of eternal filthy programme, when you have realised at last that the thing is debased, but you have nothing else, and you have to live on that for ever and

for ever. The foulness, the vileness! That evil, that debased desecration of everything that is righteous and like God. Those who are in hell fester, shut out from
glory and the purity and the holiness of the life of God and his holy angels and
his saints.
God's Way Not Ours, 52

urgency
Do we really believe that those who are not saved are going to eternal damna-
tion? If we do, is it not inevitable that we should have a concern about them and
especially those who are nearest to us?
God's Sovereign Purpose, 32

I will do my utmost to alarm you with a sight of the terrors of hell. Eternal
remorse, eternal misery, eternal wretchedness, unchangeable torment, such is
the lot of all who content themselves with just agreeing with and enjoying
the gospel, but who for some reason or other never forsake all else and
embrace it with a whole heart. God save us all from it, as He is indeed waiting to do.
Evangelistic Sermons, 161

It is when you have suffered a great deal of pain that you most appreciate the
relief. It is the man who has been healed at the very door of death who is most
grateful for his cure. It is the sinner who has had a glimpse into hell who is most
appreciative of the glories of heaven.
Assurance, 305

HEREDITY
A man is never saved by heredity – never! You are not saved because your parents were Christians or because you belong to the Jewish nation or any other
nation. Heredity does not come in at all.
God's Sovereign Purpose, 246

HERESY
And it is interesting to observe how heresies almost invariably cancel one
another out.
Studies in the Sermon on the Mount (1), 184

The Apostle Paul says, 'Be not deceived: evil communications corrupt good
manners' (1 Corinthians 15:33). He means that wrong teaching is desperately
dangerous.
The Christian Warfare, 113

It is good for us to remind ourselves that every single heresy that we can ever
think of had been thought of probably before the end of the first century. There
is nothing very modern or up to date in being heretical; it is as old as the gospel

itself. Let no one think he is wonderful and modern in denying certain of these essential doctrines!
Fellowship with God, 54

HERETICS
They were good and sincere people, as heretics often are
Christian Unity, 190

There is a sense in which it is true to say that you can prove anything you like from the Bible. That is how heresies have arisen. The heretics were never dishonest men; they were mistaken men. They should not be thought of as men who were deliberately setting out to go wrong and to teach something that is wrong; they have been some of the most sincere men that the Church has ever known. What was the matter with them? Their trouble was this: they evolved a theory and they were rather pleased with it; then they went back with this theory to the Bible, and they seemed to find it everywhere.
Studies in the Sermon on the Mount (1), 11

HISTORY
Second to the study of the Bible for the Christian, Lloyd Jones argued, is the reading of history. Behind it is the hand of God; thus there are two approaches to this subject, 'the secular' and 'the spiritual'. The discriminating Christian will see in the saga of history the wonderful outworking of God's purpose. This will give him hope and confidence for the future which, too, is in the hands of God.

I would like to lay it down as a principle that there is great value in the reading of Church history and a study of the past, and nothing surely is more important for us at this present time than to read the history of the past and to discover its message. I suggest that we should do so for the very reasons which impelled Isaac to dig again the wells which they had dug in the days of Abraham, his father. It is very foolish to ignore the past. The man who does ignores it and assumes that our problems are quite new, and that therefore the past has nothing at all to teach us, is a man who is not only grossly ignorant of the Scriptures, he is equally ignorant of some of the greatest lessons even in secular history.
Revival, 21

Whose are the voices that speak to us from the past and whisper to us from the records of antiquity? Look at them! Abel, Abraham, Jacob, Moses, David, the prophets, the apostles, Augustine, Luther, and in the centre Jesus of Nazareth, the Son of God! Does all this mean nothing to you? Can you ignore such testimony? Can you lightly reject an offer that has faced mankind steadily and unchangeably throughout the centuries, the acceptance of which has made the noblest souls the world has ever seen and which is commended by One who towers above all mankind and upon whom all history converges?
Old Testament Evangelistic Sermons, 153

I commend to you the reading of biographies of men who have been used by God in the Church throughout the centuries, especially in revival. And you will find this same holy boldness.
Revival, 197

When I get discouraged and over-tired and weary I also invariably go to the eighteenth century. I have never found George Whitefield to fail me. Go to the eighteenth century! In other words read the stories of the great tides and movements of the Spirit experienced in that century. It is the most exhilarating experience, the finest tonic you will ever know. For a preacher it is absolutely invaluable; there is nothing to compare with it. The more he learns in this way about the history of the Church the better preacher he will be.
Preaching and Preachers, 118

The whole story of the human race can be summed up in terms of what has happened because of Adam, and what has happened and will yet happen because of Christ.
Assurance, 178

In the last analysis there are only two views of history – the view stated most perfectly perhaps by Hegel, and that of the New Testament.
Evangelistic Sermons, 282

It is important to understand that there are two types of history. First there is the history that God permits. He allows men and women to do many things. But there is secondly, the history that God himself produces and that is the history that we are dealing with on Christmas Day
Authentic Christianity (4), 175–76

We should not look at history from day to day, or even from year to year, or decade to decade, rather, we should look back across the centuries. How often have people thought that Christianity was defeated! When you look back you will see that people have said, 'This is the end'. Then a revival has come. He is controlling everything and the promise of the New Testament is that he will continue to do so until the time has arrived for him to wind up world history and all its affairs.
The Life of Joy, 157

There is this unseen history which is at the back of the visible history, and which is much more important. There is this spiritual history which, as it were, underlies all secular history, and in the light of which secular history becomes relatively unimportant.
God's Way of Reconciliation, 13

HOLINESS

I am to be holy because God is holy; I am to be holy because, if I am holy, I shall thereby display the glory of God in a manner which will be well pleasing to Him.
Expository Sermons on 2 Peter, 243

The New Testament makes holiness the most reasonable and common sense thing imaginable and its whole case with respect to those who are not concerned about holiness is that they are utterly unreasonable and self contradictory.
Expository Sermons on 2 Peter, 42

God does not work through big battalions, He is not interested in numbers; He is interested in purity, in holiness, in vessels fit and meet for the Master's use. We must concentrate, not on numbers, but upon doctrine, upon regeneration, upon holiness, upon the realisation that this is a holy temple in the Lord, a habitation of God.
God's Way of Reconciliation, 472

There is no holiness teaching in the New Testament apart from this direct association with doctrine; it is a deduction from the doctrine.
The New Man, 271

Holiness is not a feeling; holiness is a life lived to the glory of God and to His eternal praise.
The Law: Its Functions and Limits, 66

To be holy is to be entirely apart from evil.
Love so Amazing, 211

Holiness is not something we are called upon to do in order that we may become something; it is something we are to do because of what we already are.
Children of God, 41

This is holiness – loving one another – and this is to be seen in terms of our whole relationship to God. It is a great doctrinal matter, and the New Testament always put the teaching about holiness in terms of ultimate doctrine.
The Love of God, 42

It is not surprising that the cross has been discounted by modern theologians; it is because they have started with the love of God without His holiness.
Fellowship with God, 108

I cannot understand how anyone who has read the Scriptures can accept and adopt any idea of passivity with respect to the way of holiness.
Spiritual Depression, 257

HOLY DAYS

It is a very good thing in the Christian life to stand back periodically and look at this great plan. That is why I think it is important to observe Christmas Day and Good Friday and Easter Sunday, and to preach on those days.
Great Doctrines of the Bible (2), 1

Many of us do not observe Ascension Day, do we? We are a little inconsistent in this: we observe Christmas, Good Friday and Easter Sunday! We observe Whit Sunday, but we do not observe Ascension Day, and it is a very essential part in all this movement of God's plan.
Saved in Eternity, 78

HOLY SPIRIT (Baptism, Charismatic Gifts)

He is a Person, He is a sovereign Lord. That is emphasised in I Corinthians 12 which deals with the question of the gifts of the Spirit. He dispenses as He decides and sees fit (verse 11). He is the third Person in the blessed Holy Trinity, and we must never speak of Him as if He were not a Person, as if He were just like the atmosphere which we can breathe in whenever we like. He is a sovereign Lord, even as the Father is and the Son is.
The Sons of God, 269

The ultimate proof of God's acceptance of Christ as our justification is the sending of the Holy Spirit.
Great Doctrines of the Bible (2), 47

Bible

As melted iron is poured into a mould, so the truth of God is a mould and the Spirit comes and melts us and we are poured into the mould to take the shape and the form of the mould of God's glorious truth and we are new men and women. God be thanked! It is the Spirit who does it through the word.
Love so Amazing, 96

What I am really saying is that the man who is 'after the Spirit' minds the things of the Spirit. In other words, the Bible is his Book.
The Sons of God, 27

The Holy Spirit always works through the word of God. Now there are many people who claim that He works directly. That was what caused the Quakers to wander off from the main party of the Puritans. They said that the word was not necessary, that the Holy Spirit spoke directly to each person, in some secret

mystical manner, by some 'inner light'. Not at all! The Holy Spirit always uses the word.
Great Doctrines of the Bible (2), 51

The Spirit applies the word. He enlightens the mind, and our minds need to be enlightened because they are darkened by sin. The Apostle says that in great detail later on in Colossians. Our minds need to be quickened, to be given a new power of vision and an ability to see unseen spiritual truth. He alone can do that and he does it through this word.
Love so Amazing, 94

believer
The first thing the Holy Spirit does to people when he comes upon them in this powerful manner is to make them think!
Authentic Christianity (1), 52

Can you not see that your need is of that heavenly oxygen – the Holy Spirit?
Authentic Christianity (1), 312

Who can understand the fact that the Holy Spirit dwells within us in our bodies, tabernacles within us? Who can understand our Lord's statement when He says that He and His Father will come and take up their abode within us? Who can understand the real meaning of Revelation 3:20, 'Behold, I stand at the door, and knock; if any man hear my voice, and open the door, I will come in to him, and will sup with him, and he with me'? But there it is – this is the teaching; that the Holy Ghost dwells within us and in our bodies. Our bodies are the temple of the Holy Ghost.
Assurance, 91–92

Any kind of teaching which would ever suggest to us that you can be a Christian without receiving the Holy Spirit is unscriptural. It is impossible for one to be a Christian and then later on receive the Holy Spirit. To be in Christ means that you are receiving the Spirit; no one can be a Christian in any sense without having already received this unction, this anointing, the gift of the Holy Spirit.
Walking with God, 120

The ultimate doctrine about the Spirit, from the practical, experiential standpoint, is that my body is the temple of the Holy Spirit, so that whatever I do, wherever I go, the Holy Spirit is in me.
Great Doctrines of the Bible (2), 11

The Holy Spirit influences me in countless ways. He is at the back of my very willing and yearning towards good.
Assurance, 94

experience

He had not been poured out under the old dispensation but he came upon specific men to enable them to accomplish given tasks. Undoubtedly God's people were made children of the kingdom because of the work of the Holy Spirit in them and upon them, but He had not been poured out in the way He was at Pentecost. The result is that the blessing is greater in scope under the New Testament.
Great Doctrines of the Bible (1), 241–42

In the Old Testament the giving of the Spirit is something unusual, and these people on whom the Spirit came were exceptional persons. But the emphasis here is upon the generality; upon this whole idea of pouring out, the largeness, and the freeness, and the fullness of the gift.
Great Doctrines of the Bible (2), 33–34

fruit

A man once said a very profound thing when he described these verses [Galatians 5:22–3] as 'The shortest biography of Christ that has ever been written'
Saved in Eternity, 169

So one of the ways in which I show that I am filled with the Spirit is not so much that I go into ecstasies and manifest certain phenomena; it is the way I behave towards my wife, when I am at home, it is this love which is 'the fruit of the Spirit'.
Life in the Spirit in Marriage Home and Work, 135

gifts

If you find yourself talking more about experiences, or gifts, than about him, you have already gone astray. The Spirit is given, and he does give gifts, yes, but they are all meant to lead us to bring glory to Christ in our esteem, in our talk, in our everything. The moment anything comes between us and the centrality of Christ, we have already gone astray.
Spiritual Blessing, 171

Have you received this gift of God's Spirit? I have reminded you of the tests; if you have them, God bless you. Now go on to covet the best gifts more and more; long increasingly for the fruit of the Spirit; and ask God to work more and more in you.
The Love of God, 101

person

'Whom no man hath seen, nor can see' (1Tim. 6:16); that is the Father. The Son is all the fullness of the Godhead manifested visibly, 'For in him dwelleth all the fullness of the Godhead bodily' (Col. 2:9); that is the Son. And what a tremendous statement that is! And the Spirit is all the fullness of the Godhead acting

immediately upon the creature. You see the difference? The fullness of the Godhead – invisible; The fullness of the Godhead – visible; the fullness of the Godhead – acting immediately and directly upon us. So thus we can say that the Spirit by His power makes manifest the Father in the image of the Son.
Great Doctrines of the Bible (2), 20

. . . [T]he Scripture everywhere speaks about the Holy Spirit as a Person, and He is indeed the third Person in the blessed Holy Trinity.[10]
The Sons of God, 287

The Holy Spirit is the greatest leveller in the world – to use a modern illustration – He is a divine bulldozer. He just flattens.
Enjoying the Presence of God, 65

power
The Holy Spirit, I say, does not exhaust; He puts power into us . . . Alcohol, or any artificial stimulus worked up by man, always leaves us exhausted and tired. Not so the Spirit! Drunkenness exhausts; the Holy Spirit does not exhaust, but energizes.
Life in the Spirit in Marriage Home and Work, 17

If it were possible to put the Spirit into a textbook of Pharmacology I would put Him under the stimulants, for that is where He belongs. He really does stimulate. He does not merely appear to do so, as alcohol does, and, thereby fools and deludes us. The Holy Spirit is an active, positive, real stimulus.
Life in the Spirit in Marriage Home and Work, 20

reception
The Apostles certainly had this power – they 'laid hands' on people, and the people received the gift of the Holy Ghost. The case of Simon the Sorcerer is interesting in this connection. We read of how he offered money in order to acquire this power (Acts 8:18,19) which was clearly confined to the apostles for a specific object and purpose; for even Philip the Evangelist did not possess it.
The Sons of God, 390

What a transformation! Water to wine! Mr Spurgeon put it like this: 'The difference between the Christian who knows what it is to have received the fullness, and the Christian who does not know that, is greater than the difference between that second Christian and the man who is not a Christian at all.' That is a tremendous statement but I believe it is true. There is, of course a striking difference between the non-Christian and the Christian, but it is not as great as the difference between the man who has been saved, the man who believes in

---

[10] Lloyd-Jones in making the above comment is critical of the Authorised Version of the Bible's rendering of the Holy Spirit in Romans 8:16 by the neuter pronoun.

Christ and believes he is forgiven but has very little more than that, and the man who is receiving the heavenly manna.
Spiritual Blessing, 88

So, again, I do not hesitate to put this question: Do you know that you have received the Spirit? I am not asking you whether you believe by faith that the Spirit is in you. I am arguing again on the basis of Scripture that when the Holy Spirit is in us we cannot help knowing it. His presence will be felt, His presence *is* felt. And as He works within us, warning us, urging us forward, enlightening us, we are aware of these things; and as He gives us those seasons of special blessing, as He moves our heart and gives us glimpses of our Lord, we know it and we rejoice in it. Our hearts are moved. It is experiential, and the emotions must be involved, the whole person is involved, the mind, the heart and the will. It is not some extravagant ecstasy. No, a true experience of the Holy Spirit leads to conduct and behaviour and action – the will and the intellect and the heart – and let us not leave any one of them out. And let us never imagine that we are being unusually spiritual because we can say, 'I felt nothing, but I went on in faith.' My friends – you *should* feel.
Great Doctrines of the Bible (2), 260

It is God's desire that we receive this gift; therefore, if we feel we lack the understanding, if we lack the power, if we lack the joy and happiness and the peace and the abounding life that the Holy Ghost gives, we have but to go to God in simplicity. We have but to confess our need and lack and ask Him for the gift of the Holy Spirit, and He is pledged to answer and to give us the gift. And having received the Holy Spirit, we shall have this understanding and begin to produce the fruit of the Spirit in our daily lives.
Life in God, 191

God knows when to give the gift, and we must never imagine that by going to a meeting or following a certain procedure it is bound to come. No; the Holy Spirit is sovereign, and He gives in His own way. It may be dramatically or suddenly or quietly; that is irrelevant, because what really matters is that we receive the gift.
The Love of God, 115

The question is, are we giving the Holy Spirit an opportunity? Are we so tied by our programmes that he is excluded? Why this formality? Why this tying down of everything? What if the Spirit should suddenly come? I do commend this matter to you very seriously.
Revival, 77

Examine again your doctrine of the Holy Spirit, and in the name of God, be careful lest, in your neat and trimmed doctrine, you are excluding and putting out this most remarkable thing which God does periodically through the Holy

Spirit, in sending him upon us, in visiting, in baptising us, in reviving the whole Church in a miraculous and astonishing manner.
Revival, 54

quenching

The quenching of the Spirit is the commoner source of trouble at the present time. I do not hesitate to assert that the state of the Christian Church today is mainly due to it. And in saying so I include the Evangelical section of the Church as well as that which is not Evangelical
The Christian Warfare, 269

It is said that, when he [Jonathan Goforth] was passing through England in 1906, the authorities responsible for a certain well-known convention [Keswick] hesitated long as to whether they would ask him to speak because they did not want meetings which might go on for hours, even through the night, such as had been happening in Korea, to happen in their convention. The matter is mentioned in the official biography, *The Life of Jonathan Goforth*, by Mrs. Goforth. In the outcome he was asked to speak at the convention, but he was given to understand that he was now not in Korea, but somewhere else! Is that not quenching the Spirit? Why should the programme, the timetable, never be upset? Why must we say that the dignity and decorum must never be interfered with? God have mercy upon us!
The Christian Warfare, 286–87

There is nothing, I am convinced, that so 'quenches' the Spirit as the teaching which identifies the baptism of the Holy Ghost with regeneration. But it is a very commonly held teaching today, indeed it has been the popular view for many years. It is said that the baptism of the Holy Spirit is 'non-experimental', that it happens to every one at regeneration.
The Christian Warfare, 280

Dislike of enthusiasm is to quench the Spirit.
Revival, 72

God save us from being so afraid of the false that we quench the Spirit of God, and become so respectable, and so pseudo-intellectual that the Spirit of God is kept back, and we go on in our dryness and aridity, and in our comparative futility, and helplessness, and uselessness.
Revival, 79

unregenerate

It is possible for the Holy Ghost to influence us to a certain point and still leave us short of regeneration.
The Final Perseverance of the Saints, 327

It is a complete fallacy to imagine that an unbeliever has never been touched by the Spirit at all. These more general influences of the Spirit are often seen in evangelistic campaigns.
The Final Perseverance of the Saints, 327–28

There is no receptacle in the natural man to receive the presence of the Holy Spirit. It is only the new nature that can receive Him.
Assurance, 92

HOMILETICS (Preaching)

Lloyd-Jones made use of hyperbole! He had a horror that sermon construction should become mechanical – forced alliteration and the like. As his sermons reveal he was not against order and preparation. The books he mentioned were authored by W.E. Sangster whose pulpit was also in the same area as the Chapel. The Methodist Westminster Central Hall probably drew the largest congregation in London.

Last, and only lastly, Homiletics. This to me is almost an abomination. There are books bearing such titles as *The Craft of Sermon Construction*, and T*he Craft of Sermon Illustration*. That to me is prostitution.
Preaching and Preachers, 118

HOMOSEXUALITY
The horrible perversions came in.
Love so Amazing, 217

HUMANISM
Of all the enemies that the Church has to fight, sin and excess and vice and lust, the most deadly and most dangerous enemy is what is generally called humanism. The more we think of one another, the more we honour one another, the more we live for one another and for this world, the less do we think of God, the less we honour God, the less we live for God's glory.
Evangelistic Sermons, 42

Here is my challenge to humanism: What has it to give to a man who has made a wreck of his life? Humanists say that a man can save himself, that all he needs is knowledge and understanding. But I know highly intelligent people who have passed through the best universities in this country who are slaves to particular sins, and would do anything if they could only stop. But they cannot.
Authentic Christianity (4), 217

HUMANITY
The whole trouble with humanity is that is has lost its true mind, it has become insane. It needs to get back the mind it once had. The mind needs to be restored to a condition which has been lost.
Christian Conduct, 106

Human beings are the most contradictory creatures on the face of the earth, on one side, brilliant in their achievements, and on the other, so often despicable in their living. Mastering the elements, they are unable to master themselves. They arrive at knowledge and understanding of great mysteries away up in the heavens, but often live like beasts and worse. What is the matter? There are warring elements and factions within them.
Authentic Christianity (1), 203

Men and women are unnatural. In their present condition they are a blot upon the landscape. They are a contradiction in creation; they are in a wrong position; they are not functioning as they were meant to function.
God's Way Not Ours, 14

I cannot accept the suggestion that there is a kind of mathematical division of human nature, and that the human nature of every individual person is merely some kind of fraction of that original totality which was in Adam. That, to me, is philosophy, and speculation, and I believe it goes too far.
Assurance, 214

Are you ready for me to hold before you now the most terrifying mirror that you have ever looked into in your life? I warn you now, if you want to be on good terms with yourself you had better read no further. Here is the mirror – sin, first of all, as it shows itself in words. How terrible, how graphic is this description! 'Their throat', he starts, 'is an open sepulchre'; that is his quotation at this point from the Old Testament. What does this mean? It means this – and it is almost too offensive a description to mention, but here we have got to expound Scripture – it is as if you opened a grave in which a body had been buried two or three weeks ago and the process of putrefaction is at its height, the stench is beyond description, foul and offensive. That is the condition of the throat of man under sin, the natural man without the grace of the Lord Jesus Christ! 'Out of the abundance of the heart the mouth speaketh' (Matthew 12:34), and because the heart is as we have seen it to be, that is the sort of thing that emanates!
The Righteous Judgement of God, 210

By nature, human beings are entirely lacking in spiritual understanding.
Authentic Christianity (3), 59

HUMILITY
It is the opposite of self-esteem, self-assertion, and pride. Humility is one of the chief of all the Christian virtues; it is the hallmark of the child of God. Humility means having a poor opinion of yourself, and of your powers and faculties. To use the word of our Lord in the Sermon on the Mount, it means to be 'poor in spirit'.
Christian Unity, 41

Humility is ever the greatest safeguard in the spiritual life.
The Final Perseverance of the Saints, 167

There is no greater 'mark' of the true saint than humility.
The Christian Warfare, 231

The world, in a sense, knew nothing about true humility until Christ came into it. That is the ultimate test. We show signs of His life in us in that way, and one of the most delicate and subtle tests is just this test of humility, the very antithesis of everything that the world represents and stands for.
Life in God, 172

I was due to preach for a weekend in a certain town and [a man] met me at the station, and then, before I had had time to say almost anything to him, he said, 'Well, of course, I am not one of the great people in this church, I am just, you know, a very ordinary, humble man. I am not a great theologian; I am not a great speaker. I do not take part in the prayer meeting, but you know I am just the man who carries the visiting preacher's bag.' 'Oh, what a wonderful man I am!' I thought. To be proud of your ignorance is as bad as to be proud of your knowledge and understanding. Any form of pride is hateful and offensive in the sight of God.
Revival, 65

What fools we are! We regard humility and rejoicing as opposites. 'I am so afraid of false rejoicing', we moan, 'I am so afraid of presumption.' Such speech means that you have misunderstood it all. There is perfect balance here; humility and rejoicing go together and must never be thought of antithetically. Ultimately it is only the man who feels quite hopeless about himself who really trusts God. And he rejoices in his salvation because God has given it to him as a free gift.
Assurance, 166

HYMNS
We can often be dishonest as we sing hymns.
The Unsearchable Riches of Christ, 161

All the greatest and the most glorious hymns are full of praise and thanksgiving.
Love so Amazing, 151

I wonder whether you have ever noticed, those of you who are interested in hymns and in hymnology, that in most hymnbooks no section is so weak as the section devoted to the Holy Spirit? Here the hymns are generally weak, sentimental and subjective. For that reason, I have always found myself in great difficulties on Whit Sunday. We are lacking in great doctrinal hymns concerning the Holy Spirit and His work.
Great Doctrines of the Bible (2), 6

The hymns we have are superficial, subjective and generally sentimental.
Great Doctrines of the Bible (2), 75

Sometimes people think that I have suddenly gone mad if I announce Christmas hymns at some other time of the year. But I have not! . . . Why should we leave them only to that particular time of the year? The gospel in its fullness should be constantly in our minds. It is glad tidings, good news!
Saving Faith, 299

– I –

IMMATURITY
I know of nothing which is more tragic than to see Christian people who remain exactly where and what they always were. They end as children, as they began.
Christian Unity, 224

IMMORTALITY
We cannot imagine ourselves coming to an end.
God's Way Not Ours, 28

IMPATIENCE
The nicest people are often the most impatient.
Banner of Truth, Issue 275

IMPERMANENCE
Your most beautiful flower is beginning to die immediately you pluck it. You will soon have to throw it away. That is true of everything in this life and world. It does not matter what it is, it is passing, it is all fading away. Everything that has life is, as the result of sin, subject to this process – 'moth and rust doth corrupt'. Things develop holes and become useless, and at the end they are gone and become utterly corrupt. The most perfect physique will eventually give way and break down and die; the most beautiful countenance will in a sense become ugly when the process of corruption has got going; the brightest gifts tend to fade. Your great genius may be seen gibbering in delirium as the result of disease . . . That is why, perhaps, the saddest of all failures in life is the failure of the philosopher who believes in worshipping goodness, beauty and truth; because there is no such thing as perfect goodness, there is no such thing as unalloyed beauty; there is an element of wrong and of sin and a lie in the highest truths. 'Moth and rust doth corrupt.'
Studies in the Sermon on the Mount (2), 89

INCONSISTENCY
Our greatest danger is to be spasmodic.
Joy Unspeakable, 222

There is nothing which is more insulting to the holy Name of God than to profess Him with your lips and deny Him in your life.
Evangelistic Sermons, 145

There is nothing so wrong and nothing so fatal, as to be living a life in compartments. Sunday morning comes and I say, 'Ah, I am a religious man. So I take up my religious bag. Then Monday morning comes and I say to myself; I am now a businessman', or something else, and I take up another bag. So I am living my life in compartments; and it is difficult to tell on Monday that I am a Christian at all. Of course I showed it on Sunday when I went to a place of worship.
Life in the Spirit, 88–89

INDIVIDUALISM
What remarkable beings we are! There are certain things of which we never speak to anyone except ourselves. Has this final and ultimate loneliness of your own nature and personality ever struck you? We are born into families and communities and yet how markedly individual we all are. We have secrets that our parents, brothers and sisters, husbands and wives, and children will never know and never discover.
Old Testament Evangelistic Sermons, 238

INFANTS (Unevangelised)
Children are not born innocent. They are born under sin, with sin in them; they are born with the guilt of Adam's guilt upon them; they have the pollution of his nature. We are born sinners, 'all under sin'.
The Righteous Judgement of God, 190

There is a teaching – and to me it is always a mystery how a man like Charles Hodge could ever have taught it – to the effect that all dying in infancy go to heaven, that they are all saved. All that I can say in regard to that is that there is not a single scripture to support that statement.
Saving Faith, 261

He can do the same [give a knowledge of Christ] to an unconscious infant and it is there I see the salvation of the unconscious infant or of men and women who may have died in a state of what we call insanity.
Saving Faith, 261

But what is there to stop the Almighty God from illuminating the man's mind, and giving him a revelation of Christ and the gospel, even in the last agony of death? . . . Do you tell me that he cannot do that? I believe He can . . . it is no more difficult for God to save an unconscious infant than it is for him to save an adult by preaching. It is God who does it in both cases.
Saving Faith, 263

Preaching is the usual method of God throughout the ages. It always will be. But he is not tied to it. For the infant, the heathen, the poor man who has lost his reason, anybody, God can exceptionally – and as it were miraculously – do the thing that he normally does by his chosen method.
Saving Faith, 272

INSENSITIVITY
As a man can be tone deaf to music, all who are not Christians are tone deaf to the spiritual.
The Sons of God, 10

INTEGRITY
There is little point in talking eloquently about the sanctity of international contracts while you are dealing with people who break their own marriage contracts and other personal contracts, for nations consist of individuals. The nation is not something abstract, and we are not entitled to expect conduct from a nation which we do not find in the individual.
God's Way of Reconciliation, 85

INTELLECT
God can use a man in spite of his being in a muddle intellectually.
God's Sovereign Purpose, 153

O the folly of modern humanity's confidence in its own intellect!
Authentic Christianity (2), 194

Intellectual pride is the last citadel of self.
Banner of Truth, Issue 275

Intellectualists are like tadpoles – all head and no body!
Banner of Truth, Issue 275

IRRELIGION
We can say the same about religion as we can about doctrine. There is no such thing as an irreligious person; everyone has his or her religion, if you mean by religion that ultimate philosophy or view of life by which people live. Now there are many who say that they do not believe in religion. But not to believe in religion is their religion!
Walking with God, 23

ISAIAH
Some people call Isaiah 'The Evangelical Prophet'. That is quite a justifiable way of describing him, because in various parts of his long book, he certainly has the gospel in some of its most glorious expressions.
Saving Faith, 214

– J –

JESUS CHRIST (Atonement)

There is no such thing as Christianity apart from Him.
Life in God, 67

There is only one way to explain Him and that is God
Enjoying the Presence of God, 20

Prophets cannot save us, psalmists cannot save us, philosophers cannot save us, politicians cannot save us, education cannot save us, nothing, no one can save us. There is only one who can – Jesus the Son of God.
Authentic Christianity (2), 93

atonement

I say with reverence that even the almighty and eternal God can never show His love in a greater manner than He did on the Cross on Calvary's hill when He delivered up His own Son for us all and kept nothing back.
The Final Perseverance of the Saints, 397

The only way of forgiveness before Christ, after Christ and always, is through Christ and Him crucified. The way of salvation in Him was ordained 'before the foundation of the world', and that fact is implicit in this and in every similar statement everywhere in the Scriptures.
Studies in the Sermon on the Mount (2), 75

In the same way, you notice that the biblical doctrine does that with our Lord and Saviour Jesus Christ. 'Had they known it,' says Paul to the Corinthians, 'they would not have crucified the Lord of glory' (1 Cor. 2:8). The Lord of glory! Now, in a sense, you cannot crucify God, but He had to have a human body before He could be crucified. Yet Paul does not say that His body was crucified, he says that 'the Lord of glory' was crucified. In other words, what happens in the one nature or the other is ascribed to the one person.
Great Doctrines of the Bible (1), 284

If I again may use language with reverence in discussing such a high and holy matter, He is there, as it were, to say to God, 'It is but right and just that You should forgive the sins of these people, for I have borne their sins and the punishment of their

sins.' The advocate turns to the Father and says, 'I must ask You to put Your law to the side. I am here just to remind You that the law has been fulfilled, that the death has been died, the punishment has been enacted; they are free because I died for them.'
Walking with God, 41

Christ', Paul says, 'died'. This is most important . . . It is not the life, it is not the teaching, it is not the miracles; but 'Christ died'. This is what he emphasises in order to show and to prove God's love towards us.
Assurance, 109

I am not foolish enough to suggest that I can understand the meaning of the death of my Lord upon the cross exhaustively. I cannot.
Great Doctrines of the Bible (1), 312

There are three main things which are the essentials of our Lord to do as our Priest in order to secure this reconciliation of sinful people with God. First, satisfaction must be offered to the offended God [propitiation]. Second, there must be a substitution of suffering and death on the part of someone who is innocent for the deserved punishment of the guilty [expiation]. And third, a community of life needs to be brought about between the one who has been offended and the offender [atonement]. Now the claim of the Scriptures is that the Lord Jesus Christ has done all that.
Great Doctrines of the Bible (1), 302

Have you ever noticed the amount of space which is given in the Gospels to the details of our Lord's death? You can almost hear the nails being hammered in.
Love so Amazing, 236

blood of Christ
There is no greater sinner in the universe than the man who has never seen his need of the blood of Christ.
Assurance, 291

All the solutions of the world are insufficient to get rid of the stain of my sins, but here is the blood of the Son of God, spotless, blameless, and I feel that this is powerful.

> There is power, power, wonder-working power
> In the precious blood of the Lamb.
>
> His blood can make the foulest clean,
> His blood availed for me.
> Charles Wesley.

That is our comfort and consolation.
Fellowship with God, 144

Our gospel is a gospel of blood; blood is the foundation; without it there is nothing.
God's Way of Reconciliation, 240

Spurgeon used to say, and I am increasingly convinced of the rightness of his dictum, that the ultimate way to test whether a man is truly preaching the gospel or not, is to notice the emphasis which he places upon 'the blood'. It is not enough to talk about the cross and the death; the test is 'the blood'
God's Way of Reconciliation, 331

You cannot get away from this blood in the New Testament. It is central; without it there is no salvation. The law of God demands sin's punishment, and the punishment is death; so our Lord came face-to-face with that demand likewise. Before He could be 'the Saviour of the world,' He had to satisfy the demands that the law makes upon guilty sinners in the sight of God. The message is that He went to the Cross; He set His face steadfastly to go to Jerusalem; He would not be delivered. He told His servants in effect, 'I could command twelve legions of angels; but if I did how could I fulfil all righteousness? I must meet the demands of the law.' He gave Himself as an offering and a sacrifice; He died passively there upon the cross, and God poured upon Him His wrath against the sin of man. He is our Saviour by His atoning death as well as by His perfect, blameless, spotless life of obedience.
The Love of God, 137–38

People hate what they call this 'theology of blood', but there is no theology worthy of the name apart from the shed blood of Christ.
Assurance, 148

divinity
Jesus Christ was not created. He is the only-begotten Son of the Father – 'begotten, not created'. He was born as a man, but not created; He was begotten of the Virgin Mary, but not created. He is not a created being. It is heresy to say that He is. The angels are created beings . . . He is the eternal Son of God. He was from the beginning; He is everlastingly in the bosom of the Father; He is one with the Father. 'In the beginning was the Word' – 'begotten, not created'.
Assurance, 237

glorification
In eternity he was God the Son, pure Deity, and he shared the glory, but now he goes back as God-Man. And as God-Man, and our representative, the glory which he momentarily laid aside at the request of the Father is restored to him, and thus as God-Man and Mediator, He again shares this ineffable glory of the eternal God.
Saved in Eternity, 77

In a sense, the final glorification of the Lord Jesus Christ was the coming of the Holy Spirit.
Saved in Eternity, 87

historicity
It is still solid history, yes, quite as definite as 55 BC when Julius Caesar conquered Britain; quite as real as 1066 and all other events of history – Jesus a person and all that we know about Him, culminating in the agony in the garden and on the cross and in the burial and the resurrection and the ascension.
Fellowship with God, 150

Jesus – the person, the one who has entered into history – thank God for a historical faith, thank God for a gospel that is based upon facts.
Fellowship with God, 51

Look at these attempts of the liberals to reconstruct Jesus – that is not the person I see in the New Testament, that is not the Saviour of my soul. What they have produced is something unreal; it does not correspond to the facts.
Walking with God, 135

I wonder whether we will not all agree that it would have been a better thing not only for the Christian Church but also for the world perhaps if our fathers and our grandfathers had faced this false teaching which came from Germany, this subtle attempt to reconstruct Jesus. Would it not have been better if they had faced it and branded it as a lie instead of trying to accommodate to it and to fit it in.
Walking with God, 136

He is not outside history; history is not working itself out apart from Him; He controls it at this moment. It is in His hands and He is unfolding it.
God's Ultimate Purpose, 440

Holy Spirit
It was at his baptism that the Holy Spirit came upon him in the form of a dove, which means that not only was He being given strength, he was being anointed for his task. He was being set aside in a very special way as the Messiah, the Anointed One, who was to deliver the people for whom He had come. Therefore, he had his ordination, the oil of the Spirit was poured upon him, and he was announced as the Messiah. So the baptism was essential; it was part of the work which he came to do, which was not only to take on our nature, but to identify himself with us in sin.
Saved in Eternity, 103–4

Bishop Westcott sums up very well the meaning of 'him hath God the Father sealed' by saying that it means 'solemnly set apart for the fulfilment of [a]

charge, and authenticated by intelligible signs'. The Father had authenticated the Son by intelligible signs – the miracles, the works, the words, everything about Him.
God's Ultimate Purpose, 247

. . . [T]he ultimate purpose of the coming of the Lord Jesus Christ into this world was to send this gift of the Holy Spirit upon His people. Must we not agree that there is a tendency for us to forget that? Is there not a tendency on our part to stop with the life and example and teaching of Jesus Christ, or to stop only with His work upon the cross, as if to say that the whole purpose of the coming of the Son of God into this world was to purchase pardon and forgiveness for us and nothing more? Thank God that we do emphasise that, and it is ever central, and must be; but the work of the Lord Jesus Christ does not end at that point. His work in the resurrection is equally vital for us; His ascension, too, is equally important; and, above all, this great event that took place on the Day of Pentecost at Jerusalem.
Life in God, 182

humanity
He really does belong, therefore, to the human race, He is one with us.
Great Doctrines of the Bible (1), 259

The need for prayer is an absolute proof of His true humanity.
Great Doctrines of the Bible (1), 274

Our Lord has been regarded only as the Prince of Peace: we have forgotten that he is also the King of Righteousness. And he insists upon both.
Spiritual Blessing, 120

So many people cannot understand why the Son of God prayed while he was here on earth. The answer is that his life as a man was dependent upon God. He looked to God for the works he was to do and received power to perform them by receiving the Holy Spirit. He was constantly being filled with the Holy Spirit that was given to him without measure, and it was in this strength and power that he offered up himself. It was through the Spirit that he offered himself up to God, and he was 'declared to be the Son of God with power, according to the spirit of holiness, by the resurrection from the dead' (Rom. 1:4).
Saved in Eternity, 166

Look at Jesus of Nazareth. He is apparently a man in the body as all other men are. He is truly in a body; it is not a phantom covering of the flesh, He is as truly man as we are, His body is as real as yours and mine. And yet, 'in him dwelleth all the fullness of the Godhead bodily.' The whole of God was in Him.
The Unsearchable Riches of Christ, 284

incarnation

There never has been a man who could understand the doctrine of the incarnation. I think of the incarnation and I take up my stand on the side of the Apostle Paul who said, 'Great is the mystery of godliness' (1 Tim. 3:16). My mind is too small to understand it, my intellect cannot span the infinities and the immensities and the eternities. My little pigmy reason and logic are not big enough to see or to take in such a conception as the self-emptying and the humiliation of the Son of God. I do not claim to understand it; who could understand an idea like that of the virgin birth? It is beyond understanding, it is beyond reason. Who can understand the doctrine of the two natures, unmixed, remaining separate, unmingled and yet both there, but still only one person? I cannot understand the doctrine of the Trinity, Father Son and Holy Spirit. I cannot and we should never try to do so.
The Heart of the Gospel, 19

Hebrews 1:3: 'and the express image of his person . . .' Now you cannot get beyond that. Language finishes at that point! But what it does say is that this baby born in Bethlehem in that stable is the very image of the invisible God! Here is the greatest thing that has ever happened in this world.
Love so Amazing, 251

He did not cease to be God, but he ceased to manifest the glory of God. Perhaps the best way of understanding this is to consider what happened on the Mount of Transfiguration, when he was transfigured before Peter and James and John. A kind of radiance came upon him, surpassing anything that had ever been seen before by those disciples. Now contrast that with what he normally appeared to be.
Saved in Eternity, 71–72

The Lord Jesus Christ, the Lord of Glory, had to be taught certain things before He could become a perfect High Priest and to represent us in the presence of God. He came into this world in order to be the Captain of our salvation, our Leader, and He had to be prepared for that work and to go through this process.
Saved in Eternity, 75

Just think of it; the Son of God, Jesus, the one through whom all things were made, the Word that is in the bosom of the Father, the Word that was God from the beginning, the eternal absolute Son enjoying all the full prerogatives of deity from everlasting to everlasting – lying helpless as a baby in a manger. And all that you and I might be saved and reconciled to God.
Fellowship with God, 155

He took humanity into His deity: that is the whole meaning of the incarnation. That is precisely what happened at Bethlehem.
Saved in Eternity, 103

He deliberately put limits upon Himself.
Great Doctrines of the Bible (1), 287

Let me hold another phrase before you: 'Jesus Christ is *come*.' What a significant statement! Do you see what it implies? It suggests that He was before; He has come from somewhere. It could be said of no one else that he has come into this world and into this life. You and I are born, but He *came*.
The Love of God, 32

judge
The judgment is in the hands of One who has been through it all; He knows all about it – He has lived in this world, as man as well as God, and has suffered under the law and under sin.
The Righteous Judgement of God, 111

New Testament
I know no Christ apart from the Christ I find in the New Testament. I have no immediacy or directness of approach. I do not believe in visions, and I cannot find Christ directly; I find Him in the Scriptures.
The Love of God, 124

person
He is always looking into the eyes of the Father.
Walking with God, 39

He is not so much man and God – He is God-Man, two in one, not intermingled – 'Jesus Christ.'
Life in God, 73

Two natures in one person and therefore that extraordinary person of whom we read in the Gospels and upon whom we meditate. This strange amazing thing – the baby in helplessness – Son of God; the boy with His understanding – Son of God; the carpenter – Son of God; always the two. Jesus, His Son.
Fellowship with God, 153

So do not waste your time in trying to picture the Lord Jesus Christ. Do not go and look at portraits of him which are wholly imaginary. There is a sense, I believe, in which nobody should ever try to paint him – it is wrong. I do not like these paintings of Christ, they are the efforts of the natural mind. No, if you want a photograph of the Lord Jesus Christ, the Holy Spirit will give it to you in the inner man. (John 14:23)
Saved in Eternity, 92–93

sin
He exposes the perversion and the twistedness of evil – the foulness and ugliness of sin. In His teaching He is undoing the lie, the works of Satan. But watch

Him as He works His miracles and His mighty deeds; what is He doing there? Well, He is just doing this great work of destroying or undoing the works of Satan.
Children of God, 67

sinlessness

The first Adam was perfect. He had not sinned, but sin was possible. It was possible for Adam not to sin, but you could not say of him that it was not possible for him to sin, because he did sin. But of the Son of God we say that not only was it possible for Him not to sin – *posse non peccare*; it was also not possible for Him to sin – *non posse peccare* – because He is the Son of God.
Great Doctrines of the Bible (1), 276

He dealt with the devil many times when he was here in the flesh. He lived untouched by the world, separate from it. The sins of the flesh he never knew. He was tempted externally in all points as are we are, yet was without sin: and he was never tempted from sin within.
Authentic Christianity (2), 184

Son of God

There are others who are described as 'sons of God' in the Scriptures. There are statements about the angels in which they are referred to as 'the sons of God'. But this One is not a 'son of God' in the sense that the angels are sons of God . . . The term [son of God] suggests a generation, a coming out of the Father, a reproduction of the Father. There are others who can be called 'sons' . . . But Christ is 'his own Son'. We who are Christians are referred to sometimes as 'the sons of God', and 'children of God'. But the One of whom Paul speaks in this verse is not a Son in the same way as you and I are sons of God. You and I are not 'his own' sons; we are sons by 'adoption'; there was a time when we were not sons. But of this One that cannot be said. He is 'God's own Son'. He always was, He always will be eternally the Son of God, not adopted.
The Law: Its Functions and Limits, 314

When we are told here that we shall be conformed to the image of his Son, it does not mean that we are to become gods, it does not mean that we are to become sons in the sense that the only begotten One is the Eternal Son of God. As we have already seen, our sonship and our relationship to God in this way, is by adoption; and therefore it is different. It is for this reason that our Lord Himself used phrases such as, 'My Father' and 'Your Father'. He never says 'Our Father'. He never puts Himself into the same category as ourselves. He taught us to pray 'Our Father' but He does not include Himself in the expression. He draws a distinction – 'My Father', and 'Your Father', 'My God', and 'Your God'.
The Final Perseverance of the Saints, 225–26

teaching
The whole point of our Lord's teaching was to show us that it was impossible. Had you ever thought of that? His teaching was just to show us that we could not do it.
Love so Amazing, 234

This man who had learning never having learned.
Authentic Christianity (3), 136

Christ never said anything accidentally. He had all the letters of the alphabet at His command.
Evangelistic Sermons, 271

JEWS

Though Lloyd-Jones was an amillennialist he did not merge his understanding of the Jew and Israel with the church – though he comes close. He believed that Christians are Jews in the spiritual sense and Israel is the Church but he still believed that God had a special place and plan for the Jews and there would be an ingathering of them into the Church of Christ. These quotations should be read in their context to fully grasp his teaching.

Who are the Jews? They are a people, a special people, chosen and separated from all others for a special possession for God Himself; the opposite of being a Gentile, an outsider, an alien from the commonwealth of Israel. They were members of God's church; members of God's family. What a privilege! Called a Jew! The highest privilege a man could ever have.
The Righteous Judgement of God, 139

It is an advantage to be a Jew, it is an advantage to have the Scriptures, as it is an advantage to be the child of Christian parents, but you are no more saved than a child who is not born into a Christian family.
The Righteous Judgement of God, 188

It is remarkable that, although they were without their country for so many centuries and nations did their utmost to destroy them completely, this nation has been preserved. The only real explanation of this is that God has not finished with them and that there is a day coming when this 'fullness of Israel' is going to be brought back to salvation, back into the Christian church, and so God's ultimate promise to Abraham is going to receive a wonderful fulfilment.
To God's Glory, 70

The key to the understanding of all the attitude of the Jews, especially their religious leaders, to our Lord Himself, is to be found in this phrase: 'They are not all Israel, which are of Israel.'
God's Sovereign Purpose, 98

There are some, and I am among them, who believe that Paul does teach in this chapter that before the end there will be large numbers of conversions among the Jews. It will be astonishing and it will rejoice the hearts of believers then alive. It will be like life from the dead. But they will not be in a special position, the nation of Israel will not be differentiated from Gentiles.
Great Doctrines of the Bible (3), 113

The Jew is not saved by being a Jew or by being circumcised. But to say that does not mean that there is no difference at all between Jew and Gentile, or that there is no advantage in being a Jew. There is a tremendous advantage in being a Jew. What is it? It is – and notice that instead of giving us a great list of things, he says, '. . . chiefly, because that unto them were committed the oracles of God'.
The Righteous Judgement of God, 165

The Jews as such have ceased to be the special people of God. There is a new nation.
God's Way of Reconciliation, 277

There is no permanent distinction for all eternity between Jew and Gentile; that is gone once and for ever.
Great Doctrines of the Bible (3), 207

There is an Israel within Israel. There is a literal, national Israel, but there is a spiritual 'Israel' within that larger body.
To God's Glory, 3

But when the Gentiles in the church see the Jews coming in also, they shall be lifted up to the heavens of delight and glory and wonder and amazement.
To God's Glory, 92

God has never promised that He would save every single Israelite who has ever lived.
To God's Glory, 226

JONATHAN EDWARDS (Hell)
If ever you find anything written by him buy it and devour it!
Great Doctrines of the Bible (1), 144

Jonathan Edwards was probably one of the greatest minds – I say it advisedly – that the world has ever known. He is certainly the greatest brain America has ever produced, a brilliant, outstanding philosopher, the last man in the world to be carried away by false emotionalism.
Great Doctrines of the Bible (2), 249

I am second to no-one in my admiration for the great Jonathan Edwards and his preaching; yet it does seem to me that Edwards in his preaching concerning hell went at times well beyond what he was warranted to do and to say by Holy Scripture. He allowed his imagination to run riot
Knowing the Times, 84

JOY
I once listened to a man preaching on 'The rainbow in the cloud' after the Flood. He was a good and able man, and a pious man; but he so disliked the type of evangelical who is glib and superficial, and he was so afraid of false joy, that though his text spoke about 'The rainbow in the cloud' he sent us out of that service under a very black cloud! He was so afraid that we might go out with a carnal joy that he concealed the rainbow and magnified the cloud!
Assurance, 166

A mateyness and a cheeriness is not Christian joy. Christian joy is that which realizes the holiness of God, the depth of sin, and Christ coming from heaven and giving Himself unto blood for ruined man. That leads to a holy joy and a thanksgiving – a joy unspeakable and full of glory.
The Gospel of God, 363

The joy of heaven is unmixed.
God's Ultimate Purpose, 310

The absence of a profound joy is, I suggest, due to the fact that we are in too much of a hurry; we are too anxious to count heads; we are too interested in results.
Saving Faith, 350

I sometimes think that it would do us all great good if we faced that statement in 1 Peter 1:8 every morning of our lives . . . Peter says, in effect: 'Whom having not seen ye love; in whom, though now ye see him not, yet believing, ye rejoice with a joy that baffles description, beyond description and full of glory'
Joy Unspeakable, 184–85

We are all too busy and too active. Even rushing round from meeting to meeting is no substitute for meditation and that thorough study of Scripture which leads to a grasping of its doctrines. If you simply desire 'spiritual' entertainment you will not know the 'joy of the Lord'; you will only be listening to someone else telling you how wonderful it is. We must reflect upon these things ourselves.
Assurance, 161

Is your salvation merely a matter of saying 'I believe my sins are forgiven', or are you rejoicing in it? Are you 'receiving of His fullness'? Are you aware of His

meeting your every need? Are you looking forward to the glory and rejoicing in anticipation of it?
Assurance, 238

It is the greatest insult that we can ever offer to the holy name of God to suggest that he desires our misery and that to obey him and live the life he would have us live is the direct road to unhappiness.
Old Testament Evangelistic Sermons, 260

The miserable Christian is guilty of unbelief. The Christian who lacks joy and assurance is either not clear about the truth, or else he is guilty of something much worse, he does not trust God who has revealed that truth to him. Shame on us! We have no right to be uncertain or joyless. To be certain is not presumption and to be joyless is not being humble.
Assurance, 165

A Christian is not merely one who is a little less miserable than he was. He is one who rejoices.
Old Testament Evangelistic Sermons, 260

You cannot really know the joy of the Lord until you are perfectly certain that all is well between you and God.
Life in God, 95

You must be made miserable before you can know true Christian joy.
Spiritual Depression, 28

JUDGMENT (Hell)
If you take this idea of judgment out of the Bible you have very little left.
The Heart of the Gospel, 98

Is there was nothing beyond death, perhaps I would not be preaching at all, but I know that there is something beyond death, and it is judgment. God is the Judge. The God who so loved the world that he sent his only Son into it, and put our sins upon him and smote him for us, he will be the Judge.
Authentic Christianity (2), 126

At the bar of God's judgment we shall not be seen in crowds but every man will be judged alone.
Old Testament Evangelistic Sermons, 16

All we can do is to read the Scriptures and observe what they teach, and submit ourselves entirely to that. It is a solemn and a terrifying matter. All will not be saved finally.
Assurance, 250

The Day of Judgment will be a revelation, a day of surprises. What appeared to us to be very great may then appear to be nothing at all; and what appeared to us to be trivial will then be seen to be of great value with the arc-light of God's love shed upon it. What a reversal of our judgments and our conceptions we shall find!
The Unsearchable Riches of Christ, 190–91

Every one of us has got to die and face God, and then there will be one of those two things – heaven or hell! Joy and bliss indescribable, or misery and wretchedness that are too awful to contemplate.
Love so Amazing, 21

If only every man and woman in the world today realised that he or she had to stand before God in the judgment it would be a very different world.
Authentic Christianity (3), 258

No man at the bar of final judgment will be able to say that any unjust demand was made of him, or that the Law is in any way unjust in punishing him.
The Law: Its Functions and Limits, 163

This judgment is final. There is no teaching in Scripture about a second chance, about a further opportunity.
Studies in the Sermon on the Mount (2), 323

The last judgment, a doctrine against which all others should be understood.
Great Doctrines of the Bible (3), 239

There is a sense in which our going out of this world into the next is a momentous event because by then our fate is sealed, but that is not the last judgment. That will be right at the very end, at the second coming, when the dead are raised, when our bodies are resurrected. It will be a great public occasion when the whole world will be assembled together and the fate of every single individual will be announced.
Great Doctrines of the Bible (3), 241

When you and I come to the judgment there will be only one real question put to us? 'What did you do about the Lord Jesus Christ?'
The Heart of the Gospel, 101

Though we are saved, though we are children of God, we shall have to appear before the judgement throne of Christ, and give an account of the deeds done in the body, whether good or bad. It is possible for us to know loss, it is possible for us to know shame.
Liberty and Conscience, 142

So many seem to imagine that, because they believe and are 'saved', that is the end; they entirely forget this matter of rewards. They go on doing the minimum in the Kingdom of God, and in the church of God, and seem to fail to understand their true relationship to Him. Never forget that everything you do, and everything you fail to do, is known to Him, and that you will have to face your own record again, and 'give an account of the deeds done in the body, whether good or bad'.
Life in the Spirit in Marriage Home and Work, 370

JUSTIFICATION

If there has been one word that has stood out more prominently, especially in the history of Protestantism, than any other, it has been this great word justification.
Great Doctrines of the Bible (2), 167

In justification we are not *made* righteous, we are *declared* to be righteous – the thing is quite different.
Great Doctrines of the Bible (2), 169

Justification means not only the forgiveness of our sins, but also that our sins have been dealt with and have been removed from us. Justification states that God regards us as righteous, as if we had not sinned. In other words, it is a stronger term than forgiveness; we may be forgiven and yet our sins remain upon us. But what God does for us in justification is to remove the guilt altogether, to remove the sin. It is not only that He does not punish us for it, but that He looks upon us as righteous, as if we had not sinned; that sin has been removed.
Fellowship with God, 138

There is no peace between man and God until a man grasps this doctrine of justification. It is the only way of peace.
Assurance, 18

To be justified means that God declares us to be righteous. It is a legal or a forensic term; it is something that God does and God alone does. He declares that He regards us as righteous, and He does so because He has attributed to us, put to our account, the righteousness of the Lord Jesus Christ. He clothes us with the righteousness of Christ, puts His robe upon us.
Assurance, 133

All our sins, all the sins of all His people, were laid upon Him; all the sins even of those yet unborn who will yet become His people were laid upon Him; in Him all who believe are justified from all sins, past, present and future!
Assurance, 257

A man who knows that he is justified by faith only is a man who should enjoy great certainty; peace with God, standing in the grace of God, rejoicing in hope of the glory of God.
Assurance, 102

. . . [J]ustification by faith is not a process; it is something that happens 'once and for ever'. Sanctification, on the other hand, is a process.
Assurance, 31

There is always something that sounds dangerous in the preaching of justification by faith only; so if our preaching does not sound dangerous in this respect, probably the gospel is not being truly preached.
The New Man, 195

We are not justified because we are regenerate, not justified because we have a new nature, not justified because we have become sanctified. That is the Roman Catholic error and heresy: But Paul's teaching is that we are justified by God, and in His sight, as we are, while 'ungodly', while sinful, without any change in our nature. Justification and regeneration, of course, generally go together, but we must never say that we are justified because we are regenerate. In our thinking the order and sequence in our minds must always be to put justification before regeneration.
Assurance, 206

It is not our regeneration that saves us. It is not the fact that we are born again that saves us. It is the righteousness of Christ that saves us. God justifies the ungodly, and the ungodly are not regenerate. It is while we are ungodly that we are declared righteous. Regeneration comes practically at the same time, but it is something different.
Assurance, 134

Justification is an act of God the Father, as we have seen; sanctification is essentially the work of God the Holy Spirit.
Great Doctrines of the Bible (2), 175

We have to fight for the great doctrine of justification by faith, it is constantly being attacked, but it would be a very grievous thing if, in asserting that, we in any way detracted from this other teaching which reminds Christian people that all their works are observed by the Lord, the righteous judge, and that what you and I do as Christians in this world will have an effect upon our life in glory in the next world.
Great Doctrines of the Bible (3), 246

– K –

KINGDOM OF GOD
If we regard the kingdom of God as the rule and the reign of God, the kingdom was here when our Lord was here in person. It is present now wherever the Lord Jesus Christ is acknowledged as Lord. But it is to come with a greater fullness when everybody and everything will have to acknowledge His lordship. So we can say that the kingdom has come, the kingdom is among us, and the kingdom is yet to come. What, then, is the relationship of the Church to the kingdom? Surely it is this: the Church is an *expression* of the kingdom but is not to be equated with it.
Great Doctrines of the Bible (3), 4

KNOWLEDGE OF GOD
The knowledge of God comes before any particular blessing that we may desire from Him.
Great Doctrines of the Bible (1), 50

Nothing is more wonderful than to know that God loves you; and no man can truly know that God loves him except in Jesus Christ and Him crucified.
Assurance, 19

If you can encompass any knowledge with your brain it means that your brain is greater than the thing that you encompass. So when man tries to understand God, and to find Him by his own searching and power and intellect and understanding, he is postulating that he is greater than God, and that God is someone open to examination. The very idea is monstrously ridiculous.
The Christian Soldier, 214

There is no such thing as a knowledge of God apart from Jesus Christ; we never arrive at God truly unless we come through Him.
Life in God, 96

If you should ask me to state in one phrase what I regard as the greatest defect in most Christian lives I would say that it is our failure to know God as our Father as we should know Him.
Studies in the Sermon on the Mount (2), 202

It is comparable to the knowledge which a man has who is in love with a woman. It is not possible for him to sit down and write out a philosophical account of his love, he cannot explain it rationally: he knows it, but here his reason ceases. The great love which reason and knowledge do not understand – that is it. We know, because we have love and love recognises love, and love attracts love. The little lamb cannot give you a rational reason why it should pick out one sheep as its mother but it knows that sheep is his mother. The Christian's knowledge of his Lord is something like that.
Saved in Eternity, 157

Genuine faith, established upon the full doctrine of the Bible, leads us to a knowledge of God which is more immediate and more direct, what the Puritans called a spiritual knowledge of God, over and above the knowledge of faith.
Saved in Eternity, 163

Knowledge of God comes before any particular blessing that we may desire from Him. The goal of all our seeking and all our worship and all our endeavour should not be to have a particular experience; it should not be to petition certain blessings; it should be to know God Himself – the Giver not the gift, the source and the fount of every blessing, not the blessing itself.
Great Doctrines of the Bible (1), 50

Do not stop at experiences. The end is to know God, and nothing less.
Faith on Trial, 111

Before everything else my chief desire is 'so that I should know Him'. Nothing surprises me so much as I look back as seeing the tendency to be satisfied with other objects. I do not refer to sins so much as to the 'poor idols of the earth' or to backsliding. It is so easy to satisfy oneself with truths about the Person. What gives more pleasure than theologising and being doctrinal about the faith, and even defending the faith? We are all ready to try to obtain and thirst after special experiences – assurance of forgiveness and salvation, being freed from special sins experiencing joy and peace, being able to live the full life and so on. All these things are part of the heritage of the Christian, but he must not live on them and be satisfied by them. To know Him is a life full of peace.
The Fight of Faith, 220

Is God real to you? When you get on your knees and pray, do you know that God is there, do you realize His presence?
God's Ultimate Purpose, 344

Do you know God? I am not asking whether you believe things about Him; but have you met Him? Have you known yourself for certain in His presence? Does He speak to you, and do you know that you speak to Him? *The Practice of the Presence of God* by Brother Lawrence tells us that this is possible in the kitchen

while you are washing the dishes, and performing the most menial tasks. It matters not where you are as long as you know that this is possible, that Christ died to make it possible. He died 'to bring us to God', and to this knowledge.
God's Ultimate Purpose, 348

If the greatest privilege that can ever come to a man is to be spoken to directly by God, it is equally true to say that there is no greater loss that a man can suffer than that God should cease to speak to him . . . The Christian is a man who ought to be wretched and miserable if he feels that he does not hear God speaking to him, if he feels he has lost contact with God.
The Righteous Judgement of God, 168–69

There is in man an innate sense of consciousness that there is a God; every man has it. The so-called atheist has it and is simply trying to argue against it, trying to buttress up something he does not want to believe in his mind, but which something within him keeps on asserting. Archaeological research has shown that the most primitive tribes in the world all have within them a sense of a Supreme God, a Supreme Being at the back of everything.
God's Ultimate Purpose, 352

LAW

The Law was never introduced as a way of salvation.
Assurance, 188

This does not mean that the Christian should not keep the Law; but he is not 'under' it. We must be clear about this. I am constituted a righteous person – that is how God regards me. I am now in His family, I am now His child, and when I sin now I am not sinning against Law, I am sinning against Love. It is no longer the action of a criminal; it is the action of a child.
Assurance, 278

Indeed the law of God was full of grace.
Studies in the Sermon on the Mount (2), 51

The best man, the noblest, the most learned, the most philanthropic, the greatest idealist, the greatest thinker, say what you like about him – there has never been a man who can stand up to the test of the law. Drop your plumb-line, and he is not true to it, he is not straight, he is not upright, he is not pure, he is not blameless: 'There is none righteous, no, not one'.
The Righteous Judgement of God, 198

The law breakers will finally be punished. Let us make no mistake about this. Those who die finally impenitent, and unbelieving in the Lord Jesus Christ, are under the condemnation of the law. And at the very end the pronouncement delivered upon them will be, 'Depart from me, ye cursed, into everlasting fire.' And it is the law that will condemn them to that.
Studies in the Sermon on the Mount (1), 196

No man at the bar of final judgment will be able to say that any unjust demand was made of him, or that the Law is in any way unjust in punishing him.
The Law: Its Functions and Limits, 163

Any view of the death of Christ which does not put it specifically and primarily in terms of the Law of God is a misinterpretation of His death.
The Law: Its Functions and Limits, 37–38

Any position which says 'law only' or which says 'grace only' is of necessity wrong, because in the Bible you have 'law' and 'grace'.
Life in the Spirit in Marriage Home and Work, 268

We must never give the impression that in the matter of our salvation the Law is put on one side, and that God says, as it were, 'I am going to make it easy for you.' That is a false and unbiblical representation of Christianity. The true doctrine honours the Law because the Law is God's Law, an expression of His eternal holy character.
The Law: Its Functions and Limits, 49–50

There is no better life than a life lived in conformity with God's Law. Anyone who lived such a life would be living the best conceivable type of life. Our Lord lived such a life. We find very often in the Psalms that the Psalmist praises the Law of God; he says that he knows more than his teachers because of God's Law; it is by means of God's Law that he has understanding and insight; it is by knowing and learning about, and attempting to keep God's Law that he has had the greatest happiness and the greatest joy in his life.
The Law: Its Functions and Limits, 164

The non-spiritual view of the Law regards it as concerned only with external actions. But the spiritual view of the Law knows that it is as much concerned about motives, desires, imaginations (that is, feelings] as it is about actions.
The Law: Its Functions and Limits, 185

Merely to be forgiven is not enough; we have to keep the Law of God.
Children of God, 54

This holy Law, this expression of God's being and character.
Children of God, 56

It does not save; it brings us to the Saviour. It is not the way of salvation; its purpose is to show us our need of salvation, and to give us some indication of how it is going to come.
The Law: Its Functions and Limits, 169

LIE
A lie cannot live in the presence of God;
Fellowship with God, 21

LIFE
The strain of life is a very serious thing. He is no friend of mankind who tries to make light of it.
The Life of Joy, 19

We can be certain that God has a plan and a purpose for our lives, and it will be carried out.
Studies in the Sermon on the Mount (2), 115

Do not carry yesterday or tomorrow with you; live for today and for the twelve hours you are in.
Studies in the Sermon on the Mount (2), 150

We proclaim what we are, finally, not by what we say, but by what we do.
The New Man, 202

One of the real difficulties in life is not to be mastered by it.
Walking with God, 10

The great question is: What do I really need to know in order to live as I should in this world?
God's Ultimate Purpose, 356

The supreme matter in this life and world for all of us is to realize our relationship to God.
Studies in the Sermon on the Mount (2), 14

Two patients who appear to be in the same condition are given identical treatment. One recovers; the other dies. What is the answer? The answer is that 'no man can add one cubit to his duration of life'. It is a great mystery, but we cannot escape it. Our times are in the hands of God, and do what we will, with all our food and drink, and our medical profession, and all our learning and science and skill, we cannot add a fraction to the duration of a man's life.
Studies in the Sermon on the Mount (2), 122

LOGIC
The Bible is full of logic, and we must never think of faith as something purely mystical.
Studies in the Sermon on the Mount (2), 129–30

I sometimes think that the whole secret of the Christian life is to know how to use the word 'therefore'. The Christian life is in many ways a matter of logic, a matter of deduction.
Assurance, 1

I simply point out in passing now that it is not unspiritual to reason and to be logical. Indeed . . . to be logical and to reason and to argue is to be highly spiritual.
Assurance, 129

LOVE

It is love alone that can appreciate love.
The Unsearchable Riches of Christ, 214

You can be aware of another's love to you by the actions of that person, but what love craves for always is a personal statement.
The Unsearchable Riches of Christ, 235

Love is all-inclusive. When you love, every part of you is involved. You cannot love in sections of your personality; love is always totalitarian in its demands and responses.
The Final Perseverance of the Saints, 185

We will agree, I am sure, that one of the real tragedies of the age in which we live is that this great word has become so debased and misused.
Children of God, 109

From the animal standpoint – men and women have an animal part of their nature, let us never forget it – we may not like certain Christians. I mean by that, there is none of this instinctive, elemental attraction; they are not the people whom we naturally like; yet what we are told is that to love them means that we treat them exactly as if we did like them.
Children of God, 110

How easy it is to fall in love with loving instead of actually loving!
Children of God, 111

It is no use asking the world to 'love one another.' It is impossible; they are incapable of doing it. We need the divine nature within us before we can truly love one another. If within the church you have failure on the part of men and women to love one another, what hope is there for the world to do this? It is utterly impossible.
The Love of God, 45

Love is not a sentiment; it is the most active, vital thing in the world.
Life in God, 30

In the natural realm those who experience true love for a person do not parade it. The people who address everyone as 'Dear' or 'Darling' obviously know nothing about true feeling, otherwise they could not use the terms so easily and freely.
The Sons of God, 368

The truth is, of course, that we are in sin and all our ideas are wrong; our conception of love is more wrong than anything else and if we begin to think of

God's love in terms of what *we* do and what *we* think, then – I say it with reverence – God help us! If we are going to attribute our sentimental, loose, unjust and unrighteous notions of love to the everlasting Godhead, then we place ourselves in the most precarious position.
Great Doctrines of the Bible (1), 333

Love does not look at itself – it is absorbed in the object of its love.
Love manifests itself by loving persons in the concrete.
The Love of God, 77

An element of incomprehension and difficulty is to be expected. Indeed there is a sense in which that is as it should be. You cannot dissect an aroma, you cannot analyse love. And that is what we are dealing with here – the love of Christ and of God.
The Unsearchable Riches of Christ, 155

Nothing is more wonderful than to know that God loves you; and no man can truly know that God loves him except in Jesus Christ and Him crucified.
Assurance, 19

Whatever one may say about the love of God in Christ Jesus there is always something more to be said.
Assurance, 140

The love of God is so great and powerful that a man feels his physical frame beginning to crack beneath it. Many Christian people, when they have suddenly had an awareness of this love of God, have literally fainted and become unconscious.
The Unsearchable Riches of Christ, 213

'Behold, what manner of love' – you cannot understand it, you cannot explain it. The only thing we can say is that it is the eternal love, it is the love of God and is self-generated, produced by nothing but itself, so that in spite of us and all that is true of us He came and died and suffered so much.
Children of God, 19

LUST
'Lust' means an inordinate affection or desire; lust means the abuse of something which is naturally and perfectly right and legitimate in and of itself.
Walking with God, 85

Modern man, far from being ruled by reason, is ruled by lust and passion.
Banner of Truth, Issue 275

There are certain desires in us that are perfectly legitimate, they have been given by God. Yes, but if we are governed and controlled by them and our whole outlook upon life is circumscribed by these things, then we are guilty of lust. *Walking with God*, 85

– M –

MAN (Adam)
There is only one explanation of man and that is God
Enjoying the Presence of God, 19

Man in unbelief is inexcusable.
Great Christian Doctrines (1), 49

Yet the doctrine of the Bible is that I can never know man truly unless I look at him in the sight of God and in the teaching concerning God.
Fellowship with God, 101

We must say now that there is nothing more remarkable in the whole of biblical doctrine than the doctrine of man, this emphasis on the greatness and dignity of man.
Studies in the Sermon on the Mount (2), 120

creation
It has been discovered in this present century that there are only four blood groups, that the whole of mankind can be divided into these four groups, and that all of them can be derived from just two persons. Then you remember that the apostle Paul told the people at Athens that God 'hath made of one blood all nations of men . . .' (Acts 17:26).
Great Doctrines of the Bible (1), 134

There are three parts to man. He was made by God, body, mind and spirit, or, if you prefer it, body, soul and spirit; and the highest is the spirit. Next to that comes the soul, and next to that the body.
Studies in the Sermon on the Mount (2), 97–98

We can say that the Scripture does draw a *distinction* between spirit and soul, even if it does not say that there is a *difference* between them. There may be a distinction without a difference. Let me put it like this: certainly the Scriptures teach us that the Spirit is that part of the spiritual or immaterial element in each of us which is related to God, and is capable of receiving the operation of the Spirit of God through His word. Spirit is that which puts us into relationship with God and enables the Spirit of God to act upon us. If there is only one

immaterial element, then a part of that immaterial element is called spirit, and it is that which, as it were, links us to God, whereas the soul is the part of the immaterial element which animates the body, which renders us capable of thinking and willing and feeling. It is also the seat of the affections. It is that part of us which links us to the body and enables us, through the body, to communicate with other people.
Great Doctrines of the Bible (1), 161

enigma
Human beings are the most contradictory creatures on the face of the earth, on one side, brilliant in their achievements, and on the other, so often despicable in their living. Mastering the elements, they are unable to master themselves. They arrive at knowledge and understanding of great mysteries away up in the heavens, but often live like beasts and worse. What is the matter? There are warring elements and factions within them.
Authentic Christianity (1), 203

Not only is nature 'red in tooth and claw', mankind is also.
Studies in the Sermon on the Mount (1), 271

Do we not have a curious feeling within us that we were not meant for the kind of thing we are experiencing, but for something bigger – an inner cry for an ampler and diviner air?
Old Testament Evangelistic Sermons, 6

True human greatness has tended to disappear as the biblical view of man has waned, for even at its best and highest the worldly, naturalistic view of man is unworthy.
Studies in the Sermon on the Mount (2), 120

You have read of Alexander the Great, so-called, one of the most skilful generals of all time, a great monarch and a mighty warrior. He conquered almost the entire known world. Do you know what the Scriptures call Him? Read your Bible right through and you will never find the name of Alexander the Great. It is not mentioned. But Alexander the Great does come into the Scriptures, and you will find the way in which God refers to him in Daniel 8. As Walter Luthi has pointed out, he who to the world is Alexander the Great, is to God 'a he-goat'
Faith on Trial, 63

Why is it that men reject the very things they say they desire most of all when the Bible offers it to them?
Old Testament Evangelistic Sermons, 146

There is a tender spirit in all men, even the hardest and the most cruel.
Old Testament Evangelistic Sermons, 101

That is the ultimate tragedy of man, that in the depth of his need and misery and shame he avoids the only One who can really help him.
Old Testament Evangelistic Sermons, 9

Man . . . is the highest point of God's great work in creation. There is nothing higher than man. Man was made 'the lord of creation', the supreme being, under God, on earth. Therefore, obviously, he is the very special object of the attacks and the onslaughts of the devil.
The Christian Warfare, 80

We have come to realise that a man can be educated and cultured and still be a beast!
Banner of Truth, Issue 275

The natural man is always play-acting, always looking at himself and admiring himself.
Banner of Truth, Issue 275

Man is not just an intellect; there is something in him which is much more powerful than his intellect, and that is what is called his heart. It does not matter how brilliant a brain a man may have, nor how highly educated he may be, he is governed much more by his instincts and by that which is elemental in him, than by his higher senses. If that were not so, educated people would never pass through the divorce courts, and they would never behave as cads, and there would be no such thing as infidelity and immorality.
The Righteous Judgement of God, 67

fall
What made them do this? Ultimately, of course, we cannot answer that question. Nobody has been able to answer it. The most we can say is that man's moral constitution, his being made in the image of God, and his possession of free will, at any rate held the possibility of his disobedience, but beyond that we cannot get, even as we could not arrive at any ultimate explanation of how Satan himself originally fell. You notice that ambition came into it, and ambition taking on a particular form; a desire for a short road to divine knowledge.
Great Doctrines of the Bible (1), 183

This image of God which was put upon man, this imprint of God's own Being, consists partly in his intellect and understanding, his power to reason, to look at himself objectively, and his capacity for communion with God. That has been defaced. Not only that, man was made lord of the creation. But he has lost much of this as the result of the Fall, and because of sin, and he is no longer like God. The image of God is not totally destroyed, but it is terribly defaced; so much so that man is no longer recognisable as one that was made in the image of God. He is ungodly
Assurance, 117

free will
In the most extraordinary way, man's being made in the image of God made sin possible for him, because of his free personality, because of his free will.
Great Doctrines of the Bible (1), 184–85

Man is never free; he is either a slave of sin and Satan or he is a slave of God and of the Lord Jesus Christ.
The New Man, 211

self
Man's troubles are in himself and not in his environment
Old Testament Evangelistic Sermons, 4

When a man truly sees himself, he knows that nobody can say anything about him that is too bad.
Banner of Truth, Issue 275

Surely, if there is one thing that stands out prominently in the whole of Scripture from beginning to end, it is the fundamental division of mankind into two great final groups, the saved, and the lost.
Assurance, 244

sin
We are all condemned felons before a holy God.
God's Way of Reconciliation, 210

Every man in the world is in one of two positions – he is either 'under sin' or else he is 'under grace'. He is either being ruled over and governed by sin, or else he is under the reign of, and is being ruled over by grace. Those, I repeat, are the only two possible positions.
Assurance, 304

Man's arrogance needs to be humbled.
To God's Glory, 280

Man in sin is unclean at his best.
The New Man, 267

There is only one thing to say about men and women in sin – they are fools.
The Glory of God, 388

Man in sin is, as it were, upside-down. The material, animal part of him is controlling him; his body is supreme and he is governed by it.
The New Man, 73

sovereignty
'Shall the thing formed' – that is what you are – 'say to him that formed it . . .' There again is the contrast: man – God! 'The thing formed' is an interesting word. It is the word from which we get our present word 'plastic': 'the thing formed' – plasma! And this is what you are, says the Apostle, you with your objection. You are only the thing formed, the plastic material, and God is the one who handles and forms and models it. Then to bring it right home to us he goes on and uses another comparison: 'Hath not the potter power over the clay, of the same lump to make . . .?' The contrast is between man and God, the thing formed and the one who forms – a lump of clay and the potter.
God's Sovereign Purpose, 191

[Men –] the pygmy creatures of time, defying the Eternal and Almighty God; they whose life is as a vapour or as a passing cloud turning their backs upon the Creator and Artificer of all things; they who were made by his hands and moulded by him out of the clay and the dust defying their Maker, the clay attempting to resist the Potter!
Old Testament Evangelistic Sermons, 190

MARRIAGE
You cannot understand marriage unless you are a Christian.
Life in the Spirit in Marriage Home and Work, 98

Marriage is not a human institution . . . God at the very beginning ordained the family as the fundamental unit, so that when we come into this world we are not left, as it were, on the cold doorsteps of life, but enter into the bosom of a family, who surround us with love and care and protection.
Singing to the Lord, 69

It is only the Christian who truly understands and appreciates marriage. I think I can say honestly that in my pastoral experience, there has been nothing more wonderful than to see the difference Christianity makes in the husband/wife relationship. Where there was a tendency to part and to drift from one another, and an antagonism and almost a bitterness and a hatred, the two people on becoming Christians have discovered one another for the first time. They have also discovered for the first time what marriage really is, though they may have been married for years. They now see what a beautiful and what a glorious thing it is.
Life in the Spirit in Marriage Home and Work, 98

We must consider marriage in terms of the doctrine of the atonement.
Life in the Spirit in Marriage Home and Work, 148

A wife worthy of the name does not need to be exhorted to take an interest in her husband's affairs; she counts it her greatest privilege to be helping her husband; she is vitally interested in all he does, and in its success.
Life in the Spirit in Marriage Home and Work, 205

I would therefore put it in this way, that it is not sufficient for us even to regard our wives as partners. They are partners, but they are more than partners. You can have two men in business who are partners, but that is not the analogy. The analogy goes higher than that. It is not a question of partnership, though it includes that idea. There is another phrase that is often used – at least, it used to be common – which puts it so much better, and which seems to me to be an unconscious statement of the Christian teaching. It is the expression used by men when they refer to their wives as 'my better half'. Now that is exactly right. She is not a partner, she is the other half of the man. 'They two shall be one flesh'. 'My better half'. The very word 'half' puts the whole case which the Apostle elaborates here. We are not dealing with two units, two entities, but dealing with two halves of one – 'They two shall be one flesh'.
Life in the Spirit in Marriage Home and Work, 213

You cannot detach yourself from your body, so you cannot detach yourself from your wife.
Life in the Spirit in Marriage Home and Work, 215

I suggest that all Christian husbands should automatically refuse every such invitation which comes to them alone and does not include their wives.
Life in the Spirit in Marriage Home and Work, 217

When two people marry and take their solemn vows and pledges before God and before men they ought to be locking a certain back door that they should never even look at again. But that is not the way today.
Faith on Trial, 29

A Christian service at a wedding should be reserved only and exclusively for Christians. It is to make a farce of it to have such a service for any others.
Life in the Spirit in Marriage Home and Work, 117

The world is full of back doors at the present time. It seems at times that the majority of people who are getting married today are already thinking of divorce even as they are getting married. That is why there is such a breakdown of morality today. Certain doors should be bolted and barred, never to be opened again. You must not look back at all, look forward. You are facing the enemy; do not think of retreat. Never toy with even the possible thought of failure; it is utterly opposed to this teaching.
The Christian Soldier, 162–63

The husband tells his wife everything. She knows his every secret, his every desire, every ambition, every hope, every project that ever enters his mind. She is one with him. He tells her things that he would not say to anybody else; she shares everything, there is nothing kept back, nothing is hidden. Such is the relationship of husband and wife.
Life in the Spirit in Marriage Home and Work, 204

We must consider marriage in terms of the doctrine of the atonement.
Life in the Spirit in Marriage Home and Work, 148

MARTYRS
Martyrs are men who know what they believe.
The Gospel of God, 21

MARY (Virgin Birth, Roman Catholicism)
What is taught in Scripture is not that Mary had been either born or made sinless, but that that portion of Mary, that cell out of Mary that was to be developed into the body of the Son of God was cleansed from sin; and that only. So Mary remained sinful, but this portion that she transmits to her Son has been delivered, set free from sin; and it is to that that the Son of God is joined. That is the human nature He takes unto Himself. It is a miracle, of course; and we are told specifically that it is a miracle. It was because she did not realize that a miracle was to happen that Mary stumbled at the announcement of the Archangel Gabriel, and his reply to her is, 'Do not try to understand this. The power of the Highest shall overshadow you, the Holy Ghost will come upon you, you are going to conceive of the Holy Ghost' who has power to work this cleansing so that the body of the human nature of the Son of God who is to be born of you shall be entirely free from sin. So we reject the so-called doctrine of the 'Immaculate Conception'; but we assert with all our power the doctrine that the human nature of the Son of God was entirely free from sin.
The Law: Its Functions and Limits, 324

But I want to emphasise this: if, as our Lord makes so plain and clear here, Mary could not direct and influence his conduct while he was here in the state of his humiliation, how much less can she do so now, in his state of exaltation. Can you not see that the very suggestion that we need to pray to Mary, that she may influence him, is blasphemous? It is to derogate from his heart of love, from his sympathy, from his understanding, from his nearness to us. The very idea that we need any intermediary detracts from the glory of his complete divinity and perfect Saviourhood.
Spiritual Blessing, 28

There is no suggestion (in the New Testament) that she is a 'co-redemptrix'. Nor can you find the immaculate conception or transubstantiation,
Christian Conduct, 247

MATERIALISM (Wealth)
All materialism is atheistic.
Studies in the Sermon on the Mount (2), 94

Man! Woman! There is something in you bigger than the world . . . you are a spiritual being. That is why all that the world can give you is not enough to satisfy you.
Authentic Christianity (3), 256

Clothing – oh, the time and the energy and the enthusiasm that goes into this. The talking and the writing; again you see it shouting at you everywhere. But you get it equally with certain people in the matter of their house and home. The lust of the eyes – how pathetic it is that human beings, endowed with the faculties that God has given, can live for things like that, this outlook of pomp and appearance and show.
Walking with God, 86–87

We worship money, we worship cars, we worship house, pleasure and one another. But it is all animal and instinctual, it is all primitive. It is all this world, and it belongs mainly to the realm to the body.
Authentic Christianity (4), 93

MATURITY
The people to whom I am drawn, the people I like, are those who give me the impression that they are hungry for God, that they have a longing in their souls for the living God. I put them before all others.
God's Way of Reconciliation, 346

Nothing builds up but the unadulterated Word of God.
Christian Unity, 203–4

To grow in some respects and not in others leads to a monstrosity; for some parts to be over-developed and others under-developed produces a lack of symmetry and form which is ugly. The Christian is to grow symmetrically 'in all things', in every respect. We are to grow up and develop, not only in our minds and understandings, but also in our hearts and feelings and our sensibility.
Christian Unity, 254–55

MEDIA
As long as the people are controlled by the standard of the cinema, the newspaper, the television and the radio you inevitably get the conditions prevailing today. Is it surprising that little boys want to shoot when they constantly see people shooting one another on the television screen, and think it is exciting and wonderful and entertaining? If you keep on telling people that the most glamorous people in the world are those who are constantly passing through the divorce court, are you surprised that others want to follow their example?
Assurance, 308–9

Incredible as it may seem, there are still people who believe what they read in the newspapers.
Banner of Truth, Issue 275

If you really want to know the truth about yourself, do not go to the newspapers. They are always praising us, always playing up to us; they would not sell

if they did not. The newspapers are liars about the fundamental problems of life, they do no know them, indeed they are partly the cause of the present muddle.
The Kingdom of God, 139–40

MEDITATION
Meditation is something that you can not put into your news columns, it is too deep, it is not sufficiently spectacular.
Revival, 81–82

Do you know what it is, when your life as a man or a woman in this world is overwhelmed by the things that are happening and you are on the point of falling and of fainting, do you know what it is to retreat into your 'inner man'? That is one of the most blessed experiences you can ever know.
The Unsearchable Riches of Christ, 128

Oh, we believe in having a quiet time, a short reading of Scripture, a hurried prayer, and we have done everything. But where is self-examination? How much talk is there about mortification of the flesh?
Revival, 82

I urge therefore that there is nothing more important in connection with prayer than preliminary meditation and consideration of what we are going to do. This is what the saints have called 'recollection', which really means that you talk to yourself about yourself and what you are doing. Our chief fault is that we do not talk to ourselves as much as we should. We must talk to ourselves about ourselves. There is little purpose in beginning to talk to God and praying unless we realize our own condition. To fail to do so means that we may be going into the presence of God in a completely false state.
The Unsearchable Riches of Christ, 269

MEEKNESS
The man who is meek never looks pleased with himself.
Studies in the Sermon on the Mount (2), 310

There was no word for meekness in Greek pagan philosophy.
God's Way of Reconciliation, 88

Meekness is essentially a true view of oneself, expressing itself in attitude and conduct with respect to others.
Studies in the Sermon on the Mount (1), 68

MEETINGS
We have become a generation of Christians that tend to live on meetings.
The Unsearchable Riches of Christ, 108

MERCY (Compassion)

'Mercy' represents the desire to relieve suffering while 'compassion' [or graciousness] refers to the feelings which are experienced in the view of suffering. In other words, compassion generally comes before mercy. Compassion means that when you see a case of suffering, then there are certain feelings that are kindled within you immediately, a sense of sorrow and a sense of pity. And mercy is what puts that into practice. Mercy is more practical than compassion; it is the desire to relieve the suffering, to do something about it and to remove it.
God's Sovereign Purpose, 156

severe

'How can you say that things which are working in opposite directions are for my good?' The old preacher answered by using the illustration of a watch. He said, 'Take your watch and open it. What do you see? You see that one wheel is turning in an anti-clockwise direction, but it is attached to another wheel that is working in a clockwise direction. You look at this machinery and you say, "This is mad, this is quite ridiculous; here are wheels turning in opposite directions; the man who made the watch must have been a madman." But he wasn't. He has so arranged this watch and put in a main-spring to govern all the wheels, that when it is wound up, though one wheel turns this way, and another that way, they are all working together to move the hands round the face of the watch. They appear to be in contradiction but they are all working together to the same end.
The Final Perseverance of the Saints, 169–70

MILLENNIUM (Jews)

Dr Lloyd-Jones was an amillennialist; that is he believed that Christ rules today through his Church thus there is no need to look for a further one thousand year – millennial – reign of Christ on earth. He set out a powerful case in his Romans series. As noted, this did not mean he denied that the Jewish nation had no special purpose prophetically in the plan of God.

———————

Nowhere in the whole of the Bible are believers exhorted to look forward to a coming millennium. Christians are exhorted everywhere to look forward to the coming of the Lord and the glory which shall be revealed. There is no injunction or exhortation anywhere to us to look forward to a coming literal thousand years of reign by the Lord and His saints here upon the earth.
The Final Perseverance of the Saints, 84

What then, is the thousand years? I suggest to you that it is a symbolical figure to indicate the perfect length of time, known to God and to God alone, between the first and the second comings. It is not a literal thousand years, but the whole of this period while Christ is reigning until His enemies are made His footstool and He returns again for the final judgement.
Great Doctrines of the Bible (3), 225

MIND

The first thing that must happen to you before you can ever become a Christian is that you must surrender that little mind of yours, and begin to say, 'Of course I cannot understand it; my whole nature is against it. I can see that there is only one thing to do; I submit myself to the revelation that God has been pleased to give'.
Assurance, 251

Take a man who is not a Christian, but then is converted. There is a sense in which he always has the same mind. A man who was rather dull and lacking ability does not suddenly become a genius because he has become a Christian! Some people seem to think that he should, but they are wrong. Your faculties and powers are not changed when you are regenerate. You have the same instrument that you had before, the same mind in terms of the capacity to think and reason and be logical.
Christian Conduct, 106

The trouble with them is that they are almost devilishly clever. The trouble is not in their minds, it is in the thing that controls their minds. The thing that matters in a person is 'the *spirit* of the mind', that essence, that ultimate power of control which determines everything else. The interior principle of the mind which directs all its processes is what must be renewed, not the mind itself. It is the direction of the mind that needs to be controlled and to be changed.
Christian Conduct, 107

The mind can be compared to a steam engine. There it is. It has great power, and is standing on rails and facing in one direction. Now what you must do, says the apostle, is to get that engine on to one of those turntables that are found in railway stations so that it is facing the opposite way. Remember, it is precisely the same engine, with exactly the same power, but it is now ready to go in a different direction.
Christian Conduct, 107

The mind, the understanding, is man's supreme gift; it is undoubtedly a part of the image of God in man.
Faith on Trial, 75

The supreme gift in man is the gift of mind. It is a part of man's original endowment, and that which differentiates him from the animal. The animal acts in the main by instinct. But man has this curious power of thinking, objective thinking, of being able to look at himself objectively, and to reason and to argue, to consider, and to be logical. All this is a part of man's original endowment, and is undoubtedly the gift of God to man.
The Christian Warfare, 83

If you are not a Christian do not trust your mind; it is the most dangerous thing you can do. But when you become a Christian your mind is put back in the centre and you become a rational being.
Studies in the Sermon on the Mount (2), 105

Our minds are never free. There is no such thing as 'free thought'. That is always an utter impossibility. I know that the Rationalist Press Association claims that the mind of man is free, but that is but the pathetic delusion of man in sin. The mind by nature, and as the result of sin, is always controlled by the world and the outlook of the world. The difference between a man who is not a Christian and a man who is a Christian is that whereas the non-Christian's mind is controlled by the world, the Christian's mind has been 'transformed' and has been 'renewed' by the Holy Spirit. The result is that the Christian man is now able to think in a spiritual manner, whereas formerly he could not do so.
The Unsearchable Riches of Christ, 292

MIRACLES (Charismatic Gifts)
Miracles are not constant and usual; they are unusual and exceptional.
The Christian Soldier, 113

A miracle does not break the laws of nature or dismiss them or set them aside; it acts above them and puts power into them. It uses them, but it uses them with all the power of God and therefore shortens everything and makes the impossible possible.
God's Sovereign Purpose, 112

The miracle is not greater than the power of the word, it is an accompanying demonstration. Indeed, in a sense it is on a lower level because it is visual, and the visual appeals to people very much more, oftentimes, than the purely spoken. So at the beginning these signs did accompany the preaching of the gospel.
Authentic Christianity (2), 207

'What is the difference between ordinary and extraordinary providence?' asks someone. I would answer that question like this: in ordinary providence God works through second causes, in accordance with the laws which He has placed in nature. But in extraordinary providences, or miracles, God works immediately, directly, and without the secondary causes. A miracle is God working, not contrary to nature, but in a supernatural manner.
Great Christian Doctrines (1), 148

A miracle by definition is supernatural. It cannot be explained in terms of the ordinary operation of the laws of nature or of secondary causes. It is God's direct and immediate action.
Great Doctrines of the Bible (1), 149

Miraculous healing is possible, thank God for it, we believe it with the whole of our being, but miracle healing is not possible just whenever you and I think it ought to take place. It is under the hand of the Lord Jesus Christ, either he wills it or he does not will it.
The Life of Joy, 230

The Lord may work miracles, he may do all sorts of amazing things, but he laid it down at the very beginning, in the Temple at Jerusalem, that he only does such things in his own time and in his own way, and to people who seek to know him and his glory.
Spiritual Blessing, 173–74

One of the early Fathers of the church put this very well when he said, 'True faith is founded on God's word, not on wonders.'
Spiritual Blessing, 179

A miracle is supernatural, beyond the natural . . . If you can explain a thing, then do so. I plead with Christians especially to do this. Do not claim that something is miraculous if it can be explained in purely natural terms.
Authentic Christianity (3), 232

There are some observations which we must make about these miracles. One is that there was never a failure in the apostolic miracles as recorded in the Book of the Acts of the Apostles. Another is that the Apostles did not work miracles every day. Again, they never made preliminary announcements that they were going to do so. That is the way in which they differ from many who claim to be working miracles today, and who claim that they can announce that they intend to do so on such and such a day. The Apostles never spoke in such a manner; and the reason for that is obvious – they never knew beforehand when they were going to work a miracle.
The Christian Soldier, 134

God has the power to work a miracle whenever he chooses. But he does not keep life going by an endless succession of miracles. A miracle is exceptional. God normally works through the laws of nature – cause and effect – but at times he acts independently of that. And that is what a miracle is. A miracle is not a breaking of the laws of nature, it is God showing at a given point, and for a given purpose, to act apart from his own laws that he has placed in nature. So a miracle is an exceptional action; the normal is for God to use the means that He Himself has brought into existence.
Saving Faith, 265

All our Lord's miracles are more than events; they are in a sense parables as well. That does not mean that we do not believe in the actual incident as a fact of history. I am simply asserting that a miracle is also a parable.
Spiritual Depression, 58

phenomena
The phenomena are to lead to him, to an understanding of who he is, and if you stop with the phenomena he will not commit himself to you.
Spiritual Blessing, 192

MISSIONARY
The greatest motive of the missionary enterprise has always been that they have known that God is the means as well as the end. They have believed that God has called them to propagate the gospel, and because of that they have sacrificed everything, even their lives, and gone and preached. The man who is most ready to sacrifice his life for the gospel is the man who knows that even death cannot separate him from the love of God and that he has the life of God in him.
Saved in Eternity, 183

In a broadcast a few years ago, a very well-known preacher said very deliberately: Missionaries should get rid of this notion that their business is to go and what they call 'preach the gospel' to people. 'That' he said, 'is not the thing to do' – he was talking in particular of Africa. He went on, 'This is what you must do, you missionaries. You must go and live amongst those people; you must enter into their politics, you must share their problems and live the Christian life among them in their political social environment. And if you do that' he said 'there may be some hope that the grandchildren of the people with whom you are living now may become Christians.' Now that is what was said by the Moderator of the General Assembly of the Church of Scotland a few years back and that is regarded as the way of propagating the Christian message. And of course we are familiar with others in this country who teach a similar kind of thing – just political, social action and nothing else. But all I would ask is: where is the good news? It is not there. It is not there at all.
Saving Faith, 301

'You can go to the heart of Central Africa and visit a tribe of people who cannot read or write and who have no learning. You can preach the gospel to them with the same confidence as you preach it in Western society, because God can enlighten them through the Holy Spirit.
God's Ultimate Purpose, 195

Have we a missionary sense with regard to our fellow citizens in this country? Does the condition of the benighted masses in other lands weigh upon us at all? Are we concerned about the missionary enterprise? Do we think about these things, do they burden us, do we pray to God about them? Are we asking, 'What can I do, how can I help, what contribution can I make?'
God's Way of Reconciliation, 23

How much of our time are we giving day by day to praying for Christians in other countries?
The Unsearchable Riches of Christ, 109

MODERNITY

Modern knowledge casts no light upon death, nor upon eternity,
Authentic Christianity (3), 182

The state of the world today is nothing but an appalling monument to human failure.
Banner of Truth, Issue 275

In this century, human ingenuity and ability have been devoted mainly to the art of destruction.
Authentic Christianity (4), 85

Modern men and women, with all their cleverness, are incapable of inventing a new sin. The worse forms of evil and vice are to be found somewhere within the Bible. Nothing new under the sun!
A Nation under Wrath, 105

This idea that the problem of humanity is different today from what it has been in the past is, of all teachings, the most ludicrous. Different? Men and women are no different at all. They are still exactly what they have always been.
Authentic Christianity (1), 142

Now that is the trouble with modern man . . . the devil has blinded his mind . . . Therefore what have I to learn from such a man? What has a man who is blinded by the devil to tell me about these matters [the ways of God]? Why should I have a dialogue with him? No, no I am sorry for him. The man is blinded, he is igno-rant, he knows nothing. I have the knowledge which alone can help him. It is not mine, it has been given to me, it has been revealed to me, it is my duty to tell him. I am doing him a disservice by letting him talk. He is not capable of expressing an opinion. He is in the dark, 'dead in trespasses and sins'.
To God's Glory, 270

This is the tragedy of modern men and women. They think they are big enough to arrive at God and to understand him; they think they can encompass the whole glory of God with their little minds. The fools! The fools! What else can you call people who try to comprehend the incomprehensible!
Authentic Christianity (4), 29

With a calm judicial detachment, conscious of his culture and learning, such a man looks on with interest at movements as they come and go, as if he will go on living for ever. Here he is, the judge on the throne of the universe. He has

forgotten that he is a mortal man and that he is approaching death, and must come face to face with it.
Authentic Christianity (3), 205

The modern world is desperately ill, and man is perhaps more unhappy than he has ever been.
Banner of Truth, Issue 275

Our central sin in this twentieth century is, of course, to believe that there have never been people like ourselves.
Fellowship with God, 62

The first thing that must happen to modern men and women is that they must be knocked off their pedestal. They must realise that they are just common human clay like all who have ever lived before them . . . they must realise that they are part of this whole process of history; and they must start looking at the whole before they concentrate over much upon their own importance and their modern problems.
Authentic Christianity (4), 25

MONASTICISM
Though you leave the world and all its prospects, and go and live as a monk or a hermit in a cell; though you have left the world, you have not left yourself – the two-thirds submerged part of the iceberg is still with you! You do not leave your sinful nature outside the monastery. Evil imaginations and thoughts are with you still; you cannot get rid of them. Stone walls do not keep them out, iron bars do not keep them out, locked doors do not keep them out; wherever you are they will be there. They are spiritual, they are unseen, they can penetrate everywhere, and they are with you in your cell. You cannot get rid of them. And for these reasons the great system of monasticism finally broke down completely.
The Christian Warfare, 36

MORALITY
It is because men and women are departing from the Bible that we have the moral muddle in society today.
Life in the Spirit in Marriage Home and Work, 334

Any appeal to the world to live a Christian life before it has become Christian, is, as we have seen, a negation of Christian teaching.
The Life of Joy, 173

The history of the human race makes it abundantly clear that religion of any sort, with its ultimate sanctions and its threat of punishment for wrong doing, has always been the greatest moral and moralizing force, the strongest keeper of law and order that the world has ever known.
The New Man, 235

You cannot have morality without godliness. The most moral periods in the history of this country have been the periods that have followed revivals, and spiritual awakening.
Revival, 151

Today, people no longer recognize the category of the moral. Modern men and women say, 'We have a new morality.' But that is simply a repetition of what the devil has suggested before. He puts an idea back into some cupboard, and brings out another one, and everybody forgets the old idea. He lets a century or two pass, then he brings the first one out again. 'Brand new!', people say. 'A new morality.' It is as old as Adam in sin!
Authentic Christianity (1), 80

MOVEMENTS
When did you last hear a sermon on the Second Coming of Christ in a holiness convention? 'But', they say, 'that is wrong. You go to a Second Advent meeting for that; you do not go to a holiness meeting for the doctrine of the Second Coming!' Thus you see how we have departed from the Scripture. We have introduced a number of special departments into the life of the church.'
Life in the Spirit in Marriage Home and Work, 167–68

We should not form movements with respect to particular doctrines; to attempt to do so is to lose balance.
The Christian Warfare, 184

MUSIC
Have you heard the kind of music they used to sing before the Reformation? Some regard it as great music, and it may be so; but it is dull, and it is negative. To me it is pagan, because it has a wail in it. There is no triumph, no victory in that 'plain song', as it is called – indeed that is exactly what it is. It lacks fullness and a sense of glory, and triumph, and victory. That element is entirely absent. As you hear it you can see the monks marching with their heads down. They are wailing. Why? Because they are in bondage. But when the Protestant Reformation came as the result of Luther's eyes being opened to this wonderful doctrine of justification by faith, he himself began to sing, and all others who saw the truth began to sing in the same way. Oh, the glory of what God has done in Christ! It dwarfs and engulfs everything else – even God's own mighty act of creation.
Assurance, 302

MYSTERY
Saving truth is no longer a mystery to the Christian; it is only a mystery to the non-Christian. To the Christian it is an open secret, because God in His grace and kindness has been pleased to unfold it and to reveal it to him.
God's Ultimate Purpose, 191

'Mystery' in the New Testament sense is a technical term pertaining to a truth which, because of its character, can never be attained unto, or arrived at, by the unaided human intellect or by mere human ability. The thing itself is clear, but because man is what he is – finite and sinful – he cannot by his own unaided intellect arrive at it or understand it.
The Unsearchable Riches of Christ, 33

MYSTICISM

In many ways, one of the greatest snares at this point is the snare of what is called *mysticism*. Mysticism can be put roughly like this: it is 'seeking the God that is in you'. It says that the Spirit of God is in all people, and therefore we must look into ourselves and surrender to the Spirit of God that is within.
Spiritual Blessing, 57

Mysticism makes *feeling* the source of knowledge of God, and not intellect; not reason; not understanding.
Fellowship with God, 90

The main criticism of the evangelical to all this can be put in this form: It is a claim to a continuation of inspiration. The mystic in a sense is claiming that God is dealing as directly with him as He was with the Old Testament prophets; he claims God is dealing with him as He did with the Apostles. Now we as evangelicals believe that God gave a message to the prophets, He gave a message to the Apostles; but we say that because God has done that, it is unnecessary that He should do that directly with us.
Fellowship with God, 94

Mysticism of necessity puts the Scriptures on one side and makes them more or less unnecessary. You will always find that persons who have a mystical tendency never talk very much about the Bible. They do not read it very much; indeed I think you will find that this is true of most mystical people . . . The danger of mysticism is to concentrate so much on the Lord's work *in* us that it forgets the Lord's work *for* us.
Fellowship with God, 94

Mystics tend to look inwards; they believe that God is resident within them and that really the way to be blessed of God and to live the spiritual life in the full sense is to look within, to dwell within, and to be sensitive to the vision that speaks to you and the light that is given you and the leading and the guidance. It is the inward process, the turning inward on one self, the belief that God is in the depths of one's being.
Walking with God, 122

Christianity is not a mystical feeling or experience only. I put it like that because there is a good deal of interest in that kind of experience at the present time. I

think you always tend to get a return to mysticism at a time of crisis or of difficulty in the history of the world. When men and women see all other powers fail on all hands, when they see that all the optimistic prophets and teachers and politicians and poets have been entirely wrong, when they are troubled and bewildered and perplexed, there is always some kind of innate tendency in men and women to turn to mysticism.
The Love of God, 26

evangelical
There is, of course, a true Christian evangelical mysticism.
God's Way of Reconciliation, 242

True mysticism emphasizes the living, experimental, experiential aspect of the Christian faith and the Christian position. If our so-called faith does not lead to any kind of experience, then I doubt whether it is Christian at all! Our faith must be living, real, and experimental.
The Christian Warfare, 122

It shines elsewhere in such statements as, 'I live, yet not I, but Christ liveth in me' (Gal. 2:20), 'I can do all things through Christ which strengtheneth me' (Phil. 4:13), 'To me to live is Christ' (Phil. 1:21). Paul speaks as a true Christian mystic in such statements.
The Unsearchable Riches of Christ, 248

How can it be expedient for the disciples that He should leave them in the flesh and go away from them in the body? How can that be true if it is not possible for the Christian to know Him immediately and directly? Obviously the supreme blessing is to be with Him, in His presence and in His company. What He is really saying is that after He has gone and has baptized them with the Holy Ghost, He will be more real to them than He was at that moment. And this is what actually happened. They knew Him much better after Pentecost than they knew Him before. He was more real to them, more living to them, more vital to them afterwards than He was in the days of His flesh. His promise was literally fulfilled and verified.
The Unsearchable Riches of Christ, 249

- N -

NATIONALISM
The fact that our parents, grandparents or forebears were great Christians does not mean that we are Christians. That was the whole tragedy of the Jews, as we have seen. Put next to birth, family, nation – none of these things matter at all. But oh, how much they have mattered throughout the centuries; how much they still matter! There are still people who think of this country as a Christian country. What utter nonsense! There is no such thing. There never has been a Christian country
God's Sovereign Purpose, 318

1. Is there such a thing as a Christian country?
   The answer is, No.
2. Are children of Christian parents of necessity Christians?
   The answer is, No.
3. Are baptised children of necessity Christians?
   The answer is, No.
4. Are all who are baptised, whether children or adults, and all who are church members of necessity Christians?
   The answer is, No.
God's Sovereign Purpose, 101

There are some people who have tried to argue that because the Apostle says, 'There is neither Greek nor Jew, circumcision nor uncircumcision, Barbarian, Scythian, bond nor free' (Colossians 3:11), that the Christian is some sort of supernationalist, but that does not follow at all. Paul does not mean that a man ceases to belong to his nation. What he does mean is that those things do not matter at all as far as salvation is concerned.
God's Sovereign Purpose, 30

In many ways, the most amazing thing that has ever happened in history is that this man, the Apostle Paul, of all men in the world, should have become the Apostle to the Gentiles. In Galatians 2 he says that God had given him this commission to the Gentiles, as He had given Peter the commission to the circumcision. It is a most astonishing thing that this intense Jew, this essential Jewish nationalist, should have had to spend the greater part of his life as the Apostle to the Gentiles.
God's Sovereign Purpose, 35

NATURE
So many people today speak of the powers of nature as if they were something independent. But they are not. There are powers and laws in nature, but not apart from God. God is in direct relationship to them, and uses them and orders them and manipulates them.
Great Doctrines of the Bible (1), 145

Christianity never does away with nature.
Life in the Spirit in Marriage Home and Work, 247

What Christianity does is to lift up and sanctify the natural.
Life in the Spirit in Marriage Home and Work, 248

You cannot explain the meanest flower without God. I remember hearing the story of a man who lived here in London who went on a holiday into the country in early September. He happened to look at a great field of wheat, ripe unto harvest. There it was in all its golden splendour, with a gentle breeze playing upon it. As he looked at it he said the only thing that anyone should say when he looks at such a sight, was 'Well done, God'.
The Unsearchable Riches of Christ, 85

NOVICE
What tragedies have happened in the life of the Church and in individual lives, because that exhortation has not been followed! Here is what is now called a 'star turn', a marvellous convert and the temptation is to put him right into the front at once. The result often is that he is ruined! He becomes proud of his past sin; he begins to boast about his past evil life because it makes him important! Do not promote a novice, says the Apostle, for, if you do, the devil is certain to trap him. Keep to this rule.
The Christian Warfare, 91

NUMBERS
God has always done His greatest work through a remnant. Get rid of the notion of numbers
The Christian Soldier, 278

NUMERICS
If we are interested in biblical numerics – an interest which is perhaps not to be entirely discouraged, though it can become dangerous if and when we tend to become too fanciful – we shall see, in addition, that the first *three* petitions (in the Lord's Prayer] have reference to God, and that three is always the number of Deity and of God, suggesting the three blessed Persons in the Trinity. In the same way, *four* is always the number of earth and refers to everything that is human. There are four beasts in the heavens in the book of Revelation, and so on. Seven, which is a combination of three and four, always stands for that

perfect number where we see God in His relationship to earth, and God in His dealing with men.
Studies in the Sermon on the Mount (2), 58

OPTIMISM

Every Christian must be an optimist. You never know when God is going to appear, you never know when the Holy Spirit is going to descend, you never know when Christ is going to deal with you and remove your burden and give your soul release. Just when you are about to convince yourself that the night is going to be endless – the dawn breaks; just when you feel sure that the struggle is all in vain and that your fighting is useless – just then, and when least expected, you are rewarded with victory.
Evangelistic Sermons, 17

ORIGINAL SIN

God created all things good. No one has ever been forced to sin.
God's Sovereign Purpose, 202

If one member of this country should be guilty of a misdemeanour in another country, that other country may well declare war against this country: and though you and I have not committed the misdemeanour we nevertheless suffer the consequences. The other country declares war, and we, therefore, legally in international law, have been constituted enemies of that country though we have done nothing at all in our own persons. It is a judicial procedure. According to the Apostle that is what has happened to us – our position before God judicially has become that of sinners.
Assurance, 272

We are not born neutral. There is no such thing as a Peter Pan who is born in complete innocence and then decides which way to go.
Assurance, 317–18

Men and women have a twist in them.
Authentic Christianity, (1) 90

ORTHODOXY

It is an appalling thought but it is nevertheless true, that there is such a thing as dead orthodoxy.
Revival, 68

You can have a dead orthodoxy. Orthodoxy is essential, but orthodoxy alone has never produced a Revival, and it never will.
The Puritans, 126

To state the Truth is not enough, it must be stated 'in demonstration of the Spirit and of power'. And that is what George Whitefield so gloriously illustrates. He was orthodox, but the thing that produced the phenomenon was the power of the Spirit upon him. He says that he felt something even at his ordination, as if he had received a commission from the Spirit Himself. He was always conscious of this – wave after wave of the Spirit would come upon him. This power of the Spirit is essential. We must be orthodox, but God forbid us to rest even on orthodoxy.
The Puritans, 126–27

You can be orthodox but dead. Why? Well, because you are stopping at the doctrines, you are stopping at the definitions, and failing to realize that the whole purpose of doctrine is not to be an end in itself, but to lead us to knowledge of the person and to an understanding of the person, and to a fellowship with the person.
Revival, 58

There have been men, also, who have clearly been perfectly orthodox – champions of the faith, and yet they have denied that very faith in the bitterness with which they have sometimes defended it. I repeat, the test of orthodoxy, while it is so vital and essential, is not enough.
The Love of God, 39

– P –

PACIFISM

I still have to meet a pacifist who understands the doctrine of the atonement!
Life in the Spirit in Marriage Home and Work, 272

To me there are no people in the world whose teaching is so opposed to the Christian faith as pacifists – I mean the people who say that you really can stop wars by applying reason and teaching. Why are they so wrong? It is because they have never realised that the cause of every kind of warfare, whether it be a quarrel between a husband and wife or between two other people, every quarrel, every fight, every lack of peace and fellowship is always due, not to a wrong mind, but to a wrong heart. Ultimately, the whole problem lies in the heart.
Authentic Christianity (2), 6

PAIN

It is one of the royal rules in medicine that pain should not be relieved by an injection of morphia until the cause of the pain has been discovered, and one of the greatest medical crimes is to break that rule. The trouble with drugs and quack-remedies is that, by lessening the pain and palliating the symptoms, they tend not only to hide the real cause of the disease, but also tend to keep the people away from the true physician. As our Lord Himself said, 'They that are whole have no need of a physician, but they that are sick', by which He meant that those who imagine themselves to be whole and to be all right are always the last to accept salvation.
Evangelistic Sermons, 184

PARENTS

It is the business of Christians to make known to their children these oracles of God, which have been entrusted to them, so that in later life the children shall say, 'I thank God I had a Christian father, a Christian mother. I cannot tell you what I owe to them. I first came into this Christian life because of what my mother taught me when I stood at her knee, or sat upon her lap; or because of something I heard my father say out of the Word of God.'
The Righteous Judgement of God, 173

PASSION

I have one passion – it is He and He alone.
The Life of Joy, 96

PASTOR

A pastor is a man who is given charge of souls. He is not merely a nice, pleasant man who visits people and has an afternoon cup of tea with them, or passes the time of day with them. He is the guardian, the custodian, the protector, the organiser, the director, the ruler of the flock.
Christian Unity, 193

Visiting is a part of a pastor's ministry; but if a man becomes just a pleasing man, a good pastor, a nice man to have in the home, one who will drink a cup of tea with you, it is tragic. What a tragedy that a prophet should end up as just a nice man and a good pastor!
The Christian Soldier, 148

PAUL

Take the apostle Paul, this outstanding genius, this most learned Pharisee, this erudite man.
Joy Unspeakable, 132

Oh, Christian Church, what has happened to you? How can you ever have forgotten these blessed words and the example of the great Apostle?
The Gospel of God, 236

It would have saved a lot of ink and a lot of trouble if everybody who became an expositor of St. Paul's epistles had reminded himself, before he started expounding, that the epistles were not written to students or to professors of doctrine at Oxford and Cambridge, but to slaves, and to common, ordinary people! 'Not many wise men . . . not many noble, are called,' said Paul (1 Cor 1:26).
Great Doctrines of the Bible (1), 42

Could a man suffering from hysteria write the epistle to the Romans and the epistle to the Ephesians?
Authentic Christianity (3), 157

Every word the Apostle uses has to be observed.
Assurance, 284

We believe that the Apostle was divinely inspired, and that there are no accidents in what he wrote, and no omissions.
The New Man, 169

We must allow ourselves to be led by him and expound his great statements in detail.
Assurance, 7

It is clear that the Apostle Paul had a constant personal struggle with physical infirmity, with weakness, disease of his eyes, and various other troubles. In the

light of this, he says, no one could attribute the character and results of his ministry to him. He suffered these things in order that it might be clear that the power that worked in him, and through him, was not his own, but the power of God through the Lord Jesus Christ, and the blessed Holy Spirit.
Christian Unity, 70

He was once Saul of Tarsus but when he became the Apostle of Christ, his temperament had not changed . . . When he became an Apostle . . . he did not suddenly become a quiet preacher. He preached with all the intensity of his mighty emotional nature. He weeps, he tells us; and at times had fears within, and was cast down. The man's temperament is exactly what it was; the zeal with which he persecuted is the same zeal with which he now preaches. The temperament remains a constant.
The Christian Warfare, 212–13

Remember that the Apostle's primary object was always a pastoral one. We must not think of him as an academic theologian. He was an evangelist and teacher, but his chief characteristic is his pastoral interest.
The Final Perseverance of the Saints, 368

Watch Paul's 'architecture', watch his structure.
Saving Faith, 230

There is one thing that the enemy cannot do, and that is, he cannot prevent Paul from praying. He can still pray. The enemy can confine him to a cell, he can bolt and bar doors, he can chain him to soldiers, he can put bars in the windows, he can hem him in and confine him physically, but he can never obstruct the way from the heart of the humblest believer to the heart of the Eternal God.
The Unsearchable Riches of Christ, 107

It would be a very great fallacy if we got the impression that the Apostle was praying for these Ephesians only because he could not preach to them.
The Unsearchable Riches of Christ, 109

I must confess that I am charmed by this man and everything he does. I admire his method, I like his style, I am drawn to his way of doing things. But particularly, and above all else, I admire his great pastoral heart. His burning desire was to help the churches.
Assurance, 283

This is pure logic, of course, and the Apostle was a master at logic.
To God's Glory, 114

I am told that I repeat my texts! Of course I do! It is the best thing I do in the pulpit. I cannot go beyond the Apostle Paul. If only I could utter these texts

properly I believe nothing else would be necessary. So I go on repeating them.
Assurance, 315

If ever a man was guilty of tautology it was the Apostle Paul. Anyone who believes the gospel is bound to repeat himself.
The Life of Joy, 13

Now one of the most fascinating studies that I know of is just to watch the working of Paul's mind, because there is never anything accidental here. He always puts the cause before its effect; he does not just rush to the details; he is always concerned about the principles. And if we are to have a true understanding of Christian doctrine, and of the message of the Christian faith, we have really got to do that. We must start with a man's state before we consider the manifestations of that state.
The Righteous Judgement of God, 97

He does not seem to have been much of a poet, but he was a brilliant logician, a master debater, an acute reasoner.
Assurance, 129–30

The Apostle regarded the preaching of the gospel as a very serious matter. There are people who are ready to run into pulpits at any time. Not so the Apostle! Had it not been that he was constrained by the love of Christ, and that he could say, 'Woe is unto me if I preach not the gospel!' he would never have preached.
Life in the Spirit in Marriage Home and Work, 347

His method is practical and experimental; he is not interested in dry-as-dust doctrine, something remote and far away; he is meeting us where we are.
Christian Unity, 50

The difference between the two writers is that the Apostle Paul always tells you what he is doing before he does it; but John does it without telling you and, as it were, leaves you to find out what he is doing!
Life in God, 23

PEACE
We shall never know 'the peace of God' until we first have 'peace with God'.
Assurance, 13

'Peace with God' is mainly an objective matter of our relationship to God and our standing with Him. 'The peace of God' is entirely subjective, it is the way I overcome the fatal tendency to anxiety and anxious care.
Assurance, 13

PENTECOST
And so the Day of Pentecost is of vital importance in Christian preaching. It is
one of the great acts of God. The day of Pentecost is equally as important as the
incarnation, the death, the resurrection and the ascension. These are the marvellous wonderful works of God, and this day is one of the most marvellous of
them all.
Authentic Christianity (2), 198

Was this therefore something once and for all? The answer is that it was once
and for all in one sense only, in that it was the first time it ever happened; but it
is not once and for all in any other sense, as I am now going to try to prove to
you. When something happens for the first time – well, you cannot go on
repeating the first time, but you can repeat what happened on that first time.
Joy Unspeakable, 433

PERFECTION
The nearer you get to the light the more you are aware of the darkness.
The Sons of God, 187–88

PERPLEXITY
To be perplexed is not sinful.
Faith on Trial, 16

It is wrong to be in a state of despair; but it is not wrong to be perplexed.
Faith on Trial, 16

PERSECUTION
I wonder whether we are prepared to face the fact that the Church of God in this
age and generation may in a sense have to go back to the catacombs. We may
have to face that; there are people who are facing that, and it is the position in
many countries today.
Walking with God, 109

PERSEVERANCE OF THE SAINTS (Eternal Security, Election)
In Christ we are not in a state of probation, and that there is no possibility of our
falling from grace.
Assurance, 236

There has been no doctrine brought to light by the Protestant Reformation
which has given more joy and comfort and consolation to God's people. It was
the doctrine that sustained the saints of the New Testament era . . . since that
time there has been nothing that has so held and stimulated God's people. It
explains some of the greatest exploits in the annals of the Christian Church. You
do not begin to understand people like the Covenanters of Scotland and the
Puritans – men who gave up their lives and did so with a sense of joy and glory

– except in the light of this doctrine. It is the explanation of some of the most amazing things that happened in the last war; it is the only way of understanding some of the German Christians who could face a Hitler and defy him.
Faith on Trial, 97–98

Not one of Christ's people will be missing, not one will be lost. We are not merely restored to Adam's condition, we are taken beyond that. The Son of God guarantees it, and the end is as certain as the beginning.
Assurance, 237

You will never find an unbeliever who accepts the doctrine of the final perseverance of the saints. Unbelievers not only do not believe it, they ridicule it and pour scorn upon it.
The Final Perseverance of the Saints, 364

If (a person] believes that one sin can put a man out of the right relationship to God, then he has never seen clearly that hitherto he has been in that right relationship, not because of anything in himself, but because of the Lord Jesus Christ and His perfect work. When a man says, 'Because I have sinned I have lost it', what he is really saying on the other side is, 'I had it because I was good'. He is wrong in both respects.
Assurance, 22

PERSISTENCE
The Christian life is narrow from the beginning to the end. There is no such thing as a holiday in the spiritual realm. We can take a holiday from our usual work; but there is no such thing as a holiday in the spiritual life.
Studies in the Sermon on the Mount (2), 226–27

PERSONALITY
Truth is sacred but a human personality is infinitely more sacred. Truth is impersonal and cannot be hurt, but personality is sensitive and can be deeply wounded. Words fail us when we try to find an epithet to describe the mean cad of a person who can stoop so low as to use another's personality to advance his own selfish ends.
Old Testament Evangelistic Sermons, 104–5

There is a type of person who parades himself and puts himself in a prominent position and is always calling attention to himself.
Studies in the Sermon on the Mount (2), 25

Have you ever observed that some of the most honoured servants of God in evangelism have been extremely ugly men? Let me commend that to you as a study. There is a danger of the evangelist relying upon the attractiveness of his own personality to produce results.
Knowing the Times, 7

PHARISEES

The modern Pharisees are those people in the churches, and often outside the churches also, who resent being made to feel uncomfortable by the preaching, who dislike feeling that they are sinners, who fight against the truth of God, and who fight against the Cross and 'the blood of Christ', They resent gospel truth because they think they are 'alive' and that sin is 'dead'. What appalling ignorance, what a tragic condition to be in!
The Law: Its Functions and Limits, 145

PHILIPPIANS

It is the most lyrical, the happiest, letter which the Apostle ever wrote.
The Life of Joy, 9

I defy you to find anywhere a more joyful letter than Paul's epistle to the Philippians. The apostle cannot contain himself.
Authentic Christianity (1), 188

PHILOSOPHY

We are all born philosophers, and the trouble with philosophers is that they claim they can understand everything. That is why philosophy, let me emphasise it again, in New Testament terms, is always the greatest enemy of revelation and Christian truth.
The Heart of the Gospel, 47

It is, and I put it dogmatically and bluntly, that the evangelical distrusts reason and particularly reason in the forms of philosophy . . . every reformation has always expressed a distrust of reason. One of the earliest examples of this is to be found in Tertullian, one of the first great theologians of the Western Church. He put it in a very striking form. What has Jerusalem to do with Athens? What has the temple to do with the porch and the academy?
Knowing the Truth, 324

I have no doubt whatsoever in my own mind that the Christian Church is as she is today, very largely because for the last hundred years so much time has been given in the theological colleges and seminaries to the teaching of philosophy. It is the greatest enemy of the Christian truth.
The Christian Warfare, 171

Philosophy has always been the cause of the church going astray, for philosophy means, ultimately, a trusting to human reason and human understanding.
Knowing the Times, 324–25

You know how often it is said of them [Plato, Socrates and the Greek philosophers] that they were Christians before Christ, that they come under this category of good people who, living up to the light they had, and holding exalted

and idealistic views, and doing good works, were undoubtedly accepted of God. But the simple answer concerning them is just to point out that they were all idolaters and worshipped idols. They were guilty of that thing which is condemned without any qualification in the Bible, in both the Old Testament and the New. They were not even God-fearers. They had a certain general philosophy and by means of that philosophy they had elaborated the teaching of the moral consciousness in a very remarkable manner, but that is useless as far as salvation is concerned.
The Righteous Judgement of God, 133–34

This is the trouble with the philosophers. They say that they do not understand how God can do this or that, they want to explain the mind of the almighty God with their pygmy minds and it cannot be done. And that is why the philosophers find it so difficult to become Christians.
Saved for Eternity, 177

That is the quest of philosophy – to span everything with the human mind. But we are now dealing with something for which the mind is utterly inadequate.
Great Doctrines of the Bible (1), 95

There are fashions in philosophy as there are in music. 'Top of the Pops' today, but not for long.
Authentic Christianity (4), 196

POLITICS
During the past one hundred years many of our nonconformist fathers forgot the gospel and really believed that the Liberal Party was going to introduce the kingdom of heaven on earth by social legislation. The Christian should never be guilty of such a colossal error.
Life in the Spirit in Marriage Home and Work, 340

There are Christians who say that you should not vote in parliamentary elections, and that you should not take any interest in this world's affairs at all. But that is not true to scriptural teaching for the Christian is still a citizen of this world and belongs to the secular realm. He knows that this is God's world, and that God has a purpose for him in it. He knows that he is a citizen of the country to which he belongs, and he is aware that he has his responsibilities. Indeed, because he is a Christian, he should be a better citizen than anyone else in the land. But he does not stop at that, he knows that he is also a citizen of another kingdom, a kingdom that cannot be seen, a kingdom that is not of this world.
God's Ultimate Purpose, 75

I have heard two statements recently that illustrate my point. I heard one man say that he did not understand how any Christian could possibly be a Conservative. But I heard another say that he really did not understand how

any Christian could possibly be a Socialist. The fact of the matter is that both were wrong; any attempt to equate the teaching of the New Testament with any one of the political parties, or any other party, is to do violence to the teaching of Christ.
God's Ultimate Purpose, 65

As Christians we are citizens of a country, and it is our business to play our part as citizens, and thereby act as salt indirectly in innumerable respects.
Studies in the Sermon on the Mount (1), 155

We are well aware that the acts of Parliament that have been passed in the last hundred years or so have righted many wrongs; but I would ask you to remember that they have, all of them, without a single exception, resulted directly from Christian activity. None of these things have been automatic. Take the movements for better education; take the hospitals; take the interest in health or the care for the aged, the abolition of slavery, the passing of factory acts – every one of these things has emanated from Christian sources.
Life in God, 162

I do not listen to a man who tells me how to solve the world's problems if he cannot solve his own personal problems. If a man's home is in a state of discord, his opinions about the state of the nation or the state of the world are purely theoretical.
Life in the Spirit in Marriage Home and Work, 233

The chaos in the world is due to the fact that people in every realm of life have lost all respect for authority, whether it be between nations or between parts of nations, whether it be in industry, whether it be in the home, whether it be in the schools, or anywhere else. The loss of authority! And in my view it really starts in the home and in the married relationship. That is why I venture to query whether a statesman whose own marriage has broken down really has a right to speak about the world's problems. If he fails in the sphere where he is most competent, what right has he to speak in others? He ought to retire out of public life.
Life in the Spirit in Marriage Home and Work, 111

It is not insignificant that certain well known evangelists are supported by numbers of millionaires and that some of them in a recent Presidential Election even went so far as to propose that a certain evangelist might be put up as Presidential candidate! They did this because of their political and economic interests.
Puritan Conference Papers 1975; The French Revolution and After, 103

POPULARITY
There is something seriously wrong with the man who is praised by everybody. There are certain preachers who are praised by evangelicals and praised by

liberals – everybody praises them. I always feel concerned about such men. 'Woe is unto you when all men speak well of you'.
Assurance, 70

PORNOGRAPHY

If you desire that pornographic literature should be published freely you are without a doubt, making 'provision for the flesh'. Men may call it great literature but it is certain to do harm. It inflames the passions, the motions of sin in the flesh. Anyone who is anxious to mortify the deeds of the body obviously makes no provision for the flesh.
The Sons of God, 190

POVERTY (Wealth)

And oh, the poverty into which He came! They could not afford to give the price of the highest offering for Him; they had to offer the two turtledoves – they could not afford any more. He was born into a very poor home; he knew something of the squalor and the need that accompanies poverty.
The Love of God, 58

The Bible nowhere teaches that poverty as such is a good thing. The poor man is no nearer to the kingdom of heaven than the rich man, speaking of them as natural men. There is no merit or advantage in being poor. Poverty does not guarantee spirituality.
Studies in the Sermon on the Mount, 143

The poor man has often been as covetous as the rich: how we fool ourselves in this respect!
The Kingdom of God, 165

POWERS (Devil, Demonism)

There are two great powers anxious to possess us and to dominate our lives. There are only two, and they are diametrically opposed to each other. It is a sheer impossibility for anyone to be under both of these powers at one and the same time.
The New Man, 205

Do you know that there are forces of evil in this world today, striving against man, trying to get him down, to ruin the soul, battling against God and heaven – these mighty, unseen spiritual forces?
The Life of Joy, 234

This world is not only a material one – there is the spiritual element surrounding it and there are forces and spirits which are evil and malign, set against God and everything that is holy.
Joy Unspeakable, 185

PRAISE
There is no better index of where we stand than the amount of praise and of thanksgiving that characterises our lives and our prayers.
Assurance, 28

It is the relative proportion of petition and praise in our prayers that tells most exactly the measure, the degree of the Holy Spirit within us.
Singing to the Lord, 65

You can never persuade yourself to say 'Abba, Father'. If you try, you will find that the words will freeze on your lips; they will not get any further.
The Sons of God, 244

Even your sin makes you sing, because you see how it has been dealt with so gloriously and so superabundantly.
Assurance, 303

If you are so filled with the Spirit, and so moved by him, that you find yourself involuntary clapping your hands, all is well. But that is very different from clapping your hands in order to induce a sense of excitement.
Singing to the Lord, 38

If we love someone we want to tell him so; we not only say it in actions we want to say it in words and we do say it. And it is exactly the same with God. The one who is in true relationship with Him praises Him.
Fellowship with God, 84

'But how can I make melody in my heart?' asks somebody. 'I don't feel like singing.' My dear friend, consider him till you do!.
Singing to the Lord, 58

Everything connected with him always leads to an outburst of praise and of singing and of thanksgiving from those who are nearest to him, those who see him, those who know him as he is.
Singing to the Lord, 48

PRAYER
approach
Do not claim, do not demand, let your requests be made known, let them come from your heart. God will understand. We have no right to demand even revival. Some Christians are tending to do so at the present time. Pray urgently, plead, use all the arguments, use all the promises; but do not demand, do not claim. Never put yourself into the position of saying, 'If we but do this, then that must happen'. God is a sovereign Lord, and these things are beyond our understanding. Never let the terminology of claiming or of demanding be used.
The Final Perseverance of the Saints, 155

Prayer is something in which we turn our backs upon everything else, excluding everything else, while, for the time being, we find ourselves face to face with God alone.
Children of God, 122

The Fathers used to use this great term – 'Pleading the promises.' You never hear it now. Why? Because people do not really pray any longer, they send little telegrams to God. They think that that is the height of spirituality. They know nothing about 'wrestling' with God and 'pleading the promises'.
Joy Unspeakable, 367

The first prayer is not prayer for statesmen, nor for friends or relatives, nor for other nations, that is not the first prayer. The *first* prayer is to plead with him to come into his Temple, to manifest his glory to show us something of the might of His power and to fill us with that power.
Spiritual Blessing, 134

I have always been comforted by this thought, that whatever I may forget in my own private prayers, as long as I pray the Lord's Prayer I have at any rate covered all the principles.
Studies in the Sermon on the Mount (2), 50

Boldness at the throne of grace is not presumption. Confidence is not cheek.
The Unsearchable Riches of Christ, 113

Oh, let me use the term, there is a holy boldness. This is *the* great characteristic of all prayers that have ever prevailed. It is, of course, inevitable.
Revival, 195

I know a number of Christians who have a universal answer to all questions. It does not matter what the question is, they always say, 'Pray about it' . . . Before we can pray truly, we must think spiritually. There is nothing more fatuous than glib talk about prayer, as if prayer were something which you can always immediately rush into.
Faith on Trial, 41

Without an element of importunity and persistence, or urgency and almost a holy violence with God, we have little right to expect that God will hear our prayer and answer it.
Joy Unspeakable, 382

Many Christians seem to think that the hallmark of spirituality is to pray to the Lord Jesus Christ. But when we turn to the Scriptures we discover that that is not really so, and that, as here, prayers are normally offered to the Father. The

Lord Jesus Christ is the Mediator, not the end; He is the One who brings us to the Father.
God's Ultimate Purpose, 328

Not so long ago I heard a man describing a visit he had paid somewhere, and he said, 'I was feeling somewhat exhausted, so I went into a cathedral and I said a prayer.' He dashed in, said a prayer, and dashed out. Is that praying? No, no; and, indeed, there are others a little nearer home to us, who rather frighten me sometimes when I hear them saying quite lightly and glibly, ' Let us have a word of prayer about it'. 'A word of prayer about it!' Almost like sending a telegram! That is not prayer.
Authentic Christianity (2), 133

There is a prayer given sometimes by the Spirit concerning which He tells you that it is going to be answered. That is 'the prayer of faith'. It is not an experiment, it is not a trying to persuade yourself, or to 'work yourself up'. It is an absolute certainty that is given by the Spirit, and you know, therefore, when you are praying and making your requests, that your prayer is answered. And it happens because the prayer was given, and the assurance of it was given, by the blessed Holy Spirit Himself.
The Final Perseverance of the Saints, 157

There are particular problems in the Christian life concerning which I say that if you do nothing but pray about them you will never solve them. You must stop praying at times because your prayer may just be reminding you of the problem and keeping your mind fixed upon it. So you must stop praying and think and work out your doctrine.
Spiritual Depression, 69

benefits
What prayer does, as it were, is to fill the lungs of the soul with the oxygen of the Holy Spirit and His power. If you want to stand on your feet and not to falter, fill yourself with the life of God.
The Unsearchable Riches of Christ, 125

difficulty
The person I am worried about is the one who has no difficulty about prayer, there is certainly something wrong about him.
Saved in Eternity, 14

If you have never had difficulty in prayer, it is absolutely certain that you have never prayed.
Banner of Truth, Issue 275

I think a case should be made for saying that the most difficult thing of all is to pray.
Children of God, 121

Everything we do in the Christian life is easier than prayer.
Banner of Truth, Issue 275

[Our Lord] says, 'What shall I pray? Shall I ask the Father to save me from this hour?' And He adds in effect, 'No, I cannot do so, because I came into the world in order to come to this hour.' Even the eternal Son of God as Son of Man knew something of this perplexity.
The Final Perseverance of the Saints, 129

importance

When a man is speaking to God he is at his very acme. It is the highest activity of the human soul, and therefore it is at the same time the ultimate test of a man's true spiritual condition.
Studies in the Sermon on the Mount (2), 46

Without an element of importunity and persistence, or urgency and almost a holy violence with God, we have little right to expect that God will hear our prayer and answer it.
Joy Unspeakable, 224

I am more than ever convinced that the trouble with many Christian people is that they do not preach to themselves. We should spend time every day preaching to ourselves, and never more so than when we get on our knees in prayer.
The Unsearchable Riches of Christ, 102

The thing that keeps one going in the Christian life is prayer – communion and fellowship with God; it is something which is absolutely essential. I would go further and say that the Christian life is really impossible without it.
Children of God, 120

Note the place that is given to intercessory prayer in the New Testament. It is extraordinary and quite amazing, and is exemplified particularly in the Apostle Paul. Notice, too, how very dependent Paul was upon the prayers of other Christians.
The Unsearchable Riches of Christ, 111

God have mercy upon all of us who are called to preach if we fail in the exercise of this ministry.
Christian Unity, 207

of faith

The 'prayer of faith' is a prayer that is given by the Spirit. You do not command it. You can never make yourself certain that you are certain to receive what you ask for. But God through the Spirit will at times give you that consciousness. Our Lord always had it.
The Christian Soldier, 328

posture
If I may use a vulgarism, you must not get up on your hind legs; you must get down on your knees.
Banner of Truth Issue, 275

The very fact that I get on my knees in prayer [and that is the value of kneeling], that very fact in and of itself is a submission. I am there submitting myself, I am abandoning myself. Now while I am talking, I am in control, and while I am discussing I am in control. Someone may be examining me, but I am still able to defend myself. When I am engaged in thought and meditation, I am still in control. But when I get on my knees in prayer, then, in a sense, I am doing nothing, I am submitting myself, I am abandoning myself before Him. It is He who is in control, it is He who is doing everything, and that is why prayer tests us in a way which nothing else can possibly do.
Children of God, 124

preparation
Great prayer is always the outcome of great understanding.
Revival, 293

But prayer is not simple.
Preaching and Preachers, 169

Prayer is not a simple thing in one sense; it may be very difficult. Prayer is sometimes an excuse for not thinking, an excuse for avoiding a problem or a situation. Have we not all known something of this in our personal experience? We have often been in difficulty and we have prayed to God to deliver us, but in the meantime we have not put something right in our lives as we should have done. Instead of facing the trouble and doing what we knew we should be doing, we have prayed. I suggest that at a point like that, our duty is not to pray but to face the truth, to face the doctrine and to apply it. Then we are entitled to pray, and not until then.
Fellowship with God, 13

Prayer is going to have an audience with the King; and there is nothing more important as you enter into the audience chamber than to know you are suitably clad, that you are sufficiently respectable, if you like, to go in.
Assurance, 262

Go through your Bible and make a list of the promises of God to you; then take them to God, use them in His presence, plead them, and you can be quite certain that you have your petition. You already possess it, and in His own time and way, God will give you a full realisation of it and a full enjoyment of it.
Life in God, 125

There are certain preliminary conditions attached to prayer. To go on our knees and to utter words is not of necessity prayer.
Revival, 43

We must get rid of this mathematical notion of prayer.
Studies in the Sermon on the Mount (2), 31

Self-examination is the high road to prayer.
Banner of Truth, Issue 275

Real prayer means taking hold of God and not letting go.
Revival, 305

One of the greatest men of prayer of the last century was the saintly George Müller of Bristol. He was an expert in prayer; and he always taught that the first thing to do in prayer is to realise the presence of God. You do not start speaking immediately . . . There must be this fellowship, this communion, this conversation. And the realisation that you are in His presence is infinitely more important than anything you may say.
The Christian Soldier, 82

We could not pray at all were it not for the Holy Spirit.
The Final Perseverance of the Saints, 138

If I, in the presence of God, and while trying to worship God actively, know there is sin in my heart which I have not dealt with and confessed, my worship is useless. There is no value in it at all. If you are in a state of conscious enmity against another, if you are not speaking to another person, or if you are harbouring these unkind thoughts and are a hindrance and an obstacle to that other, God's Word assures you that there is no value in your attempted act of worship. It will avail you nothing, the Lord will not hear you.
Studies in the Sermon on the Mount (1), 228

pulpit
What I try to do when I enter a pulpit is to forget the congregation in a certain sense. I am not praying to them or addressing them; I am not speaking to them. I am speaking to God, I am leading in prayer to God, so I have to shut out and forget people. Yes; and having done that, I shut out and forget myself.
Studies in the Sermon on the Mount (2), 29

Far from desiring people to thank us for our so-called beautiful prayers, we should rather be troubled when they do so. Public prayer should be such that the people who are praying silently and the one who is uttering the words should be no longer conscious of each other, but should be carried on the wings of prayer into the very presence of God.
Studies in the Sermon on the Mount (2), 27

The preacher should not enter his pulpit claiming to have received a revelation; his claim should be that he is a man who reads the Word and prays and believes that the Holy Spirit illumines and enlightens his understanding, with the result that he has a message for the people.
Christian Unity, 191

God knows it is very much easier to preach like this from a pulpit than it is to pray.
Studies in the Sermon on the Mount (2), 46

sovereignty
Do not try to understand, do not try to reconcile prayer with the sovereignty of God. The Bible teaches me the sovereignty of God, and, equally definitely, it teaches me the duty of prayer. I hold to that doctrine *and* I pray. I am not concerned about reconciling them. I cannot. Nobody else can. I imagine that in the glory we shall be given an explanation.
Saving Faith, 9–10

In an ultimate and absolute sense you and I simply cannot reconcile God's omniscience and foreknowledge and sovereignty with this fact of prayer that we find so clearly taught in Scripture.
Life in God, 116

scope
'The sky is the limit,' says the modern man, 'but we are praying to one who is above the sky'! Oh rend the heavens, come down, there is no limit, we are praying to the eternal and the illimitable God.
Revival, 314

'What should I pray for?' asks somebody? My dear friend, there is no limit to what you should pray for, no limit at all.
Revival, 313

stimulus
Above all – and this I regard as most important of all – always respond to every impulse to pray.
Preaching and Preachers, 170–71

The moment you feel the slightest drawing or indication of His love, act upon it at once, however it may come. You may be reading a book, for instance, and not really thinking very much about this particular matter, when suddenly you become aware of some urge or some call to prayer. The whole essence of wisdom in this matter is to put down your book immediately, no matter how interesting it may be, and begin to pray . . . The moment you feel the slightest movement or indication of His love, respond, act, yield to Him immediately. Whatever He

calls you to do, do it at once. And as you do so, you will find that He will come more frequently, and the manifestations will be plainer and clearer.
The Unsearchable Riches of Christ, 274–75

The call to the church is not so much to organise as to agonise.
Banner of Truth, Issue 275

tests
Shame on us for our puny prayers.
Revival, 314

The ultimate test of our profession of faith is our prayer life.
Authentic Christianity (2), 132

Is there an altar in your life?
Old Testament Evangelistic Sermons, 249

Have we not all known what it is to find that, somehow, we have less to say to God when we are alone than when we are in the presence of others?
Studies in the Sermon on the Mount (2), 46

Is there an 'Oh' in your praying? That is another very good test of prayer, that this 'Oh' comes in. 'Oh, Lord.' . . . That is how the prophet prayed. That is how the men of God have always prayed: this, 'Oh'. Somebody once said that a sign, the best sign, of a coming revival is that the word, 'Oh' begins to enter into the prayers of the people. 'Oh, Lord!'
Revival, 301

If you cannot pray for an hour, why cannot you?
God's Ultimate Purpose, 352

Do we pray with confidence? Do we pray with assurance? Do we pray with boldness? Are we quite certain of our introduction, or do we spend most of our time wondering whether we really have a right or not, and whether God is listening?
Assurance, 37

There has never been a man or woman of God who has been singularly used of God in this world, but that they spent much time in prayer.
Life in God, 117

If we have eternal life, if we are His children, we, I say it with reverence, have the ear of God – we can be confident that He is always waiting to listen to us.
Life in God, 119

Those who know God best are the ones who speak to him most of all.
Saved in Eternity, 31

The ultimate test of the Christian life is the amount of time we give to prayer.
Banner of Truth, Issue 275

One of the best ways in which we can test whether we are truly in fellowship and communion with God is to examine our prayer life. How much prayer life is there in my life? How often do I pray; do I find freedom in prayer, do I delight in prayer, or is prayer a wearisome task; do I never know enlargement and liberty in it?
Fellowship with God, 84

unbelievers
There is no teaching anywhere in the Bible that the Spirit helps unbelievers in this matter of prayer.
The Final Perseverance of the Saints, 145

PREACHER
call
God knows, I do not enter the pulpit because I just choose to do so. If it were not for the call of the Lord I would not be doing it. All I did was to resist that call. It is His way. He calls men, He separates them, He gives them the message, and the Spirit is present to give illumination.
Life in the Spirit in Marriage Home and Work, 172

I would not be a preacher of the gospel if it did not work. This is no profession to me. I did not come into a pulpit because I want a profession.
Not Ashamed, 39

It is utterly unscriptural for a man to set himself up as a preacher
Saving Faith, 284

A call generally starts in the form of a consciousness within one's own spirit, an awareness of a kind of pressure being brought to bear . . . some disturbance in the realm of the spirit . . . that your mind is being directed to the whole question of preaching. You have not thought of it deliberately, you have not sat down in cold blood to consider possibilities, and then, having looked at several have decided to take this up. It is not that. This is something that happens to you; it is God dealing with you, and God acting upon you by His Spirit; it is something you become aware of rather than what you do. It is thrust upon you; it is presented to you and almost forced upon you constantly in this way.
Preachers and Preaching, 104

I would say that the only man who is called to preach is the man who cannot do anything else, in the sense that he is not satisfied with anything else. This call

to preach is so put upon him, and such pressure comes to bear upon him that he says, 'I can do nothing else, I must preach.'
Preachers and Preaching, 105

A man who feels that he is competent, and that he can do this easily, and so rushes to preach without any sense of fear or trembling, or any hesitation whatsoever, is a man who is proclaiming that he has never been 'called' to be a preacher.
Preaching and Preachers, 107

We are not all meant to preach. But there is a teaching today which almost seems to say that we are. The moment a man is converted he has to give his testimony, then preach. But we are not all meant to preach. We are not all meant to go to the foreign mission field. We are not all meant to be whole-time workers in the cause of God.
God's Way of Reconciliation, 459

I think the calling of a minister, a pastor, the greatest calling in the world. There is nothing I know of that is comparable to watching the Holy Spirit dealing with people, searching them, examining them, revealing truth to them, while you watch their growth and their development.
The Gospel of God, 240

Preachers are born, not made. This is an absolute. You will never teach a man to be a preacher if he is not already one . . .
Preachers and Preaching, 119

In the New Testament this distinction is drawn very clearly; certain people only are set apart and called upon to deliver the message, as it were, on behalf of the Church in an official manner. That act is confined to the elders, and only to some of them – the teaching elders, the elder who has received the gift of teaching, the pastors and the teachers.
Preachers and Preaching, 102–3

preparation
The preacher's first and most important task is to prepare himself, not his sermon.
Preaching and Preachers, 166

As a man goes on preaching this gospel he finds he has to work more and more. In the early days of my Christian ministry I was given sermons, but now I have to work harder, and it is like that in the Christian life. I sometimes think that one of the very best signs which a man can ever have of the fact that he is preaching the gospel of Christ and not merely indulging his own fancy, is that certain people should take a violent objection to what he is saying and should feel a sense of grudge and annoyance with him for having said it.
Evangelistic Sermons, 52

responsibility

To be a preacher, an expositor of God's Book, is one of the most dangerous things in the world.
The Christian Warfare, 180

I am called, as I understand it, to speak in the name of God and the Lord Jesus Christ, by the power of the Holy Spirit, to men and women in need and in trouble.
Love so Amazing, 30–31

Our object is to know God, and to know God is to worship Him, and here am I, a little pygmy man, a preacher in time, talking about the essential nature and being of God!
Great Doctrines of the Bible (1), 52

The privileges of the preacher are very great and his responsibility is correspondingly great.
Assurance, 235

The true preacher does not seek for truth in the pulpit; he is there because he has found it.
The Sons of God, 47

A preacher who does not preach his sermon to himself before he preaches it to anybody else, is exposing himself to hypocrisy; he is in a very dangerous condition.
The Righteous Judgement of God, 146

If I cannot preach, I say again, to everybody, well then, for myself I say I cannot preach to anybody.
The Gospel of God, 253

The first business of the preacher of salvation is to call men to repentance.
The Righteous Judgement of God, 57

But the business of a preacher is not to give people intellectual treats; it is to present spiritual truth to them in a spiritual manner.
The Righteous Judgement of God, 145

There is but one thing that gives a preacher authority, and that is that he be 'filled with the Holy Spirit'.
Preaching and Preachers, 159–60

Ladies first – except in the pulpit and at prayer meetings!
Banner of Truth, Issue 275

It is a wonderful thing when a preacher can enjoy another man's preaching as much as his own. Nothing but the Holy Ghost can do that for him.
Authority, 88

[Liberal preachers] talk about learning and scholarship, but one never hears of a soul being saved under their ministry. Such teaching has all but emptied the churches. It is time that these things should be said plainly and clearly in order that we may realize the consequences that follow when we begin to set up our understanding and our reason as the ultimate sanction and the final authority.
Assurance, 222

It is especially the part of the preacher always to be applying the truth. I have never called myself a Bible lecturer for that reason. The Bible is to be preached, it is always to be applied.
To God's Glory, 148

. . . [I]t is most dangerous for a man to be a lay preacher
Saving Faith, 289

PREACHING
We must always realise when we talk to others that the heart is never to be approached directly. I go further; the will is never to be approached directly either. This is a most important principle to bear in mind both in personal dealings and in preaching. The heart is always to be influenced through the understanding – the mind then the heart, then the will,
Spiritual Depression, 62

'. . . on another occasion I stand in this pulpit labouring as it were left to myself, preaching badly and utterly weak, and the devil has come and said, 'There will be nobody there at all next Sunday', But thank God I have found on the following Sunday a larger congregation. That is God's method of accountancy. You never know. I enter a pulpit in weakness and I end with power, I enter with self confidence and I am made to feel a fool. It is God's accountancy. He knows us so much better than we know ourselves . . . His book-keeping is the most romantic thing I know of in the whole world,
Spiritual Depression, 131

PREACHING (Unction)
What is preaching? Logic on fire! Eloquent reason! . . . Preaching is theology coming through a man who is on fire . . . What is the chief end of preaching? It is to give men and women a sense of God and His presence.
Preaching and Preachers, 97

Preaching should make such a difference to a man who is listening that he is never the same again. Preaching, in other words, is a transaction between the

preacher and the listener. It does something for the soul of a man, for the whole of the person, the entire man; it deals with him in a vital and radical manner.
Preachers and Preaching, 53

It is the only thing in the universe that can deal with conditions which are utterly desperate, completely hopeless.
Spiritual Blessing, 81

affect
We wound in order to heal; we knock down in order to lift up.
The Kingdom of God, 152

The preacher is not in the pulpit merely to give knowledge and information to people. He is to inspire them, he is to enthuse them, he is to enliven them and send them out glorifying in the Spirit.
The Puritans, 376–77

If you do not agree with me that this is the most stupendous thing you will ever hear in time or in eternity, well then I despair of you.
God's Way of Reconciliation, 316

The thing that has given me greatest pleasure, and greatest encouragement of all the things I have ever been told that people say about my ministry, is this. It was said by a lady, who remonstrated, and said, 'This man preaches to us as if we were sinners!'
Revival, 71

It is still a fact that it is the old supernatural gospel that assumes nothing about modern men and women, except that they are the same as human beings have always been – that they are sinners controlled by the devil, who need to be born again and can only be saved by the blood of Christ – it is such preaching that still appeals to them because it is the only truth.
Christian Conduct, 80

Preaching is designed to do something to people.
Preaching and Preachers, 85

I once read in a paper a story which I must confess searched me to the very depth of my being. It was an account of a meeting held in the St. Andrew's Hall in Glasgow a number of years ago and the report of the meeting was given by Alexander Gammie, who was well-known as a religious writer, but he also went to political meetings and so on. He had been listening to two men speaking, and speaking on the same theme, and he later wrote: 'They were both excellent speakers, very eloquent, able men, able to marshal their arguments, state their case and so on, but', he said, 'I felt there was one great difference

between the two men . . . The first man spoke as an advocate, the second man spoke as a witness.' That is the difference! The first was like a barrister, with his brief – an advocate. He stated the case – and stated it so well because he believed in it. But the second man had got something additional, a plus – he was a witness.
Joy Unspeakable, 98

The business of Christian preaching is to tell us that whatever the circumstances may be, whatever may be awaiting us in the future, if we are right with God it will not finally matter, it will not have a devastating effect upon us.
Walking with God, 12

Let me say it once more: if the preaching of the gospel does not make you think, and think as you have never thought in your life before, it is very bad preaching.
Authentic Christianity (3), 74

approach
I cannot speak without a text
Knowing the Times, 198

Peter stood up and he preached. He did not spend hours in a study polishing his phrases, thinking of clever illustrations – oh, such a thing is so repugnant to the New Testament gospel. Here was a man, alive, and he wanted other people to be alive. Here was a man who felt the burden of souls and so he brought his whole great statement of the gospel to this focus, to this point of application. And that should be the aim of all preaching . . . Do you get tired of hearing me saying the same things, my friends? Well, I am just doing what the Apostle Peter did (2 Peter 1 verses 12–13). I am sure he was right and I am sure I am right! Our greatest trouble always is that we forget . . . And I think this is the call that comes more than ever before to ministers today. Christian people are forgetting things they have known, and that is why we are in the present muddle and confusion; and the business of preaching is to go on reminding them.
Christian Conduct, 117

I feel that oftentimes we fail to expound correctly and we misinterpret Scripture because we do not talk to it and ask it questions. It is a very good and a very rewarding thing to do that with Scripture.
The Love of God, 76

One of the most fatal habits a preacher can ever fall into is to read his Bible simply in order to find text for sermons. This is a real danger; it must be recognised and fought and resisted with all your might.
Preaching and Preachers, 172

There is all the difference in the world between having your preaching controlled by theology, and preaching theology. Our preaching should always be controlled by theology, we must always be scriptural in our presentation of the truth, but that is a very different thing from preaching theology.
Saving Faith, 140

I enter a pulpit with weakness and I end with power. I enter with self confidence and I am made to feel a fool.
Spiritual Depression: Its Causes and Its Cure, 131

congregation
If the Holy Spirit only acted on the preacher there would be no conversions. He acts also on the listeners, and that is what is put abundantly before us especially in Acts . . . This then is the dual action of the Spirit. He takes the preacher, the speaker, whether in a pulpit or in private, and gives this enabling. Then he acts upon the ones who are listening and he deals with their minds and hearts and wills. Both happen at the same time.
Authentic Christianity (2), 208

definition
Preaching, in other words, is a transaction between the preacher and the listener. It does something for the soul of man, for the whole of the person, the entire man; it deals with him in a vital and radical manner.
Preaching and Preachers, 53

goal
. . . I can forgive the preacher almost anything if he gives me a sense of God, if he gives me something for my soul, if he gives me a sense that, though he is inadequate himself, he is handling something which is very great and very glorious, if he gives me some dim glimpse of the majesty and the glory of God, the love of Christ my Saviour, and the magnificence of the gospel.
Preaching and Preachers, 98

Some of you may recall the advice that Martin Luther gave to his friend Philip Melanchthon when he was setting out on his career. 'Always preach', said Luther, 'in such a way that if the people do not come to hate their sin, they will instead hate you.'
Expository Sermons on 2 Peter, 43

. . . [P]resent-day preaching does not even annoy men, but leaves them precisely where they were, without a ruffle and without the slightest disturbance.
Evangelistic Sermons, 52–53

The more you know your Bible the easier preaching becomes.
The Cross, 65

I am not here to denounce a poor man who is a sinner like I am! I am here to tell him – if he could hear my words and God grant that he may – that he can be delivered, he can be pardoned, he can be renewed, he can start a new life in Jesus Christ.
The Kingdom of God, 152

How can a man be dull when he is handling such themes? I will say that a 'dull preacher' is a contradiction in terms; if he is dull he is not a preacher. He may stand in a pulpit and talk but he is certainly not a preacher. With the grand theme and message of the Bible dullness is impossible.
Preaching and Preachers, 87

Holy Spirit

The Holy Spirit gives to preachers fresh revelations of truth. They had always been there, but the preacher is led to see them in a progressive manner by this 'spirit of revelation'. Without this spirit of revelation the preacher would fail and become bankrupt of ideas. I am more dependent upon Him than I have ever been. The truth is so great, and my mind is so small; but the Spirit of revelation gives us understanding.
God's Ultimate Purpose, 362

Whenever there is an effectual ministry it is because of this 'working', this 'energetic working' of the power of God through the Holy Spirit. As the Apostle tells us in I Corinthians chapter 2, his preaching was 'not with enticing words of man's wisdom'. He did not depend upon any human gifts or methods or contrivances. It was 'in demonstration of the Spirit and of power'.
The Unsearchable Riches of Christ, 56

I do not even put a 'test on the meeting' by asking people to come forward at the end. Again, why not? It is because I believe that there is a type of preaching, there is an action of the Spirit, that makes the congregation cry out, 'Men and brethren what shall we do?' I do not understand this pressure brought to bear upon people to make them decide or to make them attend services.
Authentic Christianity (1), 100

We must never separate the Spirit and the Word. The Spirit speaks to us through the Word; so we should always doubt and query any supposed revelation that is not entirely consistent with the Word of God. Indeed the essence of wisdom is to reject altogether the term 'revelation' as far as we are concerned, and speak only of 'illumination'.
Christian Unity, 191

length

I am told that there are certain churches now where the poor man who comes to preach is given a programme: 11am – opening prayer; and then he will find at the end of his programme: 12 noon – benediction. He is not even given any

choice, you see. He has to stop. The service must not be too long. Now again, can you fit that sort of thing into this book of Acts?
Authentic Christianity (1), 100

method
When I preach, I do not tell stories about myself or anybody else, I do not just make people sing choruses and try to work them up – I reason with them.
Not Ashamed, 42

The true hallmark of greatness is simplicity. It is little minds that are compli-cated and involved.
Banner of Truth, Issue 275

One advantage in preaching through a book of the Bible, as we are proposing to do, is that it compels us to face every single statement come what may, and stand before it, and look at it, and allow it to speak to us. Indeed it is interesting to observe that not infrequently certain well-known Bible teachers never face certain Epistles at all in their expositions because there are difficulties which they are resolved to avoid.
God's Ultimate Purpose, 84

responsibility
A man standing in a Christian pulpit has no business to say, 'I suggest to you', or 'shall I put it to you', or 'On the whole I think', or 'I am almost persuaded'. Or 'The results of research and knowledge and speculation all seem to point in this direction'. No! 'These things *declare* we unto you.' I know that the old charge which has so often been brought up against the Church and her preach-ers is that we are dogmatic; but the preacher who is not dogmatic is not a preacher in the New Testament sense. We should be modest about our own opinions and careful as to how we voice our own speculations, but here, thank God, we are not in such a realm, we are not concerned about such things.
The Love of God, 6

Let us be very practical, for, after all, one should never expound Scripture with-out being practical. I am not a lecturer, I am a preacher. I do not believe that one should lecture on the Bible.
Assurance, 301

My responsibility is a very serious one. I shall be held responsible at the Bar of Judgement for the way I have preached this gospel.
Love so Amazing, 107

We must remember that there is a radical basic difference between preaching the Word and preaching *about* the Word. It is only the preaching of the Word which saves men.
Knowing the Times, 24

Any preacher will tell you that it is easier to preach than it is to pray.
Authentic Christianity (1), 173

The Bible is always to be preached.
God's Sovereign Purpose, 25

A ministry which merely states the truth without applying it has failed. The true preacher of righteousness urges the people to put it into practice.
Christian Unity, 205–6

If I were preaching something that I myself could understand or that you could understand it would not be a gospel. I am preaching the everlasting and eternal God.
Authentic Christianity (4), 235

No, this is the message, the message that was given to John and his fellow Apostles; I have entered into fellowship with the Apostles and I am repeating their message. But the mystic says he has received a new and fresh message and that he is in a state of direct inspiration.
Fellowship with God, 94

One of the great discoveries of this present century, and especially during the Second World War, was the importance of having a balanced diet. People are often ill, not only because they are not taking sufficient food, but also because their diet is not balanced. This is equally true and vital with respect to spiritual food. It must be a balanced diet, as our quotations have told us. It is to consist of teaching and doctrine.
Christian Unity, 204–5

In spiritual nurture there is milk, and there is strong meat; and it is a part of the business of the preacher to know the difference between the two. He must vary the diet according to the people's need – not only milk, and not only strong meat – otherwise his preaching will not be edifying. Then again, there are varying circumstances; and this Word is to be applied to every conceivable circumstance. Some of the listeners are happy, and some are sad; there are those who may be enduring persecution and tribulation; some may be celebrating a victory. There is a word for all; and a full ministry of the whole Word will meet every condition and every conceivable circumstance.
Christian Unity, 204

I tremble to think of the position of men who have been called to be stewards of the mysteries, men to whom God has entrusted His oracles, who themselves have attacked it, and undermined it, and shaken the faith of other people in it! There is nothing more terrible than that.
The Righteous Judgement of God, 171–72

unction

Preaching is in demonstration of the Spirit and of power. And a man has to realise, after he has prepared his sermons, that however perfectly he may have done so, that it is all waste and useless unless the power of the Spirit comes upon it and upon him. He must pray for that.
Revival, 124

The point Peter is making is that the gospel, 'these things', had been reported to them 'by the Holy Ghost that was sent down from heaven' – the Holy Spirit was using the preacher. That is what I mean by 'unction' and by 'power'.
Authentic Christianity (2), 207

These two: 'the Holy Spirit'; 'the word of God'. We must never separate them, and if we ever do we shall go astray. Some people put their emphasis only on the word. These are the intellectuals. 'Ah', they say 'nothing matters but the Word.' They spend their time reading and studying and they become authorities on theology and doctrine. As a result, they may become proud of their own great knowledge, and they may get the admiration of others who join in with them, but this is nothing but a little mutual admiration society. Nobody is converted; nobody is convicted. Heads packed with knowledge and understanding – useless! 'Word only', you see.
Authentic Christianity (2), 209

One of the remarkable things about preaching is that often one finds that the best things one says are things that have not been premeditated, and were not even thought of in the preparation of the sermon, but are given while one is actually speaking and preaching.
Preachers and Preaching, 84

Do we know the difference between God smiling upon us and God not smiling upon us? It is the test of a preacher. There is all the difference in the world between preaching merely from human understanding and energy, and preaching in the conscious smile of God . . . To me there is nothing more terrible for a preacher, than to be in a pulpit alone, without the conscious smile of God.
Revival, 295

I take leave to say in all humility, that there is nothing more blessed under heaven than to know something of the power of the Holy Spirit. I am sorry for those who have never known it as they have preached and tried to expound the Scriptures. There is an almost inexpressible difference between preaching in one's own strength and preaching in the power of the Spirit. This can happen also in conversation and in all the activities and endeavours of the Christian.
The Unsearchable Riches of Christ, 298

urgency
Lend me your ears! I have something to put before you that will not be easy. Listen! Listen for all you are worth. Listen for your very life.
Authentic Christianity (4), 14

How can one keep silent?
Authentic Christianity (3), 146

I turn you into members of the jury.
God's Way Not Ours, 89

visual aid
I am tempted at this point to digress and point out that a sad feature of the age in which we are living is that there is accumulating evidence that people, in spite of their education and their vaunted culture, are finding it increasingly difficult to take in truth by listening and are increasingly calling for visual aids.
Great Doctrines of the Bible (3), 28

PREDESTINATION
Have you ever considered the process involved in the salvation of the individual? 'Ah but', you say, 'There is nothing in that; the individual is saved in this way – he is taken to a meeting by a friend and he listens to the preaching of the gospel. He says, 'Yes, I will accept it, I will believe', and so he is saved. That is it, that is the process of salvation. What a poor conception of salvation! Do you not know that the programme for the salvation of every individual was all determined and decided upon before the foundation of the world?
Assurance, 333–34

My dear friends, I am not saying these things because I understand all this. I do not! Do not ask me why God ordains some and not others, I do not know. I am not told in the Bible and I know nothing except what I am told there. I will go further: I do not want to know. It is a mystery. It is a great mystery. That is the inscrutable mind of God.
God's Sovereign Purpose, 295

PREJUDICE
You do not take up a prejudice. It takes you up, and controls you.
Banner of Truth, Issue 275

The better the brain, the stronger the prejudice.
Banner of Truth, Issue 275

We are all creatures of prejudice; we are born like that as the result of sin, and we tend to start with minds which are biased. One of the most difficult things in life in any realm is to get rid of such prejudice.
Children of God, 72

There is as much bitterness and prejudice and bias in scientific circles as in any other circle. Prejudice and persecution are conditions of the spirit, and are to be found in the highest circles as well as the lowest, and equally among intellectuals and non-intellectuals.
Authentic Christianity (2), 118

PRIDE
The ultimate sin of man is pride of intellect. That is why it is always true to say that 'Not many wise men after the flesh, not many mighty, not many noble are 'called'. The wise man after the flesh wants to understand. He pits his brain against God's wisdom, and he says, 'I don't see'. Of course, he doesn't. And Christ says to him, 'Except ye be converted, and become as little children, ye shall not enter into the kingdom of heaven'. (Matthew 18:3)
Assurance, 250–51

PROMISES
There are always conditions attached to the promises of God and it is because men ignore these conditions that they fail to obtain the blessing.
Old Testament Evangelistic Sermons, 261

God's promises are always conditional.
Life in God, 22

PROPHECY
What is the difference between prophecy on the one hand and preaching and teaching on the other? Because there is a difference. And I would say that the difference can be put in one word – immediacy.
Christian Conduct, 236

I think I know something of what it is to be preaching or teaching, and suddenly to find myself prophesying. I am aware that my words are not what I prepared, but have been given at that moment and with clarity and force and directness. I am speaking, and I am listening to myself, as it were, because it is not me. The prophecy may come in the middle of a sermon, or a teaching, but it is differentiated from teaching and preaching by this immediacy, this sense that God is revealing a message.
Christian Conduct, 237

Women can prophesy; but the Scripture also tells us that it is not permitted to a woman to preach or teach.
Christian Conduct, 237

Prophecy is essentially a revelation, not in the sense of being equal to Scripture, but in the sense that a particular truth is laid upon the mind of a believer by the Holy Spirit in order that he or she may communicate it to the members of the church.
Christian Conduct, 239

You find much about prophecy in the New Testament. Paul discusses it at some length in 1 Corinthians, in connection with the various gifts that were exercised in the Church. Those were the days before the New Testament was written, when certain members of the Church were given messages and the ability to speak them by the Holy Spirit. That is what is meant by prophesying.
Studies in the Sermon on the Mount (2), 267

How did this divine afflatus come to the man? Be careful, my friends, lest with your intellectualism you dismiss the prophets and the whole phenomenon of prophecy as we have it in the Old Testament. They were certainly laid hold of. They knew something about an ecstatic condition.
Revival, 143

I knew a man whose minister had had this gift, again in the revival of 1904 and 1905. It disappeared completely afterwards, but while the revival lasted he was told beforehand of something that was going to happen in his Church, not once, but morning by morning. He would be awakened out of his sleep at half past two in the morning, and given direct and exact information of something that was going to happen during that day, and it did happen. That is another part of this mental phenomenon.
Revival, 135

The whole question of prophets is a difficult subject, and one must not speak too dogmatically about it.
Christian Unity, 188

The priest is one who represents us with God; the prophet is one who represented God with us. The prophet is one who came with a message from God to man; the priest is one who goes from man to God, one who approaches God on behalf of man.
Great Christian Doctrines (1), 297

PROVIDENCE

'The very hairs of your head are all numbered' (Matt. 10:30). There are events which appear to be quite accidental, but they are controlled by God.
Great Doctrines of the Bible (1), 97

Creation brings things into existence, providence keeps them, or guarantees their continuation in existence, in fulfilment of God's purposes. The doctrine of providence does not just mean, therefore, that God has a foreknowledge of what is going to happen, but is a description of His continuing activity, of what He does in the world, and what He has continued to do since He made the world at the very beginning.
Great Doctrines of the Bible (1), 140

I am prepared to assert that perhaps in this twentieth century of ours the most important doctrine in many ways is the doctrine of providence.
Great Doctrines of the Bible (1), 141

PSALMS
I always point out whenever I happen to preach from the book of Psalms that a psalm is a song and should therefore be always taken in its entirety. Certainly there are individual verses in the psalms which merit prolonged and separate attention but a psalm is generally composed so as to give expression to some one big prevailing thought or mood.
Old Testament Evangelistic Sermons, 181

. . . [T]he Psalms generally start with a conclusion.
Faith on Trial, 13

Imprecation is a desire expressed to God that certain evil things should happen to sinners.
To God's Glory, 45

God, in his infinite wisdom, gives his revelation in thought forms which always suit the particular age and generation in which he gives it.
To God's Glory, 51

PSYCHOLOGY
If you want psychology, go to the Scriptures.
God's Way of Reconciliation, 48

You know those great, profound psychologists of the soul, the much maligned Puritans, used to write at great length on what they called a 'false peace'; there was nothing they were more afraid of than having a false peace with God.
Fellowship with God, 109

Incidentally there is such a thing as spiritual and biblical psychology, though it is not called that very frequently.
Faith on Trial, 38

Face the Bible and its records merely from the standpoint of modern ideas and modern psychological methods and it remains a hopeless jumble of discordant facts which cannot be harmonised and which baffles all attempts at classification and order. But approach it in the light of the key called sin and you will find every door opening and the tangled skein suddenly unravelling itself. Take any case you like, the key always works; what is more, it always works in precisely the same way.
Old Testament Evangelistic Sermons, 89

. . . Several psychologists – most Freudians – developed an extensive clinical psychology practice. One even heard of missionary societies sending their candidates to be interviewed by a psychologist [or psychotherapist] in order to find whether they were fit people to be sent to the mission field . . . it was truly astonishing to find that the fashion had begun to invade evangelical circles.
Healing and the Scriptures, 146

Many who go to the psychiatrist are like the woman in the gospels – they are nothing bettered, but rather grow worse!
Banner of Truth, Issue 275

Psychology is based on pure theory. The popular psychology is, indeed, based upon insanity and the study of insanity. Freud's whole system is based upon such a study, the abnormal which is transferred to the normal and then mighty deductions are drawn.
Enjoying the Presence of God, 17

Psychology, I suggest to you, like philosophy, is one of the greatest of the enemies of Christianity.
Authentic Christianity (1), 246

PUBLICITY
'I thank my God that your faith is spoken of throughout the whole world.' They had not got newspapers, and they had not got telegrams or telephones, they had no radio or television, no press agencies or any advertising agents, and yet the news had spread throughout the whole of the Roman Empire in this way. What a lesson on Church publicity! How did it happen, do you think? Why was this spoken of throughout the whole world? How did it become known? My dear friends, the answer is a very simple one. A revival never needs to be advertised; it always advertises itself.
The Gospel of God, 179–80

PUNISHMENT (Hell)
You are going to suffer if you do not listen to God.
Old Testament Evangelistic Sermons, 8

There is no greater fallacy than to imagine that the moment a man sins he will immediately have his punishment.
Old Testament Evangelistic Sermons, 94

PURITANS
At various points in its long history, the church foolishly tried to impose upon men and women who were not Christians, the Christian teaching with regard to conduct. I believe, and I say so with great regret and reluctance, that that was one of the cardinal errors of the Puritans of three hundred years ago, as it is still the error in the thinking of many of their blind followers today.
Christian Conduct, 75

– Q –

QUAKERS

George Fox was most certainly calling attention to something vital but he went too far. He almost went to the point of saying that the Scriptures did not matter, that it was only this 'inner light' and the Spirit within that mattered, and the result of that has been that modern Quakerism – the Society of Friends – is almost entirely non-doctrinal and, indeed, at times almost reaches the point at which you would query whether it is even Christian. It is a vague general benevolence and a good spirit.
Great Doctrines of the Bible (2), 245

The extreme opposite of Roman Catholic teaching on the sacraments is the view that was originally taught and propounded by the Quakers and is still held by them, namely, their teaching that the only means of grace is the internal operation of the Holy Spirit in the believer. Quakers believe that if someone experiences the working of this 'inner light' – the Spirit of God within – nothing further is needed.
Great Doctrines of the Bible (3), 25

. . . [I]t is always dangerous to separate the Holy Spirit from the Word. Many have done this, and there have often been grievous excesses. Indeed the virtual departure of the people called Quakers from the Christian faith is due to this very thing; they put such emphasis upon the 'inner light' that they ignore the Word. They tend to say that the Word does not matter; it is this inner light that matters. And they have reached the point at which they are more or less detached from New Testament doctrines, and the Lord Jesus Christ is scarcely necessary to their system.
Life in the Spirit in Marriage Home and Work, 161

The tragedy of subsequent Quakerism – I am not speaking of George Fox himself at this point because he did hold the true doctrine – the tragedy is that in the following centuries, the Quaker movement has tended to put its exclusive emphasis upon the Spirit and has been ignoring and forgetting the doctrine concerning our Lord and Saviour Jesus Christ.
God's Way of Reconciliation, 328

– R –

RADIO

. . . [T]his is my main reason for not preaching on the radio. I once asked one of the religious directors, 'What would happen to your programmes if the Holy Spirit suddenly took over?' And he was honest enough to admit that really that question had never entered their minds.
Revival, 77

REASON

You think with your mind, and only then do you feel with your heart. You do not start with your heart, you start with your head, with your mind, with your understanding.
God's Way of Reconciliation, 163

If you and I do not reason and argue and deduce from this mighty Revelation in such a way that it leads us to glorying in God, it means either that we have not understood the truth, or even, perhaps, that we have never really become aware of it; or else that, having seen it, we do not really believe God and trust him.
Assurance, 164

I do not pretend to understand the eternal mind of God and how it works. I am not meant to do that. This is the trouble with the philosophers. They say that they do not understand how God can do this or that, they want to explain the mind of the almighty God with their pigmy minds and it cannot be done. And that is why the philosophers find it so difficult to become Christians.
Saved in Eternity, 177

Indeed, it is quite unscriptural for men and women to put their intellectual difficulties before the plain statement of Scripture.
Saved in Eternity, 178

My mind is too small to understand it, my intellect cannot span the infinities and the immensities and the eternities. My little 'pigmy' reason and logic are not big enough to see or to take in such a conception as the self-emptying and the humiliation of the Son of God. I do not claim to understand it; who could understand an idea like that of the virgin birth? It is beyond understanding, it

is beyond reason. Who can understand the doctrine of the two natures, unmixed, remaining separate, unmingled and yet both there, but still only one person? I cannot understand the doctrine of the Trinity, Father Son and Holy Spirit. I cannot and we should never try to do so.
Heart of the Gospel, 19–20

The claim of the gospel is that it is in a realm which is beyond human reasoning and understanding. It is a revelation, a statement that comes to us, an announcement; it is the gift of God. That is why instead of reasoning round and round in circles and trying to span and grasp the infinite and the everlasting, I say, go to Him!
Heart of the Gospel, 20

If I am to rely upon human reason I am already defeated. You cannot rely upon your reason; it is too small, it is too inadequate. Yet that is what men are doing today. They are relying upon their reason and criticising the Bible; they are even criticising the Lord Jesus Christ Himself! 'He was a child of His age', they say, 'He could not possibly know what we know'. That is human reason, human knowledge, set in the supreme position; and you are left without any higher authority. Our final authority cannot be reason.
The Christian Soldier, 202

We have no right to ask for reasons.
God's Sovereign Purpose, 210

Reason can take me to a certain point, and it is quite right to use it up to that point, but that will never bring me to a true knowledge of God.
Fellowship with God, 104

RECONCILIATION
Reconciliation is amazing. But this is more wondrous and more amazing. Reconciliation is not the end. Beyond reconciliation, we have access to the Father.
God's Way of Reconciliation, 316

REDEMPTION
Apart from the blood we have no redemption!
Great Doctrines of the Bible (1), 321

Redemption cannot be undone.
Life in God, 151

Our bodies have suffered as the result of the Fall. It was not merely man's spirit which fell. When Adam fell the whole man fell – body, mind, and spirit. Our very bodies are not what they were meant to be. Our bodies are weak and subject to illness and infections and coughs and colds and aches and pains and all these

things . . . All the beauty of man, the most handsome man or woman, is only relative beauty, and there are seeds of decay in it. But when we are glorified our very bodies shall be perfect, every vestige of sin will be taken out of them, and all the results and consequences of sin will be entirely removed. There will be no trace of sin left, and every one of us will be glorious in beauty.
Assurance, 51

Does he say, 'As thou hast given him power over all flesh, that he should give eternal life to all flesh'? No – 'That he should give eternal life to *as many as thou has given him*' (John 17:2). The universal and the particular are both here in one verse. This is indeed high doctrine, so high that no human can understand it, but so high and glorious, that every man who has the mind of Christ in himself, bows before it in humble Reverence, in amazement and in astonishment.
Saved in Eternity, 61

When he comes and reconstitutes the whole cosmos – not only this earth but Mars and Jupiter and the sun and the moon and all the universe – it will all be restored to its original, absolute perfection.
Authentic Christianity (1), 282

REGENERATION
I do not preach decisions – I preach regeneration.
Banner of Truth Issue, 275

Regeneration is the work of the Holy Spirit; it is a secret work of the Spirit. It is not something experimental but is a secret work, and a man only knows that it has happened to him.
Joy Unspeakable, 22

Salvation, redemption, regeneration do not merely put us back where Adam was; we are in a much higher position.
Great Doctrines of the Bible (1), 170

The difficult operation is the operation of grafting us into Christ. When you graft a new branch into a tree you take your knife and you strike that tree and then you take the branch and push it into the gash you have made. That is the difficult part of the process. Once you have put the graft in, the rest happens easily. The sap flows through the tree to the branch giving it life and strength; and so it grows. Once the actual act of grafting has been done you just wait for the results, and the fruit follows. 'How much more shall we be saved in his life!'
Assurance, 151

There is no profounder change in the universe than the change which is described as regeneration . . .
Spiritual Depression its Causes and Cure, 95

If you are in Christ you are in Christ; and if Christ 'has been made of God unto you wisdom, even righteousness and sanctification' (1 Cor. 1:30) He must be glorification to you also. You cannot divide Him and 'take' justification only, or sanctification only. It is 'all or nothing'. You must not divide these things. It is unscriptural, indeed it is impossible. It is the Person of Christ that matters. He is indivisible. We have all these in Christ.
Assurance, 54

REGRETS
There is nothing that is more reprehensible, judged by common canons of thought, than to allow anything that belongs to the past to cause you to be a failure in the present'.
Spiritual Depression, 83

If you were to feel more interest in Christ you would be less interested in yourself.
Spiritual Depression, 88

Never look back again; never waste your time in the present; never waste your energy; forget the past and rejoice in the fact that you are what you are by the grace of God, and that in the divine alchemy of his marvellous grace you may yet have the greatest surprise in your life and existence and find that even in your case it will come to pass that the last shall be first. Praise God for the fact that you are what you are, and that you are in the Kingdom
Spiritual Depression, 90

From the sheer standpoint of orthodoxy and doctrinal beliefs I find myself nearer to many a Roman Catholic than to many with the ranks of Protestantism, but where I part company and must part company with them is that they add these vial pluses – Christ, plus the Church, plus the Virgin Mary, plus the priests, plus the saints, and so on.
Spiritual Depression, 187

RELATIONSHIPS
A blood relationship is a more intimate, direct, vital, living thing than any relationship which is delimited and determined by the processes of the law and by the enactments of men.
God's Way of Reconciliation, 411

RELIGION
The formalising and externalising of religion is a great curse.
Spiritual Blessing, 126

The greatest enemy of true Christianity has always been religion.
Authentic Christianity (1), 19

In a sense, I do not know anything that is more terrible than formal thanksgiving.
Singing to the Lord, 66

other religions
I am not interested in a World Congress of Faiths. I cannot kneel down together with, and look up with people, one of whom is looking at Confucius and another at Mohammed and another at the Buddha, and another at some philosopher. I cannot! There is only One to look at, it is this blessed Son of God.
God's Way of Reconciliation, 359

You cannot have a World Congress of Faiths. Such an idea is a farce; indeed it is a denial of Christ. Christianity cannot participate in such a Congress. It cannot enter into any proposal or conference that says that Christianity is marvellous, but, after all, God gave insights to the Buddha, to Confucius, Mahomet and others and we can learn something from them. The Christian does not need to learn from such quarters, because 'all the treasures of wisdom and knowledge are in Christ'.
Christian Unity, 103

Confucianism, Buddhism, Islam, and so on. Now those religions are nothing but teachings. They do not claim to be anything else. They are teachings with regard to how people should live, philosophies which take a religious form. And the danger is that people put the Christian faith into that category.
Authentic Christianity (1), 241

Not only do I not learn from the natural unregenerate man, I do not learn from the Hindu or the Muslim, the Confucian or the Buddhist; they have nothing to tell me. The Bible and the Bible alone contains the knowledge and it is given by God . . . we are to say 'Whom you ignorantly worship Him declare I unto you'.
To God's Glory, 270

REPENTANCE
I remember a man who had been converted, but who then fell into sin. I was very ready to help him until I found that he was much too ready to help himself. In other words, he came and confessed his sin, but immediately he began to smile and said: 'After all, there is the doctrine of grace'. I felt he was too healthy; he was healing himself a little too quickly. The reaction to sin should be deep penitence.
Studies in the Sermon on the Mount (2), 291

Repentance means to think again about God and yourself and the relationship between you; but the first call is to think again about God.
The Sons of God, 44

Look back and think of the times when you were unhappy and you will find that it was almost certainly due to something you said and which you regretted perhaps for days.
Banner of Truth, Issue 275

Repentance precedes pardon and it is only to those who have become miserable because of their sin that the gracious Word of God in Christ offering pardon and joy and peace ever comes. The direct way to feasting is preliminary fasting; it is ever 'sorrow' that is turned into 'joy' by the intervention of Christ. Let us clearly grasp this fact. It is only those who have been miserable on account of their sin who can experience the joy of salvation, and, as we have already seen, it is doubtful whether there is such a thing as salvation without the joy of salvation.
Old Testament Evangelistic Sermons, 262

No one ever repents unless he has come under the influence of the Holy Spirit of God.
Authentic Christianity (3), 80

RESPONSIBILITY
God never causes sin, nor approves of it; He only permits, directs, restrains, limits and overrules it. People alone are responsible for their sin. The first chapter of James gives that particular teaching clearly.
Great Doctrines of the Bible (1), 150

I am responsible for the actions of Great Britain, for instance, in China, in the last century when they so shamefully introduced the opium trade there. Though I did not do it personally, though it was done before I was born, I am responsible for it because I am a Britisher, and I feel my responsibility and I am conscious of shame. In exactly the same way, when Christ died on that cross and endured the wrath of God against sin, I was participating in it; I was in Him, I was dying with Him. I am dead to the law, I am dead to the wrath of God.
God's Way of Reconciliation, 106

. . . [T]he doctrine of the sovereignty of God and the doctrine of human responsibility are both true and that the Apostle is stating the two doctrines here . . .
God's Sovereign Purpose, 284

RESURRECTION (After Life, Heaven)
As you look at the resurrection you are looking at a victor.
Great Doctrines of the Bible (1), 340

Putting all the ecclesiastical corpses into one graveyard will not bring about a resurrection!
Banner of Truth, Issue 275

bodily

As certainly as the Lord Jesus Christ rose from the grave, we shall rise from the grave. And we shall rise without corruption; we shall be faultless and blameless. The fact that the Head has risen is a guarantee that the body must rise. We have already risen spiritually; we shall soon rise physically, materially, bodily. Nothing can prevent this.
God's Ultimate Purpose, 445

My body will be raised; I shall still have my identity; my body will be recognisable . . . My body is the particular configuration that the atoms take in my case; and that is what is going to be raised. If we are still on earth when Christ returns there will be a mighty miracle wrought in our flesh and blood so that it becomes a glorified body.
The Sons of God, 88

There were heresies in the world then, as there are still, which taught that sin applies only to the body, that sin is something physical, and that salvation, therefore, means escaping out of the body. That is the teaching of Hinduism and of Buddhism. The great thing is to escape out of the body, to get rid of the flesh, and the moment you get out of the body, it is said, you leave sin behind. That is the exact opposite of Christian salvation which teaches not the escape out of the body, but the redemption of the body.

　　When Adam and Eve sinned, the effect of sin was that it did something to their spirit, their soul and their body. The whole person suffered. When they fell, they fell in every part, the body included and therefore to be complete, salvation must include the body as well as the soul and spirit. If it does not, the works of the devil have not been undone. Christ, we are told by John in his first epistle, came 'that he might destroy the works of the devil' (1 John 3v8).
Great Doctrines of the Bible (3), 233

If my body is not in the hereafter to be redeemed and glorified, then Christ has failed at that point. Our bodies are as they are, subject to diseases, subject to death, the place where sin dwells, and where the devil is constantly tempting us and trying us, all because of sin and the Fall; and if we are not going to reach a stage and a point at which these evils no longer pertain to the body, then I say that the work of the Saviour will prove incomplete.
The Sons of God, 87

You often hear people thank God for this whole 'principle of resurrection,' how the flowers begin to appear, and how the trees and life come into being in the Spring. Now, that has nothing to do with this blessed message of the Resurrection. We are concerned about a fact, not a principle of nature, and the fact is that there, in the Resurrection, our Lord ultimately established His conquest over the devil.
Children of God, 61

certainty

Whatever may be true of our experience, whatever may be true of the world and its darkness, whatever may be true of the seeds of decay and of illness and of death that are in our bodies, and howsoever great is the power of the last enemy, we can be certain and confident of this, that nothing can prevent the carrying out of God's purpose with respect to us. There is no power that can withstand Him; there is no might or influence that can match Him, there is no possible antagonist that can equal Him. The mightiest foes, the devil, death and hell have already been vanquished, and the resurrection of Christ is the proof of it.
God's Ultimate Purpose, 400

Hold on to the doctrine of the resurrection of the body. We shall not spend our eternity as disembodied spirits.
The Sons of God, 89

Those who say that it is immaterial and unimportant that you should believe in the literal, physical resurrection are always people who are without assurance. Indeed they are without a gospel.
The Final Perseverance of the Saints, 419

The Resurrection is a proclamation of what? . . . it is a proclamation of the fact that the world is to be judged in righteousness, that the wrath of God is to be Revealed against all ungodliness and unrighteousness of men, and that Christ is the Judge. The Resurrection is a declaration, therefore, of this tremendous doctrine of the wrath of God.
The Gospel of God, 350

REVELATION
'Oh, that I knew where I might find *him*' (Job 23:3). That is the question! I look at history, I look at providence, I look into myself, I look everywhere and yet I cannot find Him. Where can I find God? There is only one solution: I must wait upon God; and God must tell me about Himself. That is revelation; and it is the function of the Holy Spirit to give us this revelation.
God's Ultimate Purpose, 357

These Old Testament incidents, in addition to being history, are at the same time perfect parables of the great Scriptural truth that is taught in Ephesians 6 about 'standing against the wiles of the devil' and 'wrestling against principalities and powers'. It is all there in that picture of Goliath and David.
The Christian Soldier, 107

Revelation! God acted and God revealing unto us his gracious purpose. Now electricity was not discovered like that. It was discovered by much thought, investigation and enquiry and everything else in life is like that. But here is a

different order of truth, unique and separate and distinct. It is God speaking and telling us something, Revealing and manifesting himself to us.
Old Testament Evangelistic Sermons, 39

The best teaching in the world is useless unless the Holy Spirit takes hold of it and applies it and opens our understanding to it, and gives it a deep lodging place in our whole being. We have already seen in the first chapter how the Apostle had been praying for the Ephesian Christians that 'the eyes of their understanding might be enlightened'. For if the Holy Spirit did not open 'the eyes of their understanding' Paul's teaching would be quite useless and void.
The Unsearchable Riches of Christ, 110

REVELATION (Book of)
Revelation is a book that speaks to every generation of Christians and will go on doing so right until the end.
The Final Perseverance of the Saints, 19

REVIVAL
advertising
The moment a Revival breaks out, the crowd will come, and, I assure you, it will not cost you a penny. I am speaking to the Church that is spending thousands of pounds on advertising to try and attract the outsider. The moment you get Revival the newspapers will report it. Their motive, of course, will be quite wrong. They will do it because they do not like it, because they think it is ridiculous, because they think that people have gone mad, or that they are drunk. It does not matter. They will give it a free advertisement. And the crowds will come to see what is happening, as they did on the day of Pentecost in Jerusalem. What fools we are!
Revival, 208

When you are calling upon the living God and his inimitable power, you do not need the sponsorship of men. The sponsorship you are interested in is the sponsorship of the Holy Spirit.
Revival, 168

If you get a Revival in your church the man in the street, and all his friends, will come crowding in . . . He has come in because he has suddenly heard that something strange and wonderful is happening in that church.
Revival, 51

affects
There is no doubt at all but that the great evangelical awakening of two hundred years ago was the means of bringing untold blessings to millions of people who died impenitent and unbelieving. As the result of that awakening in the eighteenth century, not only were thousands of people converted,

but the whole level of life in this country was raised. As the result of that revival, the Factory Acts were passed and many other beneficial things came about.
Great Doctrines of the Bible (1), 363

There has never yet been a revival but that with the revival tide many people have been washed up on the shore who have never become true believers and do not belong to the church. The tidal movement of the Spirit seems to take them up and to carry them along.
Spiritual Blessing, 184

There is nothing more typical of the eighteenth century Revival and awakening than such words as, 'Jesus, lover of my soul, let me to thy bosom fly . . .' Into the midst of all the deism and the philosophical preaching, that had characterised the end of the seventeenth and the beginning of the eighteenth century, came this warm, devotional, vital, spiritual, preaching about the Lord Jesus Christ, and people's personal knowledge of him.
Revival, 45

The first indication of Revival is always that something begins to happen to the life of the Church. There seems to be a new quickening. The worship of the Church becomes warmer, something comes back which had gone, a warmth and a tenderness, a new concern, a new note of agony. Some old people I remember used to say that the thing they were looking for in the prayer meetings in the church was the element of 'Oh', the longing, the groaning, the waiting, the 'Oh'. And when that comes it is a sign that the cloudy pillar has come back.
Revival, 171

The Christian church would have been dead and finished centuries ago and many times over were it not for Revivals.
Joy Unspeakable, 436

There can be a lot of laughing and lightness, and obvious organisation in evangelistic campaigns. Never in a Revival, but rather awe, this Reverence, this holy fear, the consciousness of God in his majesty, his glory, his holiness, his utter purity.
Revival, 101

definition
I would define a Revival as a large number, a group of people, being baptised by the Holy Spirit at the same time; or the Holy Spirit falling upon, coming upon a number of people assembled together.
Joy Unspeakable, 55

It is generally agreed that the best way of defining a Revival is to say that it is the church returning to the book of Acts, that it is a kind of repetition of Pentecost. It is the Spirit being poured out again upon the church.
Joy Unspeakable, 36

We can define it, as a period of unusual blessing and activity in the life of the Christian Church.
Revival, 99

I would define a Revival as a repetition in some degree, or in some measure, of that which happened on the Day of Pentecost in Jerusalem, as recorded in the second chapter of the Book of the Acts of the Apostles.
Christian Unity, 71

It is just this glimpse of God, of the glory of God, passing by. That is precisely what it is . . . The God who is there in the glory, as it were, comes down and pours out his Spirit and ascends again, and we look on, and feel, and know that the glory of God is in the midst, and is passing by. It is only a touching of the hem of the garment, as it were, it is but a vision of the back.
Revival, 220

Revival, above everything else, is a glorification of the Lord Jesus Christ, the Son of God. It is the restoration of him to the centre of the life of the Church.
Revival, 47

In one sense, the whole story of the church can be described as a series of Pentecosts – I mean by that, a series of revivals.
Spiritual Blessing, 67

What is a revival? It is God pouring out His Spirit. It is this tremendous filling that happens to numbers of people at the same time. You need not wait for a revival to get it, each of us is individually commanded to seek it, and to have it, and indeed to make sure that it is there. But at times of revival God, as it were, fills a number of people together, they almost describe it as the Spirit falling upon them. That is a revival, and that is the greatest need of the Church today.
Great Doctrines of the Bible (2), 243

It has often been said, and rightly so, that every true revival of religion is a return to the first-century religion; every re-awakening that takes place is just a return on the part of the Church to that which is described in the book of the Acts of the Apostles. That is profoundly true, and if you read the histories of revivals, you will find that in a most extraordinary manner. Revivals repeat one another; there is nothing that is more fascinating than to take the outstanding characteristics of the revivals of the different centuries and you will find that they are always the same.
Fellowship with God, 61

A revival means the Holy Ghost descending upon a church or a community or a country in power and in might, in an unmistakeable manner, breaking men down and perhaps even casting them physically to the ground. It leads to agonies of repentance and longings for peace and salvation.
Authority, 90

interim
Go on with all your activities, if you wish to do so. Go on with your work. I am not saying that you should stop all your efforts and just wait. No, go on, if you like, doing all that you are doing, but I do say this – make certain that you leave time to pray for Revival, and to see that that has more time than anything else.
Revival, 210

obstacle
It is our arrogance, it is our pride, it is our tendency to set ourselves up and to define God after our own image, instead of falling and prostrating ourselves before him, it is that, which stands between us and these mighty blessings.
Revival, 42

No Revival has ever been known in the history of churches which deny or ignore certain essential truths. Such churches have always opposed, and have always persecuted, those who have been in the midst of Revival. You will also read in the history of Northern Ireland, for instance, that a hundred years ago the Roman Catholic church of that time was actually putting on sale the so-called holy water, and urging people to sprinkle it upon themselves, and even to drink it, in order to avoid, and to evade, this thing which was being called Revival.
Revival, 35

phenomena
A Revival always humbles men, abases them, casts them to the floor, makes them feel they can do nothing, fills them with a sense of Reverence and of godly fear. Oh, how absent that is amongst us.
Revival, 125

This agony, this terrible conviction – you may get that in Revival. People are in an agony of soul and groaning. They may cry and sob and agonise audibly. But it does not always even stop at that. Sometimes people are so convicted and feel the power of the Spirit to such an extent that they faint and fall to the ground. Sometimes there are even convulsions, physical convulsions. And sometimes people seem to fall into a state of unconsciousness, into a kind of trance, and may remain like that for hours.
Revival, 111

We must not be interested in, nor frightened of phenomena. I am pointing out to you that God himself has said that the glory is so glorious that men's physical

frame is inadequate. So do not be surprised when you read the reports of people fainting, or going off into a kind of dead swoon, it is a measure of the glory of God. It is beyond us, and it is not surprising, therefore, that it should sometimes lead to such consequences.
Revival, 219

At Pentecost you had miracles, speaking with tongues and many other things. They are variable, they do not always happen. But mighty things happen. Miraculous things happen, things that are beyond the explanation and the wit of men.
Revival, 116

source
You can not stop a Revival, any more than you can start it. It is altogether in the hands of God.
Revival, 236

Seek Him; stir yourself up to call upon His name. Take hold upon Him, plead with Him as your Father, as your Maker, as your Potter, as your Guide, as your God. Plead His own promises. Cry unto Him and say, 'Oh that thou wouldest rend the heavens, that thou wouldest come down.'
Revival, 316

Does our doctrine allow for an outpouring of the Spirit – 'the gale' of the Spirit coming upon us individually and collectively?
The Puritans, 302

No Revival that has ever been experienced in the long history of the Church has ever been an official movement in the Church.
Revival, 166

The church can never organise a revival – never!
Christian Conduct, 200

But as we consider the Revivals of 1857–59 may I use the expression 'the divine humour'? Where did they break out then? It was not in the capital city of Belfast in Northern Ireland, it was in a village you have never heard of called Connor. That is how God does things . . . And it was exactly the same thing two hundred years ago. It was in that little town of Northampton in New England that the Revival broke out. It was in a little hamlet called Trevecca in Wales that Howell Harris was suddenly laid hold of, and in another similar small village that Daniel Rowland was apprehended by God – places you have never heard of, that is how God does it. And this is the wonderful thing – the next Revival may break out in a little hamlet that you and I have never heard of.
Revival, 115

sovereignty

A revival happens in God's own time, and never at any other time. That, as I have shown, was the tragic blunder of Finney in his lectures on Revival. He taught that you can have a Revival whenever you like if you only do certain things, and fulfil certain conditions. It is a complete denial of the sovereignty of God. Not only that, it is proved by history to be wrong. I, in my own lifetime, have known numbers of ministers who have taken Finney's lectures on Revival and have honestly put them into practice in their preaching and in their churches, and have persuaded their people to do them. But they have not had a Revival. Thank God for that. You will never organise a Revival. It is God who gives it.

Revival, 235

Indeed we must be prepared for some strange surprises with regard to this plan. We may think at times that everything is going wrong. The churches may be empty and people will ask, 'Where is your God's plan?' The answer is that the churches have been empty many times before; but in the fullness of His time God sends a revival, and if it is His will He will send one again.

The Unsearchable Riches of Christ, 78

God always seems to do this after a period of great trial and great discouragement.

Revival, 128

urgency

We need to become desperate.

Authentic Christianity (1), 238

If I may speak for myself, I shall not feel happy and encouraged until I feel that the Church is concentrating on this one thing – prayer for Revival.

Revival, 197

REWARD

There is no reward from God for those who seek it from men.

Studies in the Sermon on the Mount (2), 17

RIGHTEOUSNESS

Righteousness is that which is acceptable to God, which is well-pleasing in God's sight; so righteousness in man must mean that man is capable of meeting God's demands and God's desideratum. It means that man so deals with himself that he is acceptable in the sight of God. It means that man meets with God's approval. It means that man is acceptable with God, because he is now like God Himself.

The Gospel of God, 299–300

But if we want to 'die the death of the righteous' we had better live the life of the righteous.
The Life of Joy, 30

You do not put on 'the breastplate of experiences', you put on the breastplate of 'righteousness'.
The Christian Soldier, 238

The business of the gospel is to make us righteous in the sight of God, to make us acceptable with God, to enable us to stand in the presence of God. Now you may have comfortable feelings, you may have had marvellous experiences, you may have had a great change in your life, and a number of wrong things may have gone out of your life, but I say that unless you have got something that enables you to stand before God, now, and in the day of judgement, you are not only not a Christian, you have never understood the gospel. This is the central purpose of the gospel – to make a man just with God, to enable us to stand with righteousness in the presence of God.
The Gospel of God, 300–1

ROMAN CATHOLICISM
There is this essential and vital distinction which the Protestant Reformers rediscovered in the Scriptures and re-emphasised as over against the Roman Catholic Church and her teaching: the distinction between the visible and the invisible church. All belong to the visible church, but all do not belong to the invisible church.
God's Sovereign Purpose, 102

There are individual Roman Catholics who are undoubtedly Christian.
Knowing the Times, 306

From the standpoint of orthodoxy and doctrinal beliefs I find myself nearer to many a Roman Catholic than to many within the ranks of Protestantism but where I part company with them and must part company is that they add these pluses – Christ, plus the Church, plus the Virgin Mary, plus the priests, plus the saints and so on. Christ alone is not enough and He does not stand in all His unique glory at the centre.
Spiritual Depression, 187

Roman Catholics dislike the doctrine of assurance of salvation, and denounce it. They do not want us to have personal certainty; our assurance must lie in the Church to which we commit ourselves. Not only so, but we have to go through purgatory they say, before we arrive at the promised rest. Everything is uncertain; and all depends upon the Church, and the prayers of the Church for us, and the lighting of candles and the payment of money for indulgences, and the work of supererogation of the saints.
God's Ultimate Purpose, 371

I cannot see a modern Roman Catholic Church in the Scriptures.
Great Doctrines of the Bible (3), 19

With the whole Roman system the Holy Spirit was ignored; the priesthood, the priests, the Church, Mary and the saints were put into the position of the Holy-Spirit.
Great Doctrines of the Bible (2), 5

Can you not see that the very suggestion that we need to pray to Mary, that she may influence him is blasphemous? It is to derogate from his heart of love, from his sympathy, from his understanding, from his nearness to us.
Spiritual Blessing, 28

If you could tell me about Roman Catholic bishops and cardinals who, as a result of the baptism of the Spirit, have tried to reform the Roman Catholic Church and have consequently been turned out or have decided to leave, then I would wholeheartedly accept the genuineness of their experience.
Christian Conduct, 247

The Bible is complete – Old Testament, New Testament – given by God. And it is all: there is nothing further. Everything, therefore, that claims to be revelation must be tested by this. So we reject the doctrine of the immaculate conception; we reject the doctrine likewise of the assumption of the Virgin, and all these various other things for which the Roman Church claims divine and unique authority. It is a violation of the Scripture teaching about itself.
The Gospel of God, 91

ROMANS
Romans is the greatest masterpiece ever written. It is a colossal and incomparable statement of Christian truth.
Christian Conduct, 3

– S –

SABBATH
The Lord's Day is a day that is meant to be given as much as possible to God.
We ought on this day to put everything aside as far as we can, that God may be
honoured and glorified and that His cause may prosper and flourish.
Studies in the Sermon on the Mount, 205

We must never discuss the keeping of the moral law. It is not to be discussed; it
is to be kept. So, I say again that [as] Sabbath observance is a part of the moral
law . . .
Liberty and Conscience, 81

It seems clear to me that the first Christians only changed to the first day of the
week because they had received some supernatural illumination, some guidance. But, whatever the case, the change is perfectly natural. What should be
more natural that that they should have decided that the great day for them to
celebrate should be the first day of the week, the day when our Lord had risen
from the dead?
Liberty and Conscience, 84

I am told that it is the custom in evangelical households for people to write their
family letters on Sunday afternoon. That is breaking the Sabbath, You can write
your letters on some other day.
Liberty and Conscience, 87

SACRAMENT
There is no transmissible grace in a sacrament.
The Righteous Judgement of God, 164

The word 'sacrament' has been used by the Christian Church for many centuries and yet I am very ready to agree with those who teach that it is unfortu-
nate that this word should ever have been used.
Great Doctrines of the Bible (3), 26

The supreme sacrament – if you like to call it such – the supreme means of grace
in the Church, is the word, the word preached and taught.
Great Doctrines of the Bible (3), 57

It is the preaching that conveys the Word to us, and the sacraments seal it, confirm it to us; certify it to us. So we must give supremacy to the preaching over against a sacrament.
The Puritans, 380

The sacraments should always be observed in connection with the preaching of the word. There should never be a service only to meet at the communion table or a service only for baptism. There must be a full church service, and the word must be preached, in order that we may safeguard ourselves from that grievous danger of all Catholicism of regarding a sacrament not only as something in and of itself, but also as the supreme means of receiving grace. I do not hesitate to take my stand with the great Protestant fathers who asserted that the preaching of the word comes first and foremost.
Great Doctrines of the Bible (3), 32

SAINTS

I do not make myself a saint, I am made a saint. I have been separated. Because I realize that I am a saint, I must live as a saint. You see, the whole process is the exact reverse of that false Roman Catholic representation, and there we have the Apostle's description of the Christian.
The Gospel of God, 166

They all seem to reach a point of exhaustion, and even physical suffering.
Spiritual Blessing, 84

To me, one of the most subtle dangers confronting most of us is that for some extraordinary reason, though we have been Protestants and have rejoiced in Protestantism for 400 years, we still seem to appropriate some of those false Roman Catholic distinctions between Christians and non-Christians. We have seen how they draw an essential difference between saints and ordinary Christians. The saints, they say, are special people, or 'spiritual Christians', as opposed to 'worldly Christians', and that is why they ask these worldly Christians to pray to the saints. But that is a distinction which is never recognised in the New Testament; indeed, it is a distinction which it denounces. The *Life of Joy*, 87

As you read the lives of the saints there is nothing which strikes you so much as the way in which they denied themselves to give their all for the sake of others. Such persons are the greatest benefactors the world has ever known and their lives are the most beautiful lives that have ever been lived, the supreme point of beauty being their utter selflessness.
Old Testament Evangelistic Sermons, 51

But the important point about the great saint is not that he spent much time in prayer. He did not keep his eye on the clock. He knew he was in the presence

of God; he entered into eternity as it were. Prayer was his life; he could not live without it.
Studies in the Sermon on the Mount (2), 28

There is no such thing as a 'perfect saint'.
Assurance, 190

There are people who seem to think that the Old Testament saints were not born again; but it is thoroughly unscriptural to say that they were not. We as Christians are Abraham's seed – we are children of Abraham, and children of faith, and the kingdom into which we have entered is the old kingdom in which Abraham, Isaac and Jacob have been for so long.
The Gospel of God, 95

In the Roman Catholic Church Christians are not accounted saints, unless they have been canonised. They are very exceptional and unusual people and are called 'Saint so-and-so'.
The Unsearchable Riches of Christ, 211

The thing the saint wants to know above everything else is that all is well between his soul and the Father. There is nothing the saint delights in more than to know God as his Father. He likes to maintain the contact and communion, to assure his heart before God and in the presence of God. The saint is in this difficult world, there are temptations from the outside and the whole world is against us, and the saint is tried – sometimes he almost despairs. So he goes to God immediately, not to ask this or that but just to make certain that all is well there, that the contact is unbroken and perfect, that he can assure his heart and know that all is well.
Saved in Eternity, 32

Affability is what most people mean by saintliness today. The man who is idealised today is a man who is an aggregate of negatives. The absence of qualities constitutes greatness today. People do not believe in true greatness any longer. They do not believe in goodness, in manliness, in truth itself. It is the smooth, nice, affable man who is popular.
Banner of Truth, Issue 275

The modern view is that men and women who have been canonised by the Church as saints have been monstrosities!
Fellowship with God, 13

SALVATION
Ah! you may admire the life of Jesus Christ and feel that His words and works were wonderful; you may shed tears as you think of Him as the babe born in that manger or as you watch Him at the end forsaken of all and crucified; you

may feel a great desire to follow Him and to imitate Him and His life, but you will never feel your whole soul and entire being going out to God in gratitude, wonder and adoration, until you are conscious of the fact that He died for you and until you have experienced His life and power flooding your own, changing it and transforming it, infusing power into it, turning your defeats into victories and liberating you from the power of sin. And that is offered to you tonight in the gospel of Jesus Christ.
Evangelistic Sermons, 201

entry
No one ever comes to Christ until the point of desperation has been reached.
God's Way Not Ours, 71

You will never know the blessings of salvation until you have cast yourself, just as you are, in utter helplessness up the sole mercy of God.
God's Way Not Ours, 93

experience
To believe that your sins are forgiven by the death of Christ is not enough. Even to be sound on the whole doctrine of justification by faith only – the great watchword of the Protestant Reformation – that is not enough. That can be held as an intellectual opinion, and if people merely hold on to a number of orthodox opinions, they are not, I repeat, in the truly Christian position. The essence of the Christian position and of the Christian life is that we should be able to say, 'Truly my fellowship is with the Father, and with His Son Jesus Christ.'
Fellowship with God, 79

The ultimate object of salvation is not merely to keep us from hell, not merely to deliver us from certain sins; it is that we may enjoy 'adoption' and that we may become 'the children of God' and 'joint-heirs with Christ'. The *'summum bonum'* is to 'see God', and while in this life, to know God intimately as our Father, and to cry 'Abba, Father'.
The Sons of God, 245

The Lord Jesus Christ did not come from heaven, and live and die and rise again, just to procure forgiveness for us and to ensure that we should not go to hell. Salvation does not stop there; it includes much more than putting us back to where Adam was before he fell.
Assurance, 235

plan
The older theologians of centuries ago used to say – and I think there is very good evidence in the Bible for what they said – that, before time, a great Council was held between the Father and the Son and the Holy Spirit about this question of the world and its salvation. And the decision of the Council was that this

matter was to be handed over to the Son, and the Son took it and said, 'Here am
I send me.'
Authentic Christianity (4), 161–62

The three blessed Persons in the eternal council were concerned about us –
Father, Son and Holy Spirit. In the first chapter of the Book of Genesis we read
that God said, 'Let us make man in our image', but, thank God, that council not
only considered the creation of man, it went on to consider also the salvation of
man. The Three Persons met in conference [I speak with reverence . . .] and
planned it. Let us get rid for ever of the idea that salvation was an afterthought
in the mind of God. It was not a thought that came to God after man had fallen
into – it was planned 'before the foundation of the world'
God's Ultimate Purpose, 53

This idea that the Lord Jesus Christ is at great pains to persuade God the Father
to forgive and accept us is utterly unscriptural and entirely false; the source and
origin of salvation is the great and eternal heart of God.
Saved in Eternity, 55

The whole tenor of scriptural teaching is entirely against the theory of a second
chance.
Great Doctrines of the Bible (3), 76

Salvation is not an afterthought.
Assurance, 106

total
It is not merely our minds that are saved, it is not merely our spirits or our
hearts, the body is also saved. It is a complete salvation, and I think that this is
of tremendous importance.
Christian Conduct, 44

'Not the righteous, sinners Jesus came to save'. Those who can swim and save
themselves will never be helped, it is only the drowning and the desperate who
can have the joy of being taken hold of by the everlasting arms of God in Jesus
Christ.
Old Testament Evangelistic Sermons, 265

There is no indication whatsoever that our Lord finally conquered the devil and
his powers in hell after His death; indeed we are told, positively, that the work
was done upon the Cross.
Christian Unity, 159

As God has arranged that the farmer should plough up the earth, and break it
up, and then put in his seed and roll it, and the seed later germinates and

sprouts and appears above the ground, and then develops and finally matures – so He does in the matter of our salvation.
Assurance, 337

Salvation, redemption, regeneration do not merely put us back where Adam was; we are in a much higher position.
Great Doctrines of the Bible (1), 170

By the grace of God, men and women, who may be muddled in their thinking and in their understanding of the mechanism of salvation, can still be saved.
Great Doctrines of the Bible (2), 58

value
How often do you think of your salvation in this way? 'The glory of God'!
Assurance, 96

Most if not all of our problems in the Christian life would be solved, if only we realised the greatness of our salvation.
Banner of Truth, Issue 275

If you ask, How is any man saved? There is only one answer: It is because God has chosen him. Why is a man lost? A man is lost because he is a wilful and a deliberate sinner, and a proud and boastful sinner, who rejects the offer of salvation.
God's Sovereign Purpose, 286

working
It is the Spirit acting upon the soul from within and producing within us a new principle of spiritual action.
Great Doctrines of the Bible (2), 71

Even when you were unconcerned, he began to interfere with your life, he came after you, and he disturbed you. God's initiating!
The Life of Joy, 169

Man can do nothing at all in the matter of his salvation – absolutely nothing.
Assurance, 114

We are saved by what he does. Our salvation is entirely his prerogative. It is entirely in his hands and he does not commit himself to all who approach him.
Spiritual Blessing, 201

There are not two ways of salvation. Salvation was by faith in Christ in the Old [Testament] exactly as in the New, and it always will be.
Saving Faith, 251

SANCTIFICATION

It does seem to me to be entirely contrary to the Apostle's doctrine to teach that we are to be sanctified in a passive manner and that we should do nothing but wait for God to do everything for us.
The Life of Joy, 167

If the 'entire sanctification' teaching were true . . . these New Testament Epistles would never have been needed.
The Sons of God, 380

My understanding of the doctrine is the motive and the controlling power in my living of the sanctified life in Christ Jesus.
Christian Conduct, 29

We do not just get born again and then remain there, static, holding on to what we have, rather giving the impression that we have lost something wonderful and that the great thrill we had at the beginning has gone. That is machinery, not life. This is a life that changes us 'from glory into glory', and it is endless and eternal.
Spiritual Blessing, 112

We must realise that experience, the experience of the greatest saints, denies this teaching of sinless perfection and we see that that is not in accordance with the teaching of Scripture.
Children of God, 80

There is no better way of preaching sanctification than preaching about Adam as he was before the Fall. That is what man was meant to be.
Life in the Spirit in Marriage Home and Work, 166

The sealing with the Spirit is not sanctification. The teaching of the Scripture is that the moment a man is 'born again' his sanctification has and must have started. The process of making him holy and separating him unto God has already begun.
God's Ultimate Purpose, 261

You must never say that at one stage you have only taken Christ as your justification, or as your righteousness, and that later on you may take Him as your sanctification. That is dividing Christ: and He cannot be divided.
The New Man, 40

God's character – if I may so put it – would be exposed to the laughter of the devil, and all hell, if any one of the chosen and the called and the redeemed did not arrive in heaven absolutely perfect and spotless.
The New Man, 143

Nowhere does the Scripture call upon you to crucify your old man; nowhere does the Scripture tell you to get rid of your old man, for the obvious reason that he has already gone. Not to realize this is to allow the devil to fool you and to delude you. What you and I are called upon to do is to cease to live as if we were still in Adam. Understand that the 'old man' is not there. The only way to stop living as if he were still there is to realize that he is not there. That is the New Testament method of teaching sanctification.
The New Man, 65

Sanctification is not an experience to be received, it is the working out of the life of God in the soul, and it starts from the moment of re-birth.
God's Ultimate Purpose, 285

If you try to imitate Christ, the world will praise you; if you become Christ-like, the world will hate you!
Banner of Truth Issue, 275

God looks at men and women in their sins, and applying to them the righteousness of Christ, declares them to be just. That is *imputed* righteousness. But in sanctification, we are discussing *imparted* righteousness. Not the righteousness that is put to my account, but the righteousness that is created within me and produced within me. Now that is a great distinction.
Great Doctrines of the Bible (2), 195

There is, therefore, an essential difference between the best moral person that the world may put forward and the Christian who is being sanctified.
Great Doctrines of the Bible (2), 196

It is something that is started by God, continued by God and perfected by God Himself. The moment, therefore, that we are regenerate and united to the Lord Jesus Christ, the process of sanctification has already started. The moment I receive the divine nature, the moment I am born again, something has come into me which is going to separate me from sin.
Great Doctrines of the Bible (2), 204

Sanctification is not an experience, it is a condition.
Great Doctrines of the Bible (2), 218

Sanctification, as we have seen, is a process that begins the moment we are regenerate; it begins, indeed the moment we are justified. You cannot be justified without the process of sanctification having already started.
Great Doctrines of the Bible (2), 247

Sanctification is of supreme importance, but where sanctification comes in is this: your effort to walk in the light is part of your sanctification and so is your confessing your sins and recognising them.
Fellowship with God, 41

We must never separate sanctification from justification; we must never separate holiness and forgiveness; we must never talk about a kind of series of separate blessings; all is one – it all belongs together.
Children of God, 57

After our sins have been forgiven and sin and guilt have been removed from us, the sin principle will remain within us, and what the New Testament means by this doctrine of sanctification is the process whereby the very principle and the activity of sin within us is being taken out of us and removed.
Fellowship with God from *Life in Christ: Studies in 1 John*, 138

The moment a man is born again and this divine seed or principle enters into him, the life has started and there is this imperceptible growth. But let a man like that be baptized with the Holy Spirit, let the rain and the sunshine of the Spirit come upon him, let the love of God be shed abroad in his heart, and you will see him springing up into life and vigour and activity; his sanctification, everything about him, is stimulated in a most amazing and astonishing manner. But, it is an indirect connection, not direct and not the same thing. There is an inevitable and intimate relationship and yet the two things must be thought of separately; otherwise there will be nothing but confusion. And the confusion has often taken place in the long history of the Christian Church.
Joy Unspeakable, 298

If God is your Father, somewhere or another, in some form or other, the family likeness will be there, the traces of your Parentage will inevitably appear.
Studies in the Sermon on the Mount, 320

SATAN (Devil, Demonism)
Satan has already been judged. He was judged by the work done on the cross; it was proclaimed by the sending of the Holy Spirit. And it is a fact. Our Lord's last great commission to His followers was, 'All power is given unto me in heaven and in earth. Go ye therefore, and teach all nations, baptizing them in the name of the Father, and of the Son, and of the Holy Ghost' (Matt. 28:18–19). He *has* this power.
Great Doctrines of the Bible (2), 48

The lie of Satan is the lie against God at the beginning.
Children of God, 64

The devil is always waiting to confuse and muddle us. He wants to destroy God's work. He can turn himself into an angel of light. He can produce counterfeits. In a very subtle way, he can insinuate his own thinking, and what starts correctly can end by being terribly wrong.
Spiritual Blessing, 158

SCHOLARSHIP
There is no such thing as pure scholarship.
The Final Perseverance of the Saints, 320

How over-awed we are by 'scholarship'!
God's Sovereign Purpose, 80

I am not dejected and I am not discouraged – I have faith in – what? Modern scholarship? Most certainly not! Scholarship denies the power of the Spirit because it is bound by human understanding. Modern scholarship would take everything from us, everything that really is the gospel.
Authentic Christianity (3), 161

SCIENCE
My dear friends, if your position is going to depend upon what scientists may or may not say, well then I tremble for you. They have their fashions, they say one thing one day and it will be denied the next.
The Gospel of God, 67

Let us be scientifically sceptical with regard to the assertions of 'Science'.
Authority, 40

Scientists *are* very fallible gentlemen
The Fight of Faith, 318

Science is very much more humble today than it was at the beginning of the century.
Great Doctrines of the Bible (1), 135

Let us never compromise the truth of God to fit any scientific theory.
Great Doctrines of the Bible (1), 139

I am not aware of any real contradiction between the teaching of the Bible and true, established scientific facts.
Great Doctrines of the Bible (1), 133

The time will soon come when that scientific theory, if it contradicts the Bible, will be replaced by another. We must never allow our position to be determined for us by the passing theories or current of so-called scientific opinion.
Great Doctrines of the Bible (1), 139

SECOND COMING
This will be the Phenomenon of phenomena.
To God's Glory, 234

The Christian knows that that Christ who is now in the heavenly places will come again to this world in a visible form, riding upon the clouds of heaven, surrounded by the holy angels and the saints who are already with Him; and those who remain on earth when He comes will be changed and will rise into the air to meet Him, and all will be 'for ever with the Lord'. He will rout His enemies, and banish sin and evil. His kingdom shall 'stretch from shore to shore' and He shall be acclaimed as Lord by 'things that are in heaven and on the earth and things that are under the earth' (Philippians 2:10). That is Christian optimism, and it means that we know that it is Christ alone who can and will conquer.
God's Ultimate Purpose, 80

It is the blessed hope, it is that to which the Church is looking forward and at the same time, of course, it is the greatest incentive to holy living.
Great Doctrines of the Bible (3), 85

I have New Testament authority for saying that it is possible for Christian people to know something of a sense of shame when they see Him as He is. The Apostle John in his First Epistle exhorts the early Christians to press forward in these respects so that they may 'not be ashamed before him at his coming'. There is clear teaching of a judgment involving rewards among believers, so we must consider this matter in the light of that teaching. The man who thinks that as long as he is forgiven, as long as he is saved, and as long as he knows that he is going to heaven, all is well, will discover that in adopting such an attitude he has been rejecting his Lord's teaching. The Lord meant him to enjoy so much more, and to use him to help others, and to use him as a pattern and an example.
The Unsearchable Riches of Christ, 254

If there is one subject about which dogmatism should be entirely excluded it is this.
Great Doctrines of the Bible (3), 97

SELF
Self is our last and our most constant enemy; and it is the most prolific cause of all our unhappiness.
Faith on Trial, 71

Sensitivity about self – is not this one of the greatest curses in life? It is a result of the Fall. We spend the whole of our life watching ourselves.
Banner of Truth, Issue 275

The curse of life is that we are all self-centred. We live for self instead of for God, and thus we are selfish, we are jealous, and we are envious.
Great Doctrines of the Bible (1), 207

You will never be able to love your neighbour as yourself until you know the truth about yourself; and you will never know the truth about yourself until you have seen yourself in the sight of God.
Authentic Christianity (4) 28

Take a statement found in the Biography of George Müller of Bristol, the founder and establisher of Müller's Homes. He says quite solemnly, 'A day came when I died to George Müller completely, utterly, absolutely; all he was and all he had and possessed and all he hoped to be. I died utterly, absolutely to George Müller.' That is the secret, the final end and the death of self! And only as we reach that state shall we know true freedom, and be able to master the wiles of the devil in this particular respect.
The Christian Warfare, 343

There is nothing so foolish as to wish you were something that you are not – a desire to be tall or to be short, a desire to be of this colour or that colour, to have this power or that power. What a foolish thing it is! How useless, for you cannot change yourself! But more, why should you want to change? It is a wonderful thing to be yourself. You are an individual made by God. These things are not accidental. There is great value in individuality.
The Christian Warfare, 310

We have motives and interests that the world knows not of, there are depths within us known only to ourselves, struggles with ourselves and our passions, suggestions and thoughts rising from some dark hidden corner in our souls!
Old Testament Evangelistic Sermons, 239

The man who does not realise that he himself is his own biggest problem is a mere tyro!
Banner of Truth, Issue 275

Consider yourself and your own experience. Face for a moment the struggles that go on within your own heart. Conjure up the vain thoughts and desires that grip you and control you from time to time. Would you like to state them all in public? Would you like the world to know all about you?
Old Testament Evangelistic Sermons, 76

So do you not think it is time you thought again about yourselves? Are you perfectly satisfied? Is all well with you? Do you not think you had better draw up a balance sheet? What are your assets? What is the value of your morality? What is the value of your knowledge? What is the value of your goodness in the sight of God? Think again, my dear friend. What have you made of life?
Authentic Christianity (1), 323

Testing, therefore, is a very vital and urgent matter because of this terrible possibility of self-delusion.
Life in God, 28

We, none of us, see the essential self of anybody, nor of ourselves. You have never really seen yourself. I wonder if you have ever thought of that? Try to think of yourself and what you look like; you cannot really do it. That is because our essential being, our personality, is invisible. When you look at another person you are seeing certain manifestations of that person but you are not really seeing the person.
Great Doctrines of the Bible (1), 172

I would say that the greatest sinners in the world are the self-satisfied, self-contained, good moral people, who believe that, as they are, they are fit to stand in the presence of God. Moreover, they are in reality telling God that He need never have sent His Son into the world as far as they are concerned, and that the Son need never have died upon the Cross. There is no greater insult to God than that; but it is precisely what they are guilty of. There is no greater sinner in the universe than the man who has never seen his need of the blood of Christ. There is no sin greater than that – murder and adultery and fornication are nothing in comparison with it.
Assurance, 291

examination
Self-examination is vital and essential. A man who does not know something of the plague of his own heart is, to say the least, a very poor specimen of a Christian.
Assurance, 159

In a certain churchyard there is a tombstone on which are to be seen the words, 'Here lies So-and-so; born a man, died a grocer'. A man is never meant to die as a grocer, he is meant to be a man. We are all souls in the sight of God.
The Christian Warfare, 320

True self-examination should drive us to Christ; and there we see the finished work which God sent Him to do, and we end by rejoicing. If your self-examination does not end in rejoicing it is wrong.
Assurance, 166

The way to treat a wound is not just to ignore it or to give it some superficial treatment; the right treatment is to probe it. It is painful, but it has to be done. If you want it to be cleansed and purified and healthy you have to apply the probe. Let us therefore probe this wound, this putrefying sore that is in the soul of every one of us, in order that we may be cleansed.
Studies in the Sermon on the Mount (2), 166

If you don't do a great deal of preaching to yourself, you are a very poor kind of Christian.
Banner of Truth, Issue 275

Self-examination is not popular today, especially, strangely enough, amongst evangelical Christians. Indeed, one often finds that evangelical Christians not only object to self-examination, but occasionally even regard it as almost sinful. Their argument is that a Christian should look only to the Lord Jesus Christ.
Studies in the Sermon on the Mount (2), 276

That is what the masters in the spiritual life have always done. Read their manuals, read the journals of the most saintly people who have adorned the life of the Church, and you will find that they have always done that. I have reminded you of John Fletcher. He not only asked twelve questions of himself before he went to sleep each night but he got his congregation to do the same. He did not content himself with a cursory general examination; he examined himself in detail, with such questions as: Do I lose my temper? Have I lost my temper? Have I made life more difficult for somebody else? Did I listen to that insinuation that the devil put in my mind, that unclean idea? Did I cling to it or immediately reject it? You go through the day and you put it all before yourself and face it. That is true self examination.
Faith on Trial, 70

A man who knows his own heart is a man who cannot be light and carefree and flippant.
The Life of Joy, 180

As Christians we should never feel sorry for ourselves. The moment we do so, we lose our energy, we lose the will to fight and the will to live, and are paralysed.
Banner of Truth, Issue 275

SELFISHNESS
Selfishness does not always take the form of greed and is not always 'grabbing'. There is another type of selfishness, the type which shows itself by its lack of concern about the lot of others.
Old Testament Evangelistic Sermons, 49–50

SENTIMENTALISM
Sentimentalism is nothing but polite emotionalism. That is the only difference. It is the difference, as it were, between emotionalism in rags and emotionalism in evening dress.
The Christian Warfare, 203

Sentiment is a pretence . . . We must never be satisfied with what just does duty for emotion, we should always desire to feel the profundity of the truth.
Assurance, 141

If a man when preaching tells an affecting story you feel something. It was not the truth that made you feel, it was the story, the illustration. That is typical of sentimentalism. It is never gripped by truth, but it is very much interested in the form in which the truth is conveyed; in other words, in the mechanism, in the presentation.
The Christian Warfare, 203

This is surely the biggest fight the Christian Church has to wage at this present hour. There has been a lowering of moral standards everywhere. We have travelled very far from the days of Puritanism. The line between the Church and the world is almost invisible, and the people of God no longer stand out in their uniqueness as they once did.
God's Ultimate Purpose, 417

SERMON (Preachers, Preaching)
People began to talk about the 'address' in the service instead of the sermon. That in itself was indicative of a subtle change. An 'address'. No longer the sermon, but an 'address' perhaps even a lecture. I shall be dealing with these distinctions later. There was a man in the USA who published a series of books under the significant title of Quiet Talks. Quiet Talks, you see, as against the 'ranting' of the preachers! Quiet Talks on Prayer; Quiet Talks on Power, etc. In other words the very title announces that the man is not going to preach. Preaching, of course, is something carnal lacking in spirituality, what is needed is a chat, a fireside chat, quiet talks and so on!
Preaching and Preachers, 16

A sermon is not a running commentary on, or a mere exposition of, the meaning of a verse or a passage or a paragraph. I emphasise this because there are many today who have become interested in what they regard as expository preaching but who show very clearly that they do not know what is meant by expository preaching.
Preachers and Preaching, 72

I have been told on excellent authority that there is a Church which is attended at certain seasons of the year by most distinguished personages, in which instructions are given to the preacher that he is not to preach for more than seven minutes.
Christian Unity, 201–2

recommendation
Read the sermons of Spurgeon and Whitefield and Edwards and all the giants. Those men themselves read the Puritans and were greatly helped by them. They seem to have lived on the Puritans. Well, let the young preacher in turn live on them, or perhaps be led by them to the Puritans.
Preaching and Preachers, 120

tape
Tape-recording – as I see it, the peculiar and special abomination at this present time.
Preachers and Preaching, 18

SERMON ON THE MOUNT

No one can really live the Sermon on the Mount until they are born again; the Sermon on the Mount is impossible to the natural man or woman.
Children of God, 12

I would rather make bricks without straw than try to live the Sermon on the Mount in my own strength.
Banner of Truth, Issue 275

There is nothing that so utterly condemns us as the Sermon on the Mount; there is nothing so utterly impossible, so terrifying, and so full of doctrine. Indeed, I do not hesitate to say that, were it not that I knew of the doctrine of justification by faith only, I would never look at the Sermon on the Mount, because it is a Sermon before which we all stand completely naked and altogether without hope. Far from being something practical that we can take up and put into practice, it is of all teaching the most impossible if we are left to ourselves. This great Sermon is full of doctrine and leads to doctrine; it is a kind of prologue to all the doctrine of the New Testament.
Studies in the Sermon on the Mount (2), 160

There is nothing more discouraging than the Sermon on the Mount; it seems to throw us right out, and to damn our every effort before we have started. It seems utterly impossible. But at the same time do we know of anything more encouraging than the Sermon on the Mount? Do we know of anything that pays us a greater compliment? The very fact that we are commanded to do these things carries with it an implicit assertion that it is possible. This is what we are supposed to be doing; and there is a suggestion, therefore, that this is what we can do. It is discouraging and encouraging at the same time; it is set for the fall and rising again. And nothing is more vital than that we should always be holding those two aspects firmly in our minds.
Studies in the Sermon on the Mount, 311

The Christian feels that that Sermon is exactly what he would expect from God, that that is how all men should live, and that if the whole world but lived in that way we should have Paradise once more.
The Sons of God, 45

If only everybody on earth today were living according to the Sermon on the Mount, we would not have the industrial, the moral and the social problems that we are now facing. There would be no wars anywhere. If only everybody lived like this!
Authentic Christianity (3), 185

If you want to have power in your life and to be blessed, go straight to the Sermon on the Mount. Live and practise it and give yourself to it, and as you do so the promised blessings will come. 'Blessed are they which do hunger and thirst after righteousness: for they shall be filled.'
Studies in the Sermon on the Mount (1), 18

SEX

He has put the sexual instinct, and the other instincts in us and they are to be used in God's way. A false asceticism is a denial of scriptural teaching and is condemned by Scripture itself.
Great Doctrines of the Bible (3), 238

There is nothing wrong in sex, but, again, if the element of excess comes in, it is bad. The world today is living for sex and nothing can be more terrible. It is worse even than the worship of the body . . . To put it bluntly and plainly, sex is given to you by God, but if you use your body and your sexuality to indulge yourself and your own appetites, you are not only violating your body, you are violating your human constitution.
Christian Conduct, 67

No one has ever been cured of immorality by reading books on the control of sex – never has been, never will.
God's Way Not Ours, 68

Sex can be used to the glory of God, just as you can eat and drink to the glory of God, and walk to the glory of God. If you think that sex cannot be used to the glory of God you have misunderstood the whole of this teaching and you are not in a Christian position.
Christian Conduct, 68

God has given us these gifts, sex included. There is nothing wrong in the erotic element in and of itself; indeed I go further, I say that it should be present. I refer to this because I am so often asked to deal with these things. I have known Christian people who very honestly, because of this wrong view of sex, and of that which is natural, have more or less come to the conclusion that any Christian man can marry any Christian woman. They say that the only thing that matters and counts now is that we are Christians. They do away altogether with the natural element.
Life in the Spirit in Marriage Home and Work, 135

sex education

I have never believed in what is called morality teaching – I mean the teaching about sex which in some quarters is now being introduced into the schools, and for this reason, that, as the result of sin, the minds of the children are not pure, and what such teaching is likely to do is to create in them a greater desire to

know about these things and to do them. They already find out about these matters surreptitiously; and the teaching will simply intensify that interest and so stimulate them to sin.
Assurance, 293–94

I have made a strong statement; but I am ready to assert that the Victorian attitude towards sex, in actual practice, was more successful than the present-day method. I am not concerned to defend Victorianism, but to expound the Scriptures; and the Scripture says that moral teaching in and of itself can be dangerous.
The Law: Its Functions and Limits, 81

No one has ever been cured of immorality by reading books on the control of sex – never has been, never will.
God's Way Not Ours, 68

There have been false teachers in the past who have said that some of these natural instincts are sinful. There have been those who have regarded the sex instinct, for instance, as inherently and essentially sinful. It is not so. It is God who put it in us as a vital part of the body. There is nothing wrong in sex. Wrong comes in when sex dominates the whole person, instead of being kept in its right position, and put to its right use.
The New Man, 75

If you are not pure, some things which are good in themselves may be harmful. That is why I never believe in giving sex-morality teaching to children in schools. You are introducing them to sin.
Sermon on the Mount, 240

There was a time when everybody would agree in condemning sexual perversion, but not today – it is almost gloried in. That is public opinion with respect to morality. You never know. A view that is right today may be wrong tomorrow.
Authentic Christianity (1), 130

SICKNESS
Our infirmities may lead us to sin, but our infirmities in and of themselves are not sinful. They are undoubtedly the result and the consequence of the original Fall of man, because there were no infirmities in man as God made him. God made him perfect. But one of the tragedies of the Fall is that everyone born into the world after the Fall of man is 'compassed by infirmities'. There are certain weaknesses, lack of powers, certain disabilities and inabilities that result from the Fall.
The Final Perseverance of the Saints, 124

He may have to apply to you the acid of 'weakness', or the acid of 'sickness' but it will be for your good. Do not misunderstand me. This does not mean that every time

we are ill it is of necessity a chastisement. The Scripture does not say that; but it does say that it may be. That has often happened. You can read many instances of it in Scripture. Paul realized that the thorn in the flesh was given him in order to keep him humble lest he be exalted over-much. (2 Corinthians 12:7–10). There are foolish and glib people who say that it is never the Lord's will that a man should be ill. The Scripture teaches that 'the Lord chasteneth whom He loveth', and this is one of His ways – 'many are weak and many are sickly among you, and many sleep'.
Life in the Spirit in Marriage Home and Work, 180

SIN
[Sin] is an invader.
Assurance, 194

[Sin] is a tyranny.
Assurance, 306

[Sin] is the greatest power in the universe apart from the power of God
A Nation Under Wrath, 130

[Sin] is moral or ethical evil; not evil in general, but a particular kind of evil.
Great Doctrines of the Bible (1), 192

[Sin] is not an intellectual problem, it is a moral problem.
Old Testament Evangelistic Sermons, 134

[Sin] is always in some sense a life of boredom.
Banner of Truth, Issue 275

If only we could see the real nature of sin, we should hate it.
Walking with God, 16

[Sin] always leads ultimately to a sense of utter hopelessness.
Walking with God, 19

In spite of all efforts the jungle is still encroaching.
Authentic Christianity (3), 106

Oh, what a robber sin is!
God's Way Not Ours, 80

The doctrine of sin has never been popular.
Fellowship with God, 12

The presence of God at once convicts of sin.
Fellowship with God, 36

All sin interrupts the life of fellowship with God.
Life in God, 134

With the whole of my being I shun sin.
Children of God, 44

Sin is the greatest power in the world, with one exception, and this is the power of God.
God's Way Not Ours, 65

The holier we become, the more anger we shall feel against sin. But we must never, I repeat, feel anger against the sinner.
Studies in the Sermon on the Mount (1), 226

Whatever we may think, we cannot be right and clear about the way of salvation unless we are right and clear about sin.
The Law: Its Functions and Limits, 151

I do not want a catalogue of your sins. I do not care what your sins are. They can be very respectable or they can be heinous, vile, foul, filthy. It does not matter, thank God. But what I have authority to tell you is this. Though you may be the vilest man or woman ever known and though you may until this moment have lived your life in the gutters and the brothels of sin in every shape and form. I say this to you, be it known unto you that through this man, this Lord, Jesus is preached unto you the forgiveness of sins.
   When sin reigns a coarsening process always follows, and increases as the grip of sin over men tightens.
Assurance, 311

Sin ultimately robs you even of the desire for evil things. The drunkard tires of drink and turns to drugs.
Banner of Truth, Issue 275

Man in sin is not free to sin. He is governed and ruled and controlled by sin.
Assurance, 306

This is a painful process; to confess my sins does not just mean that I say in general, 'Well, I am a sinner – I have never claimed to be a saint.' No, rather it comes to the details. I must confess my particular sins, I must name them one by one; it means that I must not gloss over them, I must not attempt to deny them. I must confess them, I must look at them. There must be no attempt to dismiss them as quickly as possible. Confession means facing them, not trying to balance up the sins I have committed and the good deeds I have done. No I must let the light so search me that I feel miserable and wretched – this honest facing

of the things I have done and of what I am; it means that I must confess it to God in words.
Fellowship with God, 32

The nearer a man gets to God the greater he sees his sin.
Spiritual Depression, 70

When Paul looks at his past and sees his sin he does not stay in a corner and say: 'I am not fit to be a Christian, I have done such terrible things'. Not at all. What it does to him, its effect upon him, is to make him praise God. He glories in grace and says: 'And the grace of our Lord was exceeding abundant with faith a love which is in Christ Jesus'.
Spiritual Depression, 75

consequences
The truth is that because God is God and because He is what He is – I say it with reverence – there are certain things that He must do, and one of them is that He must punish sin. God would not be God if He did not do so.
God's Sovereign Purpose, 212

The sinner has the frown of God upon him.
Assurance, 33

Man in sin is a pygmy fighting against Almighty God – like a fly pitting itself against atomic power!
Banner of Truth, Issue 275

Every Christian who falls into sin is a fool.
The New Man, 27

There is a very interesting statement about this in Paul's first letter to Timothy: 'Some men's sins are open beforehand, going before to judgment; and some men they follow after' (1 Tim. 5:24). Now this is what that means among other things. It not only means that the sins of some men are obvious and others hidden, and you are not so sure. It does mean that, but it also means the punishment; some are made plain and God punishes. Two men may commit the same sin; one has the immediate physical consequences, the other has nothing. God punishes one immediately. In the case of the other He holds it back and He postpones it.
The Gospel of God, 350

original
My very nature is polluted; there is a desire for and an inclination towards evil. Apart from my actions, my *nature* is sinful, and that is where all the sinless perfectionists who think of sin only in terms of actions go so sadly and hopelessly

astray. Before I do anything, my nature is polluted; there is a sinful propensity in me, and I need to be delivered from that. I need to be saved from it; and, blessed by the name of God, according to the Scriptures the Lord Jesus Christ as Saviour deals with that problem also! He not only saves from the guilt of sin and the power of sin but also from this terrible pollution of sin, and that is the special work of the Holy Spirit within us.
The Love of God, 14

You and I here upon the earth, with our finite and sinful minds, are confronted with a problem. It is this: Why did God decree to permit sin? And there is only one answer to that question: We do not know. We know that He did decree to permit sin, or sin would never have taken place. Why, we do not know. It is an insoluble problem. But we shall see it all clearly when we are in glory and face to face with God.
Great Doctrines of the Bible (1), 100

power
Sin, far from being a mere weakness or negation, is actually an overpowering and blinding force which defeats even the strongest human nature.
Old Testament Evangelistic Sermons, 76

No man is isolated in his rebellion against God. He can always quote great and inspiring and impressive names for support.
Old Testament Evangelistic Sermons, 93

Sin is something so terrible, according to our Lord's exposure of it, that it will not only follow us to the gates of heaven, but – if it were possible – into heaven itself.
Studies in the Sermon on the Mount (2), 21

Human nature is so sinful that even good clean instruction will do people harm. They will twist it, feed upon it and gloat over it. Sin twists even God's law so that it makes us worse than we were before and kills us.
God's Way Not Ours, 68

The Church is to be concerned about sin in all its manifestations, and sin can be as terrible in a capitalist as in a communist; it can be as terrible in a rich man as in a poor man; it can manifest itself in all classes and in all types and in all groups.
Studies in the Sermon on the Mount (1), 156

A man who says that he is entirely free from sin, that he never commits an act of sin, is a man who is guilty at some point or other of misunderstanding the meaning of sin.
The Law: Its Functions and Limits, 199

Sin and God are eternal opposites, and with all the intensity of His being God abhors sin and desires to punish it.
God's Sovereign Purpose, 211

The point about the life of sin is that you have to be healthy to enjoy it!
Banner of Truth, Issue 275

Nothing is quite so fallacious as to think of sin only in terms of actions; and as long as we think of sin only in terms of things actually done, we fail to understand it. The essence of the biblical teaching on sin is that it is essentially a disposition. It is a state of heart. I suppose we can sum it up by saying that sin is ultimately self-worship and self-adulation.
Studies in the Sermon on the Mount (2), 22

terror
The adder, or viper, which is so harmful and so poisonous, has the poison concealed in a little bag at the root of the lips. This little bag is under the upper jaw of the adder close to some fangs which lie in a horizontal position. When the adder is about to pounce upon a victim he puts back his head and as he does so, these teeth or fangs drop down and he bites the victim. As he is biting with the fangs one of them presses the bag that is full of poison and into the wound is injected this venom, this poison that is going to kill the victim! So the Bible gives an exact scientific description of how the adder kills by means of his poison.
The Righteous Judgement of God, 211

Do you notice how the Apostle personifies sin? 'Wherefore', he says, 'as by one man sin entered into the world . . .' Sin opened a door. Sin 'came in'. Sin is personified. Later he says that 'sin reigned'. What does he mean by this? It is his way of stating that sin is not merely a lack of certain qualities, not merely a negative phase, but that sin is active, sin is positive, sin is something that does things; it enters in, reigns, rules, governs and manifests a tremendous degree of activity. Clearly we have here a complete contradiction of the non-biblical view. This personification of sin is characteristic of the biblical teaching. That is not surprising, for sin entered in through the person of the devil. The other view of course does not believe in the devil. It ridicules the whole notion of the devil and laughs it to scorn. 'Fancy still believing in the devil!' they say. But here the Apostle shows that sin, as a thing most positive, must have a sufficient cause to account for it. So he personifies it to remind us that it entered in in that way.
Assurance, 193

Knowledge of sin has never prevented anybody from sinning. Indeed, the more one knows about it the more one is subject to the temptation to do it.
Assurance, 294

unpardonable
If you are troubled by the thought that you have sinned against the Holy Ghost, it follows automatically that you are not guilty of it, simply because you are troubled about it.
The Christian Warfare, 261

To be afraid that you are guilty of it is proof that you are not.
Life in God, 138

A man who has committed *the* sin against the Holy Ghost is not concerned about forgiveness; he ridicules the grace of God and the gospel.
The Sons of God, 230

Whenever anyone tells me that he [or she] is worried about his [or her] soul's salvation, I always say, 'You are a believer, for you would not be worried if you were not'. False believers are never worried. They say, 'Lord, Lord, have we not done this, that, and the other?' They may be very active and busy persons in the church; but they are never worried, never troubled, and they dislike preaching that disturbs and causes them to examine themselves.
The Final Perseverance of the Saints, 332

SLAVERY
What Christianity is interested in is the way in which a Christian slave behaves himself towards his master, and how the master behaves towards his slave. It does not deal directly with the question of slavery *per se*.
Life in the Spirit in Marriage Home and Work, 323

But in many ways . . . Christianity really solved the problem of slavery at the beginning. That is the message of the Epistle to Philemon. 'Philemon', says Paul in effect, 'I am sending back to you this run-away slave of yours, Onesimus. He happened to be in the same prison as I myself, and he has become a Christian. I am sending him back to you, not only as a slave, but now as a brother. You are a Christian, Philemon, and so is Onesimus. He is coming back to you to occupy the old position; but of course he is now a different man. Therefore though the actual situation, and the external relationship, has not changed, in reality everything has changed. Onesimus is now a beloved brother. Receive him as such'. Here we have the real solution of the problem of slavery; the two men, the master and the slave, have become Christians. But, you notice, that while it really 'solves' the problem in its essence, it leaves it in existence as a political and a social problem. That is the method of Christianity.
Life in the Spirit in Marriage Home and Work, 336

Take the case of those poor slaves in the United States of America about a hundred years ago. There they were in a condition of slavery. Then the American Civil War came, and as the result of that war slavery was abolished

in the United States. But what had actually happened? All slaves, young and old, were given their freedom, but many of the older ones who had endured long years of servitude found it very difficult to understand their new status. They heard the announcement that slavery was abolished and that they were free: but hundreds, not to say thousands, of times in their after lives and experiences many of them did not realize it, and when they saw their old master coming near them they began to quake and to tremble, and to wonder whether they were going to be sold. They were free, they were no longer slaves; the law had been changed, and their status and their position was entirely different; but it took them a very long time to realize it. You can still be a slave experimentally, even when you are no longer a slave legally. You can be a slave in your feelings when actually in respect of your position you have been emancipated completely. So it is with the Christian.
The New Man, 25–26

SOCIETY

The church cannot change conditions: and she is not meant to change conditions. And the moment she tries to do so she is in many ways shutting the door of evangelistic opportunity.
Life in the Spirit in Marriage, Home and Work, 329

The trouble today is that the leaders of the Christian church are spending too much of their time in dealing with these things directly. They are always preaching about them, sending messages and protests to governments, taking part in processions. Direct action! The Bible never does that . . .
Life in the Spirit in Marriage, Home and Work, 323

SOCIETY (Gospel)

Lloyd-Jones rarely touched on specific social issues and relief work; this did not demonstrate a lack of concern. Rather he believed that the greater good for society is served through increasing the number of Christians which, historical record affirms, brings about social awareness and reform. Some might feel that he overreacted against the social gospel and failed to proclaim a holistic gospel.

From the standpoint of the optimism of the world, the New Testament is a profoundly pessimistic book; it takes a realistic view of man and his condition, and it tells us that any solution that is merely superficial can never adequately meet the position with which we are confronted.
The Life of Joy, 139

Rich nations have too much corn; they dump it into the sea or burn it. What makes people do things like that when other nations are starving? There is only one answer – they do not live under God.
Authentic Christianity (3), 254

The great hope for society today is an increasing number of individual Christians. Let the Church of God concentrate on that and not waste her time and energy on matters outside her province. Let the individual Christian be certain that this essential quality of saltness is in him, that because he is what he is, he is a check, a control, an antiseptic in society, preserving it from unspeakable foulness, preserving it, perhaps, from a return to a dark age.
Studies in the Sermon on the Mount (1), 158

There is no question but that we are living in an age when there is a ferment of evil working actively in the whole of society. We can go further – and I am simply saying something that all observers of life are agreed about, whether they are Christians or not – and say that in many ways we are face to face with a total collapse and breakdown of what is called 'civilisation' and society.
Life in the Spirit in Marriage Home and Work, 238

The fact that we have become Christians does not abolish our relationship to social, political and economic conditions.
Life in the Spirit in Marriage Home and Work, 321

The church has always led the way in matters of philanthropy and kindness to widows, to the poor, to children, to the suffering, the wounded and those who are treated harshly by life.
Authentic Christianity (3), 250

SOUL
You cannot see people's souls, but you know that each person has a soul and expresses that fact through the body, through behaviour and life, the invisible manifesting itself through the visible.
Great Doctrines of the Bible (3), 7

In all of us there is what we call the soul, but what is the soul? A famous doctor once said that having dissected many human bodies he had never come across an organ described as 'the soul' – thereby, of course, betraying a pathetic ignorance of the spiritual definition of the soul. The soul is immaterial; it is not a substance, nor is it an organ; and no man dissecting the human frame should ever seek for it. The soul is a spiritual entity and quality. But I say that my soul is in me and that my soul will go out of my body.
The Love of God, 86

What is going to happen to you when you die – you have got to, your soul will go on, you will face God.
Heart of the Gospel, 80

sleep
Paul is not looking forward to a 'sleep of the soul', he is looking forward to 'being with Christ, which is far better'; and that agrees with what we are told

everywhere else. Why then are the Christian dead referred to as being asleep? I answer that it is a term which is used to describe an incomplete condition, an intermediate state. At the final 'glorification', when the resurrection of the body takes place and man is fully saved in every respect, it will no longer be incomplete but full and complete. There is a sense in which that cannot happen until the glorification of the body. The body at death as it were 'falls on sleep', it is not yet revived and alive and active. So I take it that 'sleep' refers mainly to the condition of the body. The body is asleep, waiting. It is no longer active, as it will be in the state of glorification; there is an intermediate condition.

The Final Perseverance of the Saints, 88

What makes men and women Christians is something that is done to them by God, not something they do themselves.

Life in God, 12

SPIRITUAL WARFARE
Our life in this world is a spiritual warfare, whether we want it or not; it is inevitably so, because of Satan.

You see that clearly in the life of the Son of God Himself, how constantly He was attacked and besieged by Satan. Satan only left Him for a season after the temptation in the wilderness; then he came back. Because Satan is the god of this world and governs and orders it. The whole life of the Christian is, of necessity, one of spiritual conflict.

Life in God, 179

People who have no sense of conflict at all in their lives are patently just not Christians; they are in the sleep of death spiritually.

Life in God, 45

Let me say regarding the monastic or Catholic view, before I come to criticise it, that whatever we may say against monasticism, it at any rate has seen very clearly that the world is something that has to be fought. So there is a sense in which I would almost say that I would sooner have a monk or an anchorite who is separating himself from the world and dwelling in a cave or a hilltop because he realises he is in the fight of faith than a smug, glib, self-satisfied individual who has never realised there is a fight to be fought.

Life in God, 45

As Christian people, as soon as we come into the Christian life we become part of this mighty conflict between the forces of God and the forces of hell, and we are involved in it whether we like it or not. What he does here is to try to enlighten these people with regard to that; he warns and prepares them to meet and withstand it.

Walking with God, 105

The first thing we have to realize is that the Christian life is a warfare, that we are strangers in an alien land, that we are in the enemy's territory. This is a warfare that you and I have to wage.
The Christian Warfare, 20

We must get rid of the notion that we are only wrestling against 'flesh and blood' on earth. Our wrestling is essentially in the spiritual realm, the realm of the heavenlies. It is simply another way of emphasising . . . that we must always think of the enemy who is fighting against us as one who is not only personal, with his personal agents, but also as one who lives in the realm of the spirit.
The Christian Warfare, 64

SPIRITUALITY

'Walk in the Spirit, and ye shall not fulfil the lust of the flesh' (Galatians 5:16). These two things, Paul says, are opposite to one another; as the one goes up the other goes down. A good illustration of this is provided by those little weather instruments that people used to have, with a little wooden man and a little wooden woman attached to a little wooden house. The man came out when the weather was wet and cold, and the woman when it was fine. They could not be both out at the same time. So it is in the Christian life. 'The flesh lusteth against the Spirit, and the Spirit against the flesh', so, 'Walk in the Spirit, and ye shall not fulfil the lust of the flesh'. Build up the spiritual man that is in you – walk, live your life 'in the Spirit'.
The Sons of God, 144–45

And I suppose there is no more delicate and subtle test of our growth in grace, and our true spirituality, than just this: how much of your time is spent in praying for yourself? How much of your time is spent in praying for others?
The Gospel of God, 192

You find great people in the Bible, You see them in despair, and then you see them rejoicing and happy – what accounts for the charge? It is invariably a question of their relationship to God. Look at a man like David . . . When he obeys God he sings the twenty-third psalm, when he disobeys and rebels, he is down in the depths of Psalm 51
Authentic Christianity (2), 224

You cannot make short cuts in the spiritual life.
Fellowship with God, 41

STOICISM

Christianity is not Stoicism which is mere resignation. Stoicism puts up with things, bears them, just manages not to give in. With courage and a tremendous effort of the will Stoicism goes on and just gets through. That is Stoicism; bearing it, putting up with it, not failing, not breaking down. That is not the Christian's reaction.
Assurance, 63

STUPIDITY
To be ignorant is not the same thing as to be stupid, but stupidity usually leads
to ignorance.
Faith on Trial, 83

SUFFERING
The New Testament, far from promising us a life of ease, and a life in which
there will be no difficulties and problems, rather does the opposite.
The Final Perseverance of the Saints, 441

Whenever the Word talks about the glory it immediately talks about the suffering.
The Final Perseverance of the Saints, 11

There is no more important, and no more subtle, test of our profession of the
Christian faith than the way we react to the trials and the troubles and the tribu-
lations of life in this world.
The New Man, 60

The Christian's reaction is not merely to put up with the trial, it is not just to be
happy in spite of it, it is not to be happy in the midst of it: it is to rejoice on
account of it, because of it.
Assurance, 65–66

It is only when a trial or tribulation comes that we are forced to see our true condition, and how perhaps we have been drifting away from our Lord. So trials
are good for us in that they bring us not only to a better knowledge of Him but
to a better knowledge of ourselves also.
Assurance, 68

When things have gone wrong and you find yourself in trouble, it is always
good to ask questions. Do not grumble or complain. Instead ask 'I wonder
whether I stood in need of this? Is this perhaps a bit of chastisement that I am
receiving from the hands of God?'
Singing to the Lord, 77

Tribulation means trouble, it means affliction, it means pressure. The deriva-
tion of the word is this: in the old days, when they wanted to separate the
wheat from the chaff, they would put the garnered wheat on a floor, and they
had great flails, with which they used to beat the wheat. In this way they
would separate the chaff from the wheat, and in so doing they were, as it
were, bruising it. They used a *tribulum* and hence the term 'tribulation' – as if
you are being struck. We still use the term in that sense. We talk about being
'struck' by misfortune, being beaten and battered and bruised by the things
that happen to us in this life. Well, that is what is going to happen to these

people for all eternity – tribulation; this tremendous kind of beating and bruising.
The Righteous Judgement of God, 87–88

Think of a man sitting at a table with a pair of scales before him. On one of the scales are his sufferings. The man looks at them and sees that they are very heavy. But then he puts on the other scale the very heavy weight of the glory yet to be, and what seemed so heavy before appears now to be as light as a feather. It is not that it is light in and of itself; it only becomes light in contrast with the far greater weight in the other scale pan
The Final Perseverance of the Saints, 45

SUPERFICIALITY
It is possible for us to go through this world, Christian people, saved, sins forgiven, and yet living on such a low level that we know nothing about the great conflicts that are described in the Scriptures and in the lives of the saints.
Joy Unspeakable, 377

SYSTEMATIC THEOLOGY
To me there is nothing more important in a preacher than that he should have a systematic theology, that he should know it and be well grounded in it. This systematic theology, this body of truth which is derived from the Scripture, should always be present as a background and as a controlling influence in his preaching. Each message which arises out of a particular text or statement of the Scriptures, must always be a part or an aspect of this total body of truth . . . the doctrine in a particular text, we must always remember, is a part of this greater whole.
Preaching and Preachers, 66

- T -

TEARS
When did you last weep because of your distance from God? Some of us have forgotten how to weep, my friends. When did we last weep for joy, out of sheer joy and the sense of the glory of God?
Revival, 78

I read of George Whitefield, preaching, and as he was preaching about the glories of grace and of salvation, the tears were pouring down his cheeks, and those who listened to him were weeping too.
Revival, 79

TEMPER
A Christian should never lose his temper, and most certainly he should not lose his temper over God's truth. And if we cannot discuss this great question that is before us without becoming heated, then the thing that we must consider first is our own selves and our own temper. We are not fit to face truth at all! If we cannot consider the truth in a balanced and a controlled manner we are indeed in a very serious condition.
God's Sovereign Purpose, 145

My friend, as a Christian you have no right to lose your temper. The New Testament Epistles tell you not to do so. Control yourself, 'Let not the sun go down upon your wrath.'
The Christian Warfare, 217

TEMPERAMENT
If I had to choose one or the other, I would prefer the man who may even be a little morbid, but who does know the plague of his own heart, to the glib, superficial, light-hearted kind of Christian who has never yet known and realized the foulness and the vileness of his own nature and the depth of sin within him.
Assurance, 159

As for the Christian, his temperament is not changed; but he can control his temperament, and should control his temperament, and must control his temperament.
The Christian Warfare, 213

There has been and there is no type of person who is not represented in the Christian church – volatile and phlegmatic; emotional and logical; sentimental and intellectual; aesthetic and mundane; ethereal or practical; artistic or scientific, credulous or sceptical, mercurial or dull – all, all have been and are today found within the fold of the Christian church. How thoroughly dishonest it is to talk glibly about the religious temperament and make-up and ignore facts which have stood the test of nearly two thousand years!
Old Testament Evangelistic Sermons, 183

It is the devil who would have us believe that we are all fundamentally different, it is of the very essence of the Christian religion that face to face with God we are all one and the same.
Old Testament Evangelistic Sermons, 165

Salvation has nothing whatever to do with temperament.
Banner of Truth, Issue 275

All moodiness is wrong for the Christian; we must snap out of it.
Banner of Truth, Issue 275

Some people are born nice people, some are not. Some people are born with such an easy, almost phlegmatic nature and temperament that they can like almost anybody. They seem to like Christian people; they seem to like being in Christian society. They do not like the noise and bustle of the world. But they are not Christians; they are just born with that temperament.
Life in God, 29

There is no profounder change in the Universe than the change which is described as regeneration; but regeneration – the work of God in the soul by which he implants a principle of divine and spiritual life within us does not change a man's temperament. Your temperament still remains the same. The fact that you have become a Christian does not mean that you cease to have to live with yourself . . . Paul was essentially the same man after his salvation and conversion as he was before.
Depression, 95

TEMPTATION

It is an entire fallacy to say that we cannot be tempted unless there is something within us that responds to it. After all, when Adam was tempted his nature was not sinful. When Adam was tempted he had a perfect human nature; Adam and Eve were tempted in a state of perfection. So obviously temptation can have force and power though the nature of the tempted one is not evil.
Revival, 324

Obviously the higher you go in spiritual experience, or in the spiritual realm, the more likely you are to be attacked by the devil. No one has ever been tempted in this

world in the way in which our blessed Lord and Saviour was tempted; and it has been the universal testimony of the saints throughout the centuries that, the closer their walk with God, the more furious was the attack of the adversary upon them.
The Sons of God, 370

When you are tempted to sin, remember that your body is 'the temple of the Holy Ghost'. We approach these matters so negatively, and for that reason we fail so frequently. People come to me and say, 'I am praying God to deliver me from this sin . . .' But what they really need is to realise that the Holy Ghost is dwelling in their hearts. That is the way to meet the devil. We must not be negative, we must not merely pray to be delivered. Realize who is dwelling in your body, then you will find it difficult to abuse or misuse that body.
The Sons of God, 61

The 'evil day' means a satanic attack. There are days in the lives of Christian people when hell is, as it were, let loose, when the devil seems to marshal all his forces against us from all directions. It is something unusual and exceptional. There is no need to be alarmed, for it is all catered for; but let us not forget it. The greatest saints have given descriptions of these evil days, when the devil, having failed to catch them along the usual lines, made an unusual effort so that they were not given a moment's peace. It might go on for weeks with scarcely any intermission at all. The evil day.
The Christian Warfare, 370

Some of the greatest saints have had a terrible conflict with the devil on their death bed . . . reminding them of their past sins, reminding them of all they have not done, the poverty of their work and their service – showing it to be nothing! In the time of their physical weakness, and with death staring them in the face, the devil tries to shake them. The only answer to give him is still the same; it is 'the breastplate of righteousness'.
The Christian Soldier, 256

The Lord Jesus himself was tempted. The devil put thoughts into His mind. But He did not sin, because He rejected them. Thoughts will come to you and the devil may try to press you to think that because thoughts have entered your mind you have sinned. But they are not your thoughts, they are the devil's. He put them there. It was the quaint Cornishman, Billy Bray, who put this in his own original manner when he said, 'You cannot prevent the crow from flying over your head, but you can prevent him from making a nest in your hair!' So I say that we cannot prevent thoughts being insinuated into our mind; but the question is what do we do with them? We talk about thoughts 'passing through' the mind, and so long as they do this, they are not sin. But if we welcome them and agree with them then they become sin. I emphasize this because I have often had to deal with people who are in great distress because unworthy thoughts have come to them. But what I say to them is this, 'Listen to what you

are telling me. You say that the thought "has come to you". Well, if that is true you are not guilty of sin. You do not say, "I have this thought"; you say, "the thought came".' That is right. The thought came to you, and it came from the devil and the fact that the thought did come from the devil means that you are not of necessity guilty of sin. Temptation in and of itself is not sin. All wool-gathering is Satan taking control of our thoughts.
Banner of Truth, Issue 275

TESTIMONY
Why are Christian converts less ashamed than others to refer to their past? Why are they so free to speak about it? Simply because they know it is gone and no longer counts. It is their way of saying good-bye to it.
Evangelistic Sermons, 19

The greatest testimony to the truth of the gospel of Christ is to be found in Christian people living the life – 'living epistles'.
The Gospel of God, 185

There is nothing more marvellous about one person being saved than another; there is nothing more marvellous about a man who has been a terrible drunkard being saved, than a man who has never had a drop of drink in his life; there is no difference at all, none whatsoever. But, you see, people are interested – 'Oh, was it not a wonderful testimony?' they say. 'Did you hear it?' My dear friend, I could easily prove, if you pressed me, that it is much more difficult to save the person who has not been a drunkard, because he does not know that he is not righteous. The drunkard does know it, he is terribly aware of it, poor fellow. You see how we pervert the whole gospel through being unscriptural and by pandering to the flesh and the carnal excitement of meetings.
The Righteous Judgement of God, 200

THEOLOGY
The business of the Christian faith is not to give us a knowledge of theology. You can have a great knowledge of theology and still not know God. I am the last man to decry theology, one of the greatest troubles is the lack of a knowledge of theology, but I say you may have a knowledge of theology and still be a stranger to the love of God.
Old Testament Evangelistic Sermons, 40

True theology always moves the heart.
Christian Conduct, 31

But apart from all that, I repeat that the big principle is that biblical teaching starts with the fundamental postulate that popular opinion is not the determining factor.
Christian Conduct, 82

Oh, you can boast of your understanding of theology, you can feel proud of yourself. But your real reason for studying and reading is to show off your great knowledge. I have known people who have had, it seems to me, nothing but a purely technical interest in the Bible. They are clever at turning up this and that verse and comparing them. They have topics and words all neatly classified. In a minute they can give you an analysis of a whole book of the Bible. But that is not true knowledge of the Scripture.
Spiritual Blessing, 188

THINKING
Generally speaking, the truly great thinker is a humble man. It is 'a little learning' that 'is a dangerous thing'.
Studies in the Sermon on the Mount (1), 49

While I draw a distinction between rational thinking and spiritual thinking, I am not for a moment suggesting that spiritual thinking is irrational. The difference between them is that rational thinking is on ground-level only; spiritual thinking is equally rational, but it takes in a higher level as well as the lower level. It takes in all the facts instead of merely some of them.
Faith on Trial, 34

One of the tragedies of the modern world is that reading has become a substitute for thinking in the case of the vast majority of people.
God's Way of Reconciliation, 65

May God enlighten us, and teach us how to think in a Christian way, and to view everything in the light of these great principles that are enunciated in the Word of God!
Life in the Spirit in Marriage Home and Work, 342

Generally speaking men are not wrong because they think but because they do not think.
Faith on Trial, 73

The secret of success is to think and to understand.
Life in the Spirit in Marriage Home and Work, 208

TIME
I wonder what the result would be if we all kept a chart for one week and put down on paper the amount of time which we spent in reading God's word and things which help us to understand it, and the time we spent reading newspapers and novels or watching films?
The Life of Joy, 178

When a revival comes we shall experience what has always been experienced, we shall be taken out of time, we shall forget time. We may start our service at the usual time, but God alone knows when it will end.
Revival, 78

The whole trouble with the man who is not a Christian, that is, the worldly man, is that to him this present life and this world are the only life and the only world. He knows nothing except what can be called chronological time, time as measured by the clock or by the calendar. His whole outlook is circumscribed entirely by the temporal, by the present, by the seen, and by the visible; and to him there is no division of time at all. His view is that you come into this world, you live in it, and you go out of it. That is all he knows about time. But that is not the view of the Christian; and it is because of this that the Christian is able to face suffering in a way that no one else can.
The Final Perseverance of the Saints, 29

I find it difficult to understand people who have to resort to crossword puzzles and things like that in order to find a fascinating matter of arrangement!
Great Doctrines of the Bible (2), 59

TOLERANCE
There is a danger that we may confuse sentimentality and a doctrinal laxity and looseness for a true spirit of charity. The New Testament uses the language of which I have just been reminding you and here it is in its essence – *liars*. So then, how do we reconcile these things? Well, there is a very real distinction drawn in the New Testament between what we are to endure for ourselves and our response when the truth is attacked. The Sermon on the Mount tells us to 'turn the other cheek'; quite right, there is no inconsistency between what John says here with that teaching. With regard to ourselves and our own personal feelings we are to endure anything and everything; we are not to stand up for ourselves; we are not to call people liars who attack us in person. But where the truth is concerned, where doctrine is involved, where the whole essence of the gospel comes in, and especially the person of the Lord Jesus Christ, we are to stand and be strong and we are not to hesitate to use language like this.
Walking with God, 133

Anything that robs me of my salvation and my standing with God is a lie, and I must denounce it with all my being.
Walking with God, 138

TRADITION
There is nothing which is quite as blind and so utterly foolish and unintelligent as to ignore the past entirely and to jettison everything that has been handed on by tradition simply because it comes on to us from the past. That a thing has been believed for centuries does not prove that it is true, but it certainly ought

to cause us to think seriously and ponder long before we lightly throw it over-board.
Old Testament Evangelistic Sermons, 152

TRINITY

Do we realize, I wonder, as we should, that the doctrine of the Trinity is in a sense the essence of the Christian faith? It is this doctrine which, of all others, differentiates the Christian faith from every other faith whatsoever.
God's Way of Reconciliation, 311

The whole Christian position, in a sense, depends upon the doctrine of the blessed Holy Trinity. If we do not believe in that we cannot be Christian; it is impossible.
Great Doctrines of the Bible (1), 256

It seems to me that there is only one thing to do, and that is to acknowledge that we stand before the mystery which is revealed in the Bible. We cannot hope to understand it. We cannot hope to grasp it with our minds; it is entirely beyond us and above us. We are simply meant to look at it with wonder, with awe and with worship and be amazed at it.
Great Doctrines of the Bible (1), 84

The scriptural truth, the Christian truth, insists upon our saying that there are three Persons, and yet we must not say that there are three Gods. This is a great and eternal mystery.
Great Doctrines of the Bible (1), 90

Do not try to understand this; no one can understand this ultimate mystery. But it is the truth which we find in the Scriptures. God is One – there is one Godhead. But there are three Persons in the Godhead. This does not imply three Gods, not Tritheism but Monotheism – three Persons in the one and Eternal Godhead. This truth is clearly in the mind of the Apostle here. We recognise the Spirit; we recognise the Son; we recognise the Father; but we say that the Three are one God.
Christian Unity, 134

Do not try to understand it: no one can do so; it baffles the understanding, we can but recognise it and adore in wonder. That is why as Christians we are Trinitarians, and not Jehovah's Witnesses, or Unitarians. It is the Scriptures that lead us to be Trinitarians. We should glory and rejoice in this, because what we deduce from it is that the three blessed Persons in the Holy Trinity are con-cerned about us and our salvation. The Father planned it all; the Son came to execute it; and the Spirit applies it. What a wonderful plan of salvation! So we can attribute different aspects of the work to the Father or the Son or the Spirit,

because the undivided Three are involved; and all the glory for all the work must be given to the three blessed Persons.
The Sons of God, 84

There is no doctrine higher than the doctrine of the blessed holy Trinity.
God's Way of Reconciliation, 323

In what sense is God the Head of Christ? The answer is what we sometimes call the Economic Trinity. The Father, Son and Holy Spirit are co-equal and co-eternal. How then can the Father [God] be the Head of Christ? For the purpose of salvation the Son has subordinated Himself to the Father, and the Spirit has subordinated Himself to the Son and to the Father. It is a voluntary subordination in order that salvation may be carried out.
The Christian Warfare, 109

The three Persons in the Trinity are equal, but for the sake of your salvation and mine [that is what the Apostle is talking about] the Son subordinates Himself to the Father. He says, 'Here am I: send Me.' So He came in the form of a servant and He was dependent upon His Father. But then in turn the Holy Spirit subordinates Himself to the Son and to the Father. The Spirit 'shall not speak of himself' – which does not mean that He will not say things about Himself so much as that He is not going to originate things Himself – 'He shall glorify me', and 'He will bring to your remembrance all that ever I have said unto you.' The Spirit, co-equal with the Son and the Father, subordinates Himself to that task.
God's Sovereign Purpose, 230

To deny the Son is also to deny the Father. I lose everything if I deny the doctrine of the Son. It is the eternal Father who has planned salvation; it is the Son who came and worked out that plan; and it is God the Holy Spirit who opens our eyes to it and who makes it real and actual in us all.
Walking with God, 139

The doctrine of the Trinity is the most distinctive doctrine of the Christian faith.
Great Doctrines of the Bible (1), 84

For the purposes of our salvation you have what has sometimes been called the economic Trinity. A division is made among the three Persons, and, for the purposes of this work and of this salvation there is a kind of subjugation of the three Persons. The Father creates; the Father elects; the Father planned salvation. The Son was sent by the Father to work out this salvation. The Holy Spirit was sent by the Father and the Son to apply the salvation.
Great Doctrines of the Bible (1), 90

We have often had to refer to that great meeting that was held in eternity, when God the Father, God the Son, and God the Holy Spirit met in council, and the

work of salvation was divided up between them. The Son volunteered to take unto Himself human nature, to give a perfect obedience to the law, and to die for the guilt and punishment of the sins of men and women. And the Holy Spirit volunteered to take upon Himself the work of applying that redemption.
Great Doctrines of the Bible (2), 43

Christianity is Trinitarian through and through. That sounds strange does it not but the way we differentiate between Christianity and every other religion or cult, or anything that pretends to be Christian, is by asking: Is it or is it not Trinitarian?
Authentic Christianity (2), 193

TRUTH
Truth is like a cube, and you must see all the facets. The failure to do that, I think you will find as we analyse ourselves is the trouble with most of us.
Faith on Trial, 46

A truth which is only held in the intellect becomes hard, and arid and dry; and a man of whom this is true can never speak the truth in love.
Christian Unity, 251

The denial of the truth is as old as the truth.
Authentic Christianity (1), 127

There is no contradiction between the truth of God and true science; there is much contradiction between the truth of God and the theories of men. But such theories are not true science; they belong to philosophy and the realm of speculation.
Life in the Spirit in Marriage Home and Work, 335

– U –

UNBELIEF
Unbelief is terribly positive and active, a state and condition of the soul, with a very definite mentality: and the Bible indeed does not hesitate to put it like this: 'Unbelief is one of the manifestations of sin; it is one of the symptoms of that fell and foul disease.'
Heart of the Gospel, 84

There is nothing new about unbelief.
Authentic Christianity (2), 3

Unbelief is the antithesis of reason.
Authentic Christianity (2), 121

Unbelief is nothing but sheer nonsense.
Authentic Christianity (2), 199

The problem of unbelief is the same today as it was in the first century, and as it was before that. Unbelief has been a universal problem ever since the Fall. Unbelief is not the consequence of modern knowledge, but neither is it based upon reason, intelligence and understanding.
Authentic Christianity (3), 182

'Blind unbelief' – Ah, that is the enemy! Unbelief is always blind. It cannot see and especially it cannot see afar off.
To God's Glory, 74

UNBELIEVERS
The difference between being a Christian and not being a Christian is not one of degree, it is one of essence and quality, so that the most unworthy Christian is in a better position than the best man outside Christianity.
Saved in Eternity, 135

You must not allow the devil to depress and discourage you because you occasionally fall into sin or because you say, 'I am not satisfied with my achievements.' If there is this struggle in a spiritual sense, then, according to the New Testament, that of itself is proof that you have eternal life.
Life in God, 108

UNCONVERTED
Our hearts should be filled with compassion as we think of people who are not Christians.
Assurance, 312

UNCTION (Preaching)
May we all seek that 'unction' and 'anointing' from 'the holy One', for the matter with which we are dealing is beyond the realm of grammar and intellectual dexterity.
The Law: Its Functions and Limits, 188

You can have a highly educated, cultured ministry, but it will be useless without this power. You can have men who can speak and expound learnedly, and do many other things, but if this power is not present it will end in nothing better than entertainment. 'I long to see you that I may impart unto you . . .' I have got it. I know I can give it. The Apostle was conscious – he was aware – of his power. Without this power we are advocates and not witnesses, and we are called to be witnesses.
The Gospel of God, 223–24

What things we have experienced! To a preacher there is nothing so wonderful as to feel the unction of the Holy Spirit while preaching, and to hear of souls being brought under conviction of sin, and then experiencing the new birth.
Letter to members Westminster Chapel, May 30 1968

Regarding preaching as I do as an activity under the influence and power of the Holy Spirit, we have to emphasise this point because the preparation is not finished just when a man has finished his preparation of the sermon. One of the remarkable things about preaching is that often one finds that the best things one says are things that have not been premeditated, and were not even thought of in the preparation of their sermon, but are given while one is actually speaking and preaching.
Preaching and Preachers, 84

But this is not confined to the New Testament, thank God. Read the biographies of the great preachers in the Church throughout the centuries, and especially in times of revival and re-awakening, and you find this kind of thing repeated endlessly. A man who is preaching suddenly becomes aware that the Spirit of God has come upon him, and has taken hold of him. He is taken out of himself, he is given a luminosity and an understanding and a power and an ability to speak with conviction; and tremendous things happen. The man himself is very conscious of it, so are those who are listening to him.
Life in the Spirit in Marriage Home and Work, 44

. . . [God] can give this power, and he can withdraw it
Joy Unspeakable, 139

When a man is filled with the Holy Spirit people feel it. Even people who do not believe what the preacher says know that power is there, they feel a reality, a strength, a force, they feel something dealing with them . . .
Authentic Christianity (2), 6

UNDERSTANDING
If you are in trouble about the understanding of this gospel, ask God to give you his Spirit in all his fullness, and you will begin to understand.
Saved in Eternity, 90

Ask him so to give you his Holy Spirit that your eyes will be open to these precious, glorious truths. The Holy Spirit was sent in order to make these things real to us. If we but realized these things then we would inevitably be praising with the whole of our being, and our whole life would be to his praise. The Holy Spirit will enable us to realize these glorious things.
Saved in Eternity, 80

To recognise the Lord Jesus Christ is not a matter of intellect, because the greatest brain can never come to see it and believe it. It is a spiritual truth and something which is spiritually discerned.
Saved in Eternity, 88

Who can understand the doctrine of the Trinity? Who can understand the doctrine of two natures in the Person of the Lord Jesus Christ, and yet say that there is only one Person? Understand! The root of all trouble is this desire to understand, and to say, 'I cannot accept and believe unless I understand'. You will never understand this.
Assurance, 211

You may remember the story of the poor woman leaving a service in a famous Church in Edinburgh where a great and learned professor had been preaching. Somebody asked her on the way out whether she had enjoyed the sermon, and on saying that she had asked her further, 'Were you able to follow him?' To which she replied, 'Far be it from me to presume to understand such a great man as that'!
Preachers and Preaching, 122

As it was with the manna in the wilderness, so spiritual understanding has to be collected freshly day by day. Unless we realize our dependence upon the Holy Spirit the Word will not speak to us. If we read the Word of God without praying for enlightenment, we shall probably get very little out of it. We must never depart from this consciousness of our dependence upon the Spirit's power and enlightenment.
God's Ultimate Purpose, 367

Is our spiritual knowledge greater today than it was a year ago? Looking back across let us say ten years in the Christian life, can you say that your spiritual knowledge is greater than it was? I am not asking whether you have a greater knowledge of the letter of the Scripture, as you may have an increasing knowledge of Shakespeare; I am not asking if you have memorized a large number of biblical verses. I am asking whether your spiritual knowledge and understanding have grown? Is your grasp of truth more profound? Do you really feel that you are being led ever onwards, as it were from chamber to chamber in a great mansion, and discovering fresh treasures of wisdom and knowledge?
God's Ultimate Purpose, 368

UNEVANGELISED (Infants)
The position of the heathen who have never heard the gospel is, in essence and in principle, no different at all from the position of infants that die almost as soon as they are born.
Saving Faith, 261

But what is there to stop the Almighty God from illuminating the man's mind, and giving him a revelation of Christ and the gospel, even in the last agony of death? . . . He can do that to a heathen who has never heard the gospel. In His own mysterious manner by the Holy Spirit God can give that man the knowledge of Christ which is adequate to save him.
Saving Faith, 263

UNGODLINESS
'Christ died for the ungodly'. He did not die for that Pharisee who stood forward in the Temple and said, 'I thank thee that I am not as other men are . . . or even as this publican'. (Luke 18:11)
Assurance, 119

There is no such thing as a naturally godly person.
Assurance, 120

What is there to be said really for the ungodly life? Examine it exactly as it is without all its trimmings and fineries. What has it to give to the soul?
Old Testament Evangelistic Sermons, 108

Ungodliness means anything in us that fails to glorify God and to worship Him and to make Him supreme in our own lives, and in the lives of others.
The Righteous Judgement of God, 18

UNITY
'singleness of heart' – melted into one in Christ Jesus.
Authentic Christianity (1), 200

I have to say this: I have no fellowship with a man who says that he is a Christian, unless he believes that the eternal Son of God was made flesh; unless he believes that God has sent forth His own Son and made him of a woman; that the eternal Son, the everlasting Christ, took unto Himself human nature. I cannot say that there is such a thing as Christianity while there is any doubt or hesitation concerning this, and unless I am greatly mistaken, if we do not fight on this matter and stand on this truth, we shall find that we shall have betrayed the Christian message, and the whole of the glorious Christian salvation.
The Gospel of God, 111

It is being said that men and women may receive the Spirit in all His fullness and continue as Roman Catholics, believing in transubstantiation and in all the magic of the Mass, and the sacramental views of the Roman Catholic Church. What people believe is not important; what matters is that they have the Spirit within them. Such talk is becoming quite common at the present time. People are saying that you can have true unity in spite of profound disagreement concerning vital and essential doctrines. But I want to put it to you again this is a complete denial of the teaching of this one verse, Romans 12:5, even without going any further. You cannot have unity unless it includes unity of mind and of thinking.
Christian Conduct, 192

You do not start with fellowship, you must start with doctrine. There is no fellowship apart from the doctrine. The order is absolutely vital.
Christian Conduct, 193

We are not merely to speak lovingly, or simply to be nice and friendly; we are to speak the *truth* in love. Truth must always come first. The result is that it is quite impossible to discuss unity with a man who denies the deity of Christ. Although he may call himself a Christian I have nothing in common with him. If he does not acknowledge this one Lord, born of the Virgin, who worked His miracles, and died an atoning death, and rose literally from the grave in the body, I cannot discuss the unity of the Church with him. There is no basis for the discussion of unity.
Christian Unity, 268

We must never start with the visible church or with an institution, but rather with the truth which alone creates unity
Knowing the Times, 159

The unity amongst Christians is a unity which is quite inevitable because of that which is true of each and every one. I sometimes think that that is the most important principle of all. With all this talk about unity, it seems to me, we are forgetting the most important thing, which is that unity is not something that man has to produce or to arrange: true unity between Christians is inevitable and unavoidable. It

is not man's creation; it is, as we have been shown so clearly, the creation of the Holy Spirit Himself. And my contention is that there is such a unity at this moment among true Christians. I do not care what labels they have on them, the unity is inevitable; they cannot avoid it, because of that which has become true of every single individual Christian.
God's Way of Reconciliation, 354

When holiness is the main characteristic, the unity looks after itself.
God's Way of Reconciliation, 432

To me one of the major tragedies of the hour, and especially in the realm of the church, is that most of the time seems to be taken up by the leaders in preaching about unity instead of preaching the gospel that alone can produce unity.
Banner of Truth, Issue 275

UNIVERSALISM

What makes it still more serious is that one of the best-known theologians in the world at the present time [1961], a man described by the late Pope as the 'greatest theologian since Thomas Aquinas' [I refer to Dr. Karl Barth] teaches this 'Universalism'. This is not surprising because, in spite of his supposed biblicism, he is in reality philosopher rather than theologian.
The Final Perseverance of the Saints, 218

The Bible nowhere teaches us that all are going to be saved.
Assurance, 246

There is nothing in Scripture anywhere to suggest what is called 'universalism, the teaching, very popular today, that at the final consummation every human being who has ever lived anywhere will be saved.
The Final Perseverance of the Saints, 217

– V –

VESTMENTS
. . . [Y]ou find people are dressing up in vestments all for processions and appearances – the lust of the eyes, the outward show.
Walking with God, 87

Why does anyone wear a clerical collar? How did that ever arise? To what extent should we by external experience, either clothing or the wearing of badges or anything like that, make it known that we are Christian or ministers of the gospel?
Saving Faith, 195

VIRGIN BIRTH (Mary, Roman Catholicism)
If you really do believe that the babe in the manger in Bethlehem is the second Person in the Trinity – and that is the truth – then I cannot see that there is any difficulty about this doctrine of the virgin birth. Indeed, I would find myself in much greater difficulty if I did not have the doctrine of the virgin birth to believe.
Great Doctrines of the Bible (1), 262

When it came to the question of the incarnation, the male was put on one side and God used the woman only. I have come across a very beautiful phrase which I think will help you to remember this: 'As the Lord's divine nature had no mother, so His human nature had no father.' I think that puts it very well.
Great Doctrines of the Bible (1), 262

WAR

I repeat again what I have often said, that I regard the two World Wars which we have experienced in this century as God's punishment of the apostasy of the last century. I see no other adequate explanation.
Revival, 151

Nations, like individuals, are not governed by common sense. I repeat, war is sheer madness; there is nothing to be said for it. Why then do the nations fight and prepare for war? The answer is that they are not governed by their minds and intellects but by the two-thirds that is underneath the surface, the part of the iceberg that you do not see – greed, avarice, national pride, the desire to possess and to become greater than others.
The Christian Warfare, 30

What I see in the two world wars I would put in this form: it is God turning to men and to the world and saying: 'You claimed that you could make a perfect world without me. You claimed that you had so outgrown me that you could carry on without me. You have said that I am unnecessary. You have relegated me to heaven and I have allowed you to see what you are, and what you make of life when you try to live without me. I am allowing you to reap the consequences of your own sin. I am showing you that sin is always followed by destruction; and that these two wars are but pictures and illustrations, in the field of history, of the final judgment of man, by my only-begotten Son, the Lord Jesus Christ'.
Old Testament Evangelistic Sermons, 69

I began preaching in the 1920s when people were still optimistic. There had been one World War but they said, 'It is alright, we'll never do that again.' They were preaching with optimism and I began preaching chaos and sin and man as he is, and I prophesied that war would come. Of course I did. There was nothing clever about that, I simply believed my Bible . . . While man is sinful there will be wars, and it is just idle fancy and nonsense to imagine that while man and women are self-centred and selfish they will do anything else but fight one another in some shape or form.
Enjoying the Presence of God, 67

WEALTH

A man was blessed in the Old Testament, and seen to be blessed, by the number of oxen and sheep and camels he possessed. You do not find that in the New Testament; indeed you find almost the exact opposite. In the Old the truth is conveyed in an external, physical, material manner; in the New it is spiritual. In the same way one belonged to the nation of Israel by physical descent; but you do not belong to the Kingdom of God by physical descent but as the result of a spiritual rebirth.
Assurance, 227–28

At the final bar of judgement the gravest charge that will be made against us Christians will be that we were so unconcerned.
Banner of Truth, Issue 275

John gives us an abundant illustration in the case of this man who shuts up his 'bowels of compassion' – who has no pity. Here is a man who has received this world's goods; then he sees a brother in Christ who is in need, and he has no pity on him. He does not do anything about it, and he goes on as if he had not seen it. Now there is no need to argue; there is no love of God in that man, because he is thinking only of himself.
Children of God, 116

The more Christian a person is, the simpler will that person's life be.
Banner of Truth, Issue 275

The trouble with this young man was the power of money, what he could do with it and what he could bring to pass through it. Money is power and this young man knew it. That is why a rich man is in a very dangerous position because the trouble with all of us ultimately is that we desire power.
The Kingdom of God, 164

There is nothing wrong in having wealth in and of itself; what can be very wrong is a man's relationship to his wealth. And the same thing is equally true about everything that money can buy.
Studies in the Sermon on the Mount (2), 81

It is not an accident that the Puritans of the seventeenth century, especially the Quakers, became wealthy people. It was not because they hoarded wealth, it was not because they worshipped mammon. It was just that they were living for God and His righteousness, and the result was that they did not throw away their money on worthless things. In a sense, therefore, they could not help becoming wealthy. They held on to the promises of God and incidentally became rich.
Studies in the Sermon on the Mount (2), 145

One of the greatest temptations to a man who becomes a Christian is to become respectable. When he becomes a Christian he also tends to make money, and resents the suggestion that he should share that money . . .
Puritan Conference Papers 1975; The French Revolution and After, 103

WICKEDNESS

But then the prophet goes on to say this: 'The wicked are like the troubled sea when it cannot rest, whose waters cast up mire and dirt'. There is the picture, there is the explanation – 'like the troubled sea'. Why is the sea always restless, always in motion? Why are there waves, why is there ebb and flow? The scientists tell us that the answer is that the sea is being acted upon by two opposing forces. There is first of all the moon. The moon partly controls the movements and the motions of the sea. On the other hand there is the magnetic force in the heart of the earth, a tremendous magnetic pull. On the one hand is the pull and the influence of the moon, and the converse influence of the magnetic powers in the centre of the earth on the other. And the result is that the sea is in constant motion; you have the waves and the billows, the ebb and flow; and then occasionally there comes a gale, the wind rises and begins to blow upon the sea and raises the billows, and you have a terrible storm. 'The wicked are like the troubled sea when it cannot rest, whose waters cast up mire and dirt.' Have you ever walked along a beach after a storm, and seen the mud and the dirt and the bits of wood and the various other things cast up? They are the flotsam and the jetsam, the filth and the mire left upon the sea shore after the ending of the storm. What a perfect description it is!
God's Way of Reconciliation, 300

WILL

The vital question is this: What is it that determines a man's will? And the moment you ask that question it comes back to one of two things: it is either God's purpose, or else it is pure accident, a matter of glands, a matter of upbringing, a thousand and one factors entirely beyond our own control.
God's Sovereign Purpose, 208

We must understand clearly that God through the Holy Spirit does not work or act upon us mechanically. God does not force our wills; God does not compel anyone against his will to believe the gospel. That is not His way of working. We are not treated as automata. What happens is that God persuades the will; He makes the truth attractive to us. So no man has ever believed the gospel against his will; he has been given to see it in such a way that he desires it, he admires it, he likes it.
God's Ultimate Purpose, 239

WISDOM

You can teach man knowledge, you can impart information to him, but you cannot make him wise. It is one of the most difficult things confronting a teacher,

but, thank God, it is something for which we can pray. It is something that the Holy Spirit can give us, and that is why the Apostle prays for it.
The Life of Joy, 53

The source of knowledge is study; the source of wisdom is discernment. You get your knowledge by studying, but you do not get wisdom that way.
Great Doctrines of the Bible (1), 65

What does wisdom mean? It means the ability to deal with a situation. A man may have great knowledge but if he lacks wisdom his knowledge is going to be no use to him.
To God's Glory, 259

WORD
The moment you separate the Spirit and the Word you are in trouble.
The Christian Warfare, 328

The Spirit and the Word must be kept together always. The Spirit has provided for us the instruction found in the Word, but we cannot use it without Him. It can be a dead letter to us: 'the letter killeth, but the Spirit giveth life.' What is needed is the Spirit opening the Word, and opening my mind and opening my heart. As long as you keep the two together as the Apostle does here, you cannot possibly go wrong; but if you separate them the devil has already 'divided in order that he may conquer', as it were . . . he has done that very often in the long history of the Christian Church.
The Christian Soldier, 329

WORLD
If God withdrew His power from the world it would collapse immediately; it is the Spirit of God that gives life and being and sustenance, to all things.
God's Ultimate Purpose, 421

The word 'world' can be defined as life and activity which, as the result of the Fall, is controlled by the devil.
Christian Conduct, 73

The fate of man and the fate of the whole cosmos are inextricably linked; and one follows the other.
The Final Perseverance of the Saints, 50

People *qua* people are not against us: but 'the world' is against us, and the 'world' means that outlook, that whole organisation, that tremendous power of evil in which we are living, as it were, and which is everywhere round and about us. Our business is to be 'in the world, but not of it'. These 'powers' are the rulers, the governors, the controllers of that mind, that outlook, which we call 'the world'.
The Christian Warfare, 59

The world is as it is today because when Adam sinned all sinned, and ever since, sin and death have been universal and have come upon the whole of mankind. It is a mystery, it is an astounding fact.
Assurance, 212

The world has gone mad on singing, and the more it sings the less it thinks.
Spiritual Blessing, 229

The whole world lies in the power of the evil one. It is lying in his bosom; he is there clasping it, and he is controlling its whole outlook and all its activities and everything that happens in it.
Life in God, 161

Let us have a right view of the world; let us have a right view of its history; let us understand what is happening to the world at this present time; let us look ahead and see what it is destined for; let us never rest our affection on it. And as we go on, let us remember its subtle insinuations, and let us beware of its defilement and sin.
Life in God, 177

The Christian is a citizen in this world; but let us be careful that the world does not enter into us again and get us back.
Life in God, 176

The world cannot be improved in an ultimate sense, but that does not mean that we do not do our utmost to control evil and its manifestations and its effects in it.
Life in God, 175

The world as we know it, without God and without Christ, is but awaiting the end that is surely coming. If reform were possible, reform would take place; but there is no ultimate reform – the world will be destroyed.
Life in God, 175

worldliness
The world, let me emphasise it again, is everything that stands between us and glorifying God only, utterly and absolutely.
Life in God, 37

You can go away and spend your day on the top of a mountain, but you cannot get away from the world; it is in you.
Life in God, 48

The world is in us the moment we begin to live. It is no use trying to fight the world immediately – that cannot be done. Monasticism recognises that and says, 'Run away from it.' So what do I need? I need emancipation.
Life in God, 53

The tragedy of the twentieth century especially has been that the Church in her folly has been trying to accommodate herself to the world, thinking that by so doing she could attract it. But the world expects the Christian to be different, and it is right – this is the New Testament emphasis. It is nothing but a departure from New Testament doctrine that ever tries to make the Church ingratiate herself to the world; the Church is meant to be, and is, essentially different.
Life in God, 157

WORSHIP
But after all, although order and dignity are splendid, the one element which is needed above everything else is life.
Knowing the Times, 24

The 'service' of God means the worship of God
Christian Conduct, 57

Worship and service are interchangeable terms. Indeed, we ourselves say both that we going into the house of God to worship God and that we are going to a service in the house of God.
Christian Conduct, 57

The whole of my life is to be a worship of God.
Christian Conduct, 57

Our coming together in public worship should be a foretaste of heaven. Public worship should be a gathering of the first fruits, a sampling of what is to be our lot in heaven
God's Ultimate Purpose, 308

Praise is really the chief object of all public acts of worship. We all need to examine ourselves at this point. We must remember that the primary purpose of worship is to give praise and thanksgiving to God. Worship should be of the mind and of the heart. It does not merely mean repeating certain phrases mechanically; it means the heart going out in fervent praise to God. We should not come to God's house simply to seek blessings and to desire various things for ourselves, or even simply to listen to sermons; we should come to worship and adore God. 'Blessed be the God and Father' is always to be the starting point, the highest point.
God's Ultimate Purpose, 50

It is God who decided and who has revealed how He is to be worshipped, not man, and they should have observed God's way instead of turning to their own inventions.
God's Sovereign Purpose, 68

True emotion produced by the Holy Ghost always leads to humility, to reverence, to a holy love of God. A man may sing, or may dance for a while; but that does not persist. It is temporary and due to the weakness of the body; but what is permanent, and what proves genuineness, is that the man is filled with a sense of awe.
God's Ultimate Purpose, 287–88

There are people who seem to think that the right thing to do in the House of God is just to go on singing choruses and a certain type of hymn until you are almost in a state of intoxication. Indeed, the whole service is with a view to 'conditioning'. You come under an emotional influence and you do feel better.
Faith on Trial, 44

There are musical instruments that are sensuous, that belong to the world. Saxophones and instruments of that type have no place in Christian worship: their sound is primitive, lacking the thoughtfulness and wisdom that characterises Christian music.
Singing to the Lord, 38

It is very interesting to notice that as men and women know less and less about a living spiritual experience, the more formal does their worship become. This has been most striking during the present century. Increasingly non-conformists have been introducing a liturgical element into their worship. This is because of the low level of spirituality. Conversely, when people come to a living experience of God they rely less and less upon forms, even if they are found in Roman Catholicism.
The Sons of God, 242

Our coming together in public worship should be a foretaste of heaven.
God's Ultimate Purpose, 308

In this world we are simply in a kind of singing rehearsal. We are all just being prepared for the mighty festival of music and song that takes place in heaven.
Singing to the Lord, 60

WRATH
The ultimate trouble with people who do not believe in the doctrine of the wrath of God is that they do not believe the biblical revelation of God. They have got a God of their own creating. Generally, people who reject the biblical doctrine of the wrath of God also reject the biblical doctrine of redemption and of salvation. They are quite consistent. If you do not believe in God's wrath there is no real need for the sacrifice on Calvary's hill.
God's Sovereign Purpose, 212

No man will really seek salvation until he is clear about this doctrine.
The Righteous Judgement of God, 93

Here is a doctrine that the natural man abominates. He feels that it is insulting to him. He has always been like this. Go back again and read the histories and you will find in all periods of deadness and of declension that people did not believe in sin in that way. They did not believe in the wrath of God. And I suppose there are no two things in connection with the Christian faith that are so abominated today, as the doctrine of sin, and the doctrine of the wrath of God.
Revival, 40

The ultimate proof of the wrath of God upon sin is the death of our Lord upon the Cross on Calvary's hill. It is the greatest manifestation of the love of God. It is at the same time the greatest manifestation of the wrath of God. Many things met at Calvary.
To God's Glory, 53

The Jesus whom people put up against the Old Testament, he taught about the wrath of God . . . and I know of nothing that is so terrifying in the whole of the Bible than in the last book, in Revelation 6, which tells us of those men and women who at the end, when they see him they will call to the mountains, and the rocks to fall upon them and to hide them – from what? From the wrath of the Lamb, the incarnation of his love. It is his wrath that is the most terrifying thing of all.
Revival, 41

If I did not believe in the doctrine of the wrath of God, I would not understand the death of Christ upon the cross, it would be meaningless to me.
A Nation Under Wrath, 173

– Z –

ZEAL

There are many Christians who, quite unbeknown to themselves, are living on their own activities, living on their busy-ness, living on the organizations to which they belong, living according to a certain routine that is prescribed for them by someone else.
The Christian Warfare, 357

It is obvious that you can have a wrong zeal. Zeal may be mistaken and may even be dangerous.
Saving Faith, 16

Dr Martyn Lloyd-Jones Book List

A Nation Under Wrath, Eastbourne: Kingsway, 1997
Alive in Christ, Wheaton: Crossway, 1997
Authentic Christianity Vol. 1 (Acts 1-3), Edinburgh: Banner of Truth Trust, 1999
Authentic Christianity Vol. 2 (Acts 4–5), Edinburgh: Banner of Truth Trust, 2001
Authentic Christianity Vol. 3 (Acts 5:17–6:8), Edinburgh: Banner of Truth Trust, 2003
Authentic Christianity Vol. 4 (Acts 7:1–29), Edinburgh Banner of Truth Trust 2004
Authority, London: IVP, 1966
Banner of Truth, Issue 275, August/September 1986
Children of God: Studies in 1st John, Wheaton: Crossway 1993,
Christmas Sermons: An Exposition of the Magnificat, Bridgend: Bryntirion Press, 1998
Enjoying the Presence of God, Eastbourne: Crossway Books, 1991
Ephesians:
> *God's Ultimate Purpose* (Ephesians 1), Edinburgh, Banner of Truth Trust, 1978
> *God's Way of Reconciliation* (Ephesians 2), Edinburgh: Banner of Truth Trust, 1981
> *The Unsearchable Riches of Christ* (Ephesians 3), Edinburgh: Banner of Truth Trust, 1979
> *Christian Unity* (Ephesians 4:1-6), Edinburgh: Banner of Truth Trust, 1980
> *Darkness and Light* (Ephesians 4:17-5:17), Grand Rapids: Baker Book House, 2003
> *Life in the Spirit* (Ephesians 5:18-6:9), Edinburgh: Banner of Truth Trust, 1975
> *The Christian Warfare* (Ephesians 6:10-13), Edinburgh: Banner of Truth Trust, 1976
> *The Christian Soldier* (Ephesians 6:10-20), Edinburgh: Banner of Truth Trust, 1977

Evangelistic Sermons at Aberavon, Edinburgh: Banner of Truth Trust, 1990
Expository Sermons on 2 Peter, Edinburgh: Banner of Truth Trust, 1983
Faith on Trial, London: IVP, 1981
First Book of Daily Readings, London: Epworth Press, 1970
From Fear to Faith, London: Inter-Varsity Press, 1953

Great Doctrines of the Bible, Vols. 1, 2, 3 (now in a single volume), Wheaton: Crossway Books, 2003
God the Father, God the Son, London: Hodder & Stoughton, 1996
God the Holy Spirit, London: Hodder & Stoughton, 1997
God's Way Not Ours, Edinburgh: Banner of Truth Trust, 2003
Healing and the Scriptures, Nashville: Oliver-Belson Books, 1988
Heirs of Salvation, Bridgend: Bryntirion Press, 2000
I am Not Ashamed: Advice to Timothy, London: Hodder and Stoughton, 1986
Joy Unspeakable, Eastbourne: Kingsway, 1995
Knowing the Times, Edinburgh: Banner of Truth Trust, 1989
Let everybody Praise the Lord (Ps 107), Bridgend: Bryntirion Press, 1999
Life in Christ: Studies in 1 John
 Fellowship with God, Wheaton: Crossway, 1993
 Walking with God, Wheaton: Crossway, 1993
 Children of God, Wheaton: Crossway, 1993
 The Love of God, Wheaton: Crossway, 1994
 Life in God, Wheaton: Crossway, 1995
Not Against Flesh and Blood, Bridgend: Bryntirion Press, 2001
Out of the Depths, Bridgend: Evangelical Press of Wales, 1986
Old Testament Evangelistic Sermons, Edinburgh: Banner of Truth Trust, 1995
Preaching and Preachers, London: Hodder and Stoughton, 1971
Prove All Things, Eastbourne: Kingsway, 1985
Revival, Wheaton: Crossway Books, 1987
Romans:
 The Gospel of God (Romans 1), Edinburgh: Banner of Truth Trust, 1985
 The Righteous Judgement of God (Romans 2:1-3:20), Edinburgh: Banner of Truth Trust, 1989
 Atonement and Justification (Romans 3:20-4:25), London: Banner of Truth Trust, 1970
 Assurance (Romans 5), London: Banner of Truth Trust, 1971
 The New Man (Romans 6), Edinburgh: Banner of Truth Trust, 1979
 The Law: Its Functions and Limits (Romans 7:1-8:4), Edinburgh: Banner of Truth Trust, 1975
 The Sons of God (Romans 8:5-17), Edinburgh: Banner of Truth Trust, 1975
 The Final Perseverance of the Saints (Romans 8:17-39), Edinburgh: Banner of Truth Trust, 1975
 God's Sovereign Purpose (Romans 9), Edinburgh: Banner of Truth Trust, 1991
 Saving Faith (Romans 10), Edinburgh: Banner of Truth Trust, 1997
 To God's Glory (Romans 11), Edinburgh: Banner of Truth Trust, 1998
 Christian Conduct (Romans 12), Edinburgh: Banner of Truth Trust, 2000
 Life in Two Kingdoms (Romans 13), Edinburgh: Banner of Truth Trust, 2002
 Liberty and Conscience (Romans 14), Edinburgh: Banner of Truth Trust, 2003
Sanctified Through Truth, Eastbourne: Kingsway, 1989
Saved in Eternity, Illinois: Crossway, 1988
Singing to the Lord, Bridgend: Bryntirion Press, 2003

Spiritual Depression: Its Cause and Its Cure, Norfolk: Pickering and Inglis, 1976
Spiritual Blessing, Eastbourne: Kingsway, 1999
Studies in the Sermon on the Mount, Grand Rapids: Eerdmans, 1987
The All Sufficient God, Edinburgh: Banner of Truth Trust, 2005
The Assurance of Our Salvation (Studies in John 17), Wheaton: Crossway, 2000
The Cross, Eastbourne: Kingsway, 1986
The Doctor Himself and the Human Condition, London: Christian Medical Fellowship, 1982
The Heart of the Gospel, Eastbourne: Crossway, 1991
The Kingdom of God, Wheaton: Crossway, 1992
The Life of Joy, London: Hodder and Stoughton, 1989
The Path to True Happiness, Grand Rapids: Baker Book House, 1999
The Plight of Man and the Power of God, London: Hodder and Stoughton, 1942
The Puritans: Their Origins and Successors, Edinburgh: Banner of Truth Trust, 1991
The Miracle of Grace, Grand Rapids: Baker Book House, 1986
The Sovereign Spirit, Wheaton: Harold Shaw Publishers, 1985
True Happiness: Exposition in Psalm 1, Bridgend: Bryntirion Press, 1997
Truth Unchanged, Unchanging, Bridgend: Evangelical Press of Wales, 1990
Unity In Truth, Darlington: Evangelical Press, 1991
Walking With God Day by Day, Wheaton: Crossway Books, 1993
Water in the Desert, Bridgend: Bryntirion Press, 1991
What is an Evangelical? Edinburgh: Banner of Truth Trust, 1992
Why Does God Allow War? Wheaton: Crossway Books, 2003
Why Does God Allow Suffering? Wheaton: Crossway Books, 1994

Also consulted

Brencher, J., *Martyn Lloyd-Jones (1899-1981) and Twentieth Century Evangelicalism*, Milton Keynes: Paternoster, 2002
Murray, I. (ed.), *D. Martyn Lloyd-Jones: Letters*, Edinburgh: Banner of Truth Trust, 1994
Murray, I , *D. Martyn Lloyd-Jones: The First Forty Years (1899-1939)*, Edinburgh Banner of Truth Trust 1983
Murray, I., *D. Martyn Lloyd-Jones: The Fight of Faith (1939-1981)*, Edinburgh: Banner of Truth Trust, 1990

Papers from the Annual Puritan Conference
Westminster Chapel Record 1940ff
Evangelical Library www.evangelical-library.org.uk
– 020 7935

Note

The Martyn Lloyd-Jones Recording Trust has on record a great deal of Lloyd-Jones taped ministry.

MLJ Recordings Trust,
2 Caxton House,
Wellesley Road,
Ashford,
Kent.
TN24 8ET
United Kingdom
+44 (0)1233 662 262

The International Christian College, Glasgow, Scotland offers courses as part of its undergraduate programme in preaching. Besides general theology it has specialisms in Children's Ministry, Youth Ministry, Cross Cultural and Urban Ministry. Post graduate study and research is available leading to three differing MTh degrees also an M.Phil and PhD. All ICC qualifications are validated by the University of Aberdeen. It is an approved college for an increasing number of denominations and independent churches and helps to train missionaries for a variety of societies besides offering sabbatical courses. The web page has full details www.icc.ac.uk; 0044 (1)41 552 4040: college@icc.ac.uk

---

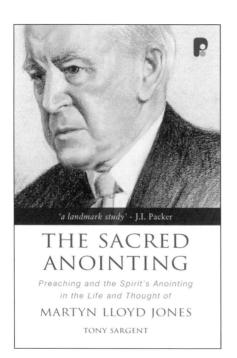

'a landmark study' - J.I. Packer

THE SACRED
ANOINTING

Preaching and the Spirit's Anointing
in the Life and Thought of

MARTYN LLOYD JONES

TONY SARGENT

Also by Tony Sargent

THE SACRED ANOINTING

Preaching and the Spirit's Anointing in the Life and Thought of Martyn Lloyd-Jones

ISBN: 978-1-84227-478-1